MW00643278

way, we know that the Church will grow and flourish for many years into the future. In fact, the structure that Jesus established for the Church will remain until the end of time; that is, until God's Kingdom of justice and peace is fully achieved. As members of the Church through our Baptism, we are part of something much greater than ourselves: something that existed long before us and that will endure far after we are gone. ✴

CATHOLICS MAKING A DIFFERENCE

© Milwaukee Journal photo courtesy of the Department of Special Collections and University Archives, Marquette University Libraries. The photo was taken in Milwaukee in February 1968.

When many people hear the word *Church,* they often think of a church building. When Dorothy Day (1897–1980) thought of the word *Church,* she pictured something completely different. She imagined a church in the streets, serving the poorest and most vulnerable people of her time.

Dorothy worked with a friend, Peter Maurin, to begin publishing a newspaper that promoted workers' rights. They called the paper *The Catholic Worker* and sold it for a penny a copy. Soon after, Day opened her New York City apartment to offer food, shelter, and hospitality to anyone who needed it. What began as a newspaper soon grew into a movement. In time, Catholic Worker Houses of Hospitality opened throughout the United States and around the world. Today, two hundred Catholic Worker Houses live out the Church's mission to bear witness to the Gospel by serving those in need. If you want to purchase a copy of *The Catholic Worker,* it still sells for a penny!

HMMMMM. . .
How does being a part of the Church connect you to something greater than yourself?

THE CHURCH FOUNDATIONS AND MISSION

High School Framework Course 4

CARRIE J. SCHROEDER, MDiv, EdD

saint mary's press

Thanks and Dedication

A very special thank you to our student contributors: Hannah from Cotter High School in Winona, MN; Rosa from Totino-Grace High School in Fridley, MN; Colin from Father Judge High School in Philadelphia, PA; Richard from Mater Dei High School in Santa Ana, CA; and Olivia from New Smyrna Beach High School in New Smyrna Beach, FL.

For Rev. Michael P. Norkett (1940–2018). A partner in ministry, and truly the best of what the Church can be.

The Subcommittee on the Catechism, United States Conference of Catholic Bishops, has found that this catechetical high school text, copyright 2020, is in conformity with the *Catechism of the Catholic Church* and that it fulfills the requirements of Core Course 4 of the *Doctrinal Elements of a Curriculum Framework for the Development of Catechetical Materials for Young People of High School Age.*

Nihil Obstat: Dr. John Martens, PhD
              Censor Librorum
              October 7, 2019

Imprimatur: † Most Rev. Bernard A. Hebda
             Archbishop of Saint Paul and Minneapolis
             October 11, 2019

The nihil obstat and imprimatur are official declarations that a book or pamphlet is free of doctrinal or moral error. No implication is contained therein that those who have granted the nihil obstat or imprimatur agree with the contents, opinions, or statements expressed, nor do they assume any legal responsibility associated with publication.

Cover image: © Markus Pfaff / Shutterstock.com

The content in this resource was acquired, developed, and reviewed by the content engagement team at Saint Mary's Press. Content design and manufacturing were coordinated by the passionate team of creatives at Saint Mary's Press.

Printed in the United States of America

1168 (PO6464)

ISBN 978-1-64121-027-0

CONTENTS

UNIT 1: The Church:
Christ's Living Presence in the World 8

CHAPTER 1: Founded by Christ: The Church Begins 10

   Article 1: Rooted in the Past, Growing toward the Future 11

   Article 2: The Seeds of the Church: Jesus' Preaching and Ministry 16

   Article 3: The Church Is Born: Jesus' Death and Resurrection 22

   Article 4: Matthew's Message: Where Two or Three Are Gathered 25

CHAPTER 2: Animated by the Holy Spirit: The Church Grows and Flourishes 30

   Article 5: The Holy Spirit Is Sent: Pentecost 31

   Article 6: The Holy Spirit Sustains: The Early Church 35

   Article 7: The Holy Spirit Sanctifies: The Church Today. 40

   Article 8: Focus on Pope Francis: "The Joy of Love" 43

UNIT 2: The Marks of the Church 54

CHAPTER 3: The Church Is One 56

Article 9: The Church: Willed by God to Be One 57

Article 10: One in Faith 61

Article 11: One in Worship 65

Article 12: One in Leadership and Witness 69

Article 13: Divisions, Wounds, and Brokenness 72

CHAPTER 4: The Church Is Holy 80

Article 14: The Church: Both Human and Divine 81

Article 15: Grace: A Gift and an Opportunity 85

Article 16: The Communion of Saints 88

Article 17: Mary: Model of Holiness 92

Article 18: Focus on Pope Francis: "Rejoice and Be Glad" 95

CHAPTER 5: The Church Is Catholic 102

Article 19: Breaking Boundaries, Cultivating Connections 103

Article 20: Evangelization: The Gospel Reaching Far and Wide 107

Article 21: Inculturation: The Gospel Taking Root 112

CHAPTER 6: The Church Is Apostolic 120

Article 22: The Apostolic Tradition 121

Article 23: Sent Forth by Jesus 126

Article 24: The Apostolate of the Laity 130

Article 25: Matthew's Message: The Great Commission 134

UNIT 3: Images of the Church 146

CHAPTER 7: The Church in Scripture 148

Article 26: Old Testament Images 149

Article 27: New Testament Images: The Gospels 157

Article 28: New Testament Images: The Epistles 162

CHAPTER 8: Traditional and Contemporary Images of the Church.................. 170

Article 29: Marian Images 171

Article 30: Vatican II Images 177

Article 31: Pope Francis: The Church in the Heart of the Action 182

CHAPTER 9: The Church and Other Religions.................................190

Article 32: What Are Ecumenism and Interreligious Dialogue? 191

Article 33: The Church's Relationship with Judaism 196

Article 34: Matthew's Message: The Jewish Gospel 201

Article 35: The Church's Relationship with Islam 206

Article 36: Focus on Pope Francis: "The Joy of the Gospel" 212

UNIT 4: Ministry in the Church.....................228

CHAPTER 10: The Ministry of Leadership...........................230

Article 37: The Structure of the Church 231

Article 38: Matthew's Message: The Ministry of the Pope...................236

Article 39: The Ministry of Bishops 240

Article 40: The Ministry of the Magisterium 244

Article 41: The Ministry of Priests and Deacons 248

Article 42: Lay Ministry..254

CHAPTER 11: Mission and Holiness 262

Article 43: The Universal Call to Holiness 263

Article 44: Focus on Pope Francis: "The Light of Faith".....................268

Article 45: Priest, Prophet, and King 272

Article 46: Consecrated Life 278

UNIT 5: The Social Mission of the Church 294

CHAPTER 12: The Gospel Message of Service and Justice 296

Article 47: Reading the Signs of the Times 297

Article 48: A Call to Conversion: The Parables 301

Article 49: Matthew's Message: The Corporal Works of Mercy 307

Article 50: The Washing of the Feet 313

CHAPTER 13: Strength in Numbers: Catholic Service Organizations 320

Article 51: Serving the Least among Us 321

Article 52: Apostolic Religious Orders 330

Article 53: Focus on Pope Francis: "On Care for Our Common Home" 336

CHAPTER 14: The Gift of Oneself: Gospel-Centered Volunteer Service 346

Article 54: The Church Unified in Service and Liturgy 347

Article 55: Making a Difference Now 352

Article 56: Making a Difference in the Future 359

Article 57: Being the Church in the World 364

APPENDIX: Challenge Questions 378

GLOSSARY 383

INDEX 391

ACKNOWLEDGMENTS 399

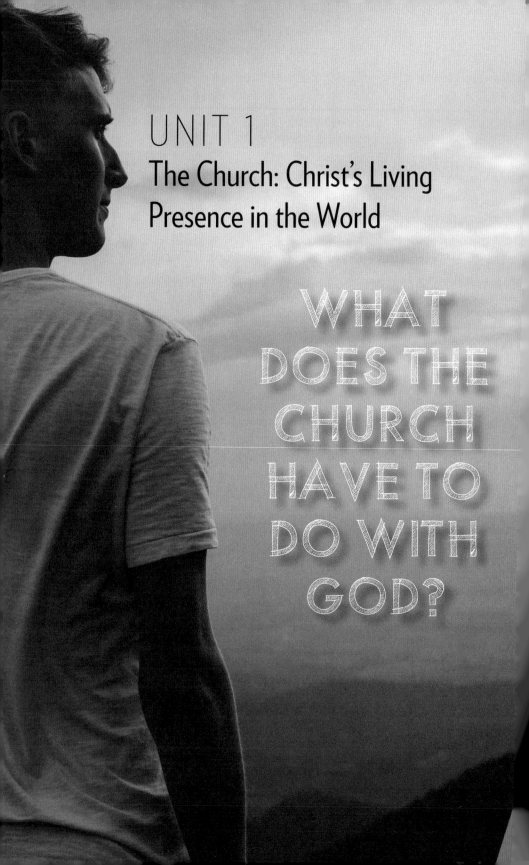

UNIT 1
The Church: Christ's Living Presence in the World

WHAT DOES THE CHURCH HAVE TO DO WITH GOD?

LOOKING AHEAD

CHAPTER 1   Page 10

Founded by Christ:
The Church Begins

CHAPTER 2   Page 30

Animated by the Holy Spirit:
The Church Grows and Flourishes

In the Gospels, Jesus laid the foundation for the Church and gave the tools to the Apostles to continue his mission. In the Acts of the Apostles, we learn how the Apostles and early disciples carry on Christ's mission and form the early Church. However, since Jesus is the Second Person of the Holy Trinity, he is God, and so the Church continues God's work!

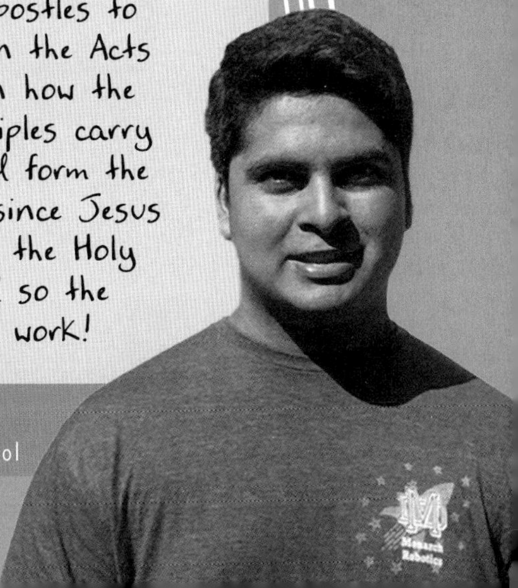

RICHARD
Mater Dei High School

CHAPTER 1
Founded by Christ: The Church Begins

HOW DID THE CHURCH GET STARTED?

SNAPSHOT

Article 1   Page 11
Rooted in the Past, Growing toward the Future

Article 2   Page 16
The Seeds of the Church: Jesus' Preaching and Ministry

Article 3   Page 22
The Church Is Born: Jesus' Death and Resurrection
• Pre-read: John 19:31–37

Article 4   Page 25
Matthew's Message: Where Two or Three Are Gathered
• Pre-read: Matthew 18:15–20

Article 1
Rooted in the Past, Growing toward the Future

Have you ever tried to create a family tree, with the names of all your ancestors? If so, did you talk with your parents, grandparents, aunts, and uncles in order to get information? Did you find any facts that surprised you? Did you hear stories that helped you understand yourself or your family better?

Looking back at our family's history can be amazing and rewarding. From our families, we inherit not only physical traits and personal characteristics but also our values and beliefs. Learning about where we have come from can give us insights into who we are now and who we may yet become in the future.

One of the many images often used to describe the **Church** is a family of faith or the family of God. Like our personal families, the Church stretches back centuries into the past, is living and thriving today, and will endure into the future.

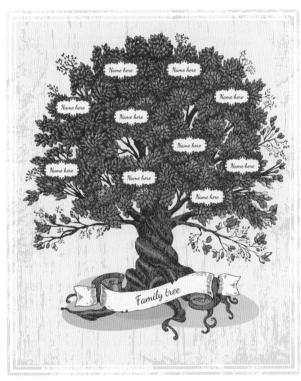

Creating a family tree can help you discover your ancestors and understand your family history.

© Tatsiana Tsyhanova / Shutterstock.com

Church ➤ The term *Church* has three inseparable meanings: (1) the entire People of God throughout the world; (2) the diocese, which is also known as the local Church; and (3) the assembly of believers gathered for the celebration of the liturgy, especially the Eucharist.

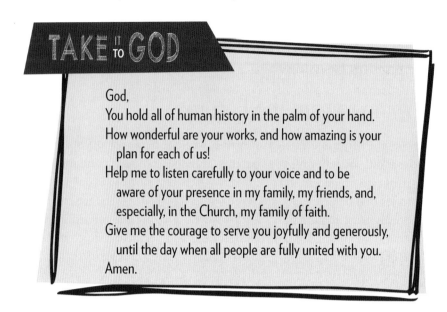

TAKE IT TO GOD

God,
You hold all of human history in the palm of your hand.
How wonderful are your works, and how amazing is your
      plan for each of us!
Help me to listen carefully to your voice and to be
      aware of your presence in my family, my friends, and,
      especially, in the Church, my family of faith.
Give me the courage to serve you joyfully and generously,
      until the day when all people are fully united with you.
Amen.

The Past: A Plan in the Very Heart of God

"God loves you." How often have you heard that? You may have heard it so often that you take it for granted. But think about it for a moment. God, the Creator of all things, the source of all that is, loves and cares for you. And he has loved and cared for every human person who has ever lived and ever will live. He wants us, and all of creation, to be united with him.

When human sinfulness destroyed our union with God and with one another, God sent Jesus, his own beloved Son, to redeem us through the **Paschal Mystery** and to establish the Church as the means of our salvation.

Throughout **salvation history**, we can see hints of God's eternal plan for the Church. God called Abraham and promised that he and his wife, Sarah, would have many descendants, giving rise to a great nation, Israel. After Moses led the Israelites from slavery in Egypt, they gathered at Mount Sinai to renew their covenant with God and receive his Law. Through the **covenant**—a sacred commitment—God claimed them as his own chosen people. When Moses went up the mountain to meet God, God spoke to him and said,

---

Paschal Mystery ➤ The work of salvation accomplished by Jesus Christ mainly through his Passion, death, Resurrection, and Ascension.

salvation history ➤ The pattern of specific events in human history in which God clearly reveals his presence and saving actions. Salvation was accomplished once and for all through Jesus Christ, a truth foreshadowed and revealed throughout the Old Testament.

"This is what you will say to the house of Jacob; tell the Israelites: . . . 'Now if you obey me completely and keep my covenant, you will be my treasured possession among all peoples, though all the earth is mine. You will be to me a kingdom of priests, a holy nation" (Exodus 19:3-6).

© artmig / Shutterstock.com

After Moses led the Israelites out of slavery in Egypt, he went up Mount Sinai to receive God's Law and renew the Israelites' covenant with God.

The Israelites struggled to be faithful to the covenant. Over and over again, they sinned, and over and over again, God forgave them. God sent the prophets to call the people back to faithfulness and to teach them how to live in unity, justice, and holiness. Recall the stories of Isaiah, Jeremiah, Ezekiel, and others, who warned the Israelites of the consequences of their infidelity, guiding and encouraging them to live a life in accordance with the covenant.

Finally, when the time was right, God sent Jesus Christ, who gathered a family of faith and established the Church according to God's divine purpose and mission. Jesus chose the Twelve Apostles as the Church's first leaders, with Peter foremost among these leaders, and he alone gave the Church divine authority, power, and responsibility.

---

covenant ➤ A solemn agreement between human beings or between God and a human being in which mutual commitments are made.

Jesus chose the Twelve Apostles to help him carry out his mission to spread the Good News.

After Jesus' Paschal Mystery had been accomplished, he ascended into Heaven. He was no longer physically present in an ordinary manner with his followers, though he remains physically present in a sacramental manner in the Eucharist. Emboldened by the Holy Spirit, the Apostles went out to spread the Good News. As Christian communities were formed, the Church, then, became the way Jesus' disciples could continue to experience his living presence.

The Present and the Future: Salvation Now and Always

From its origins in Jesus' earthly ministry with a few hundred followers, to the globe-spanning institution today, the Church is an essential way in which we encounter God's grace and experience his saving love. The Church's liturgy and sacraments unite us with God and with all our brothers and sisters in faith, restoring the unity and blessedness that had once been lost by sin.

When you created your family tree, did you think about how it will continue growing in the future? Through marriage and children, your family tree will likely continue adding new members, nieces, nephews, and perhaps, someday, your own children—as a new generation begins. In much the same

TAKE IT TO GOD

God,

You hold all of human history in the palm of your hand.

How wonderful are your works, and how amazing is your plan for each of us!

Help me to listen carefully to your voice and to be aware of your presence in my family, my friends, and, especially, in the Church, my family of faith.

Give me the courage to serve you joyfully and generously, until the day when all people are fully united with you.

Amen.

way, we know that the Church will grow and flourish for many years into the future. In fact, the structure that Jesus established for the Church will remain until the end of time; that is, until God's Kingdom of justice and peace is fully achieved. As members of the Church through our Baptism, we are part of something much greater than ourselves: something that existed long before us and that will endure far after we are gone. ✳

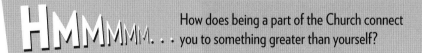

HMMMMMM... How does being a part of the Church connect you to something greater than yourself?

Article 2

The Seeds of the Church: Jesus' Preaching and Ministry

As usual, Alyssa was running a little late as she drove across town to the elementary school to pick up her little sister. When she finally got there, Nadia was bubbling with enthusiasm, as if kindergarten were the Most. Exciting. Thing. Ever.

"We planted seeds! We're making flowers! But it might take awhile. That's what my teacher said."

The sunflower seed in the paper cup! Alyssa remembered doing that when *she* was in kindergarten, almost ten years ago. She had planted her seed in the dirt and then stared at it, waiting for the flower to appear. Her teacher had laughed a little as she explained that the flower was still inside the seed and would take time to grow. So, every day, she had checked her paper cup on the window sill and watered it if the soil was dry. Sure enough, little green sprouts appeared, then a stalk, and then leaves. Alyssa remembered being amazed when, one day, she saw a tiny bud—the beginning of her sunflower that had been there, in the seed, all along.

God the Father's plan for the Church was present since the very beginning of time. This plan came from God's desire to be fully united with us and to redeem us. Yet who would carry out this plan on Earth, within human history? Who would plant the seeds that, one day, would grow into the Church as we know it today? The answer is Jesus Christ, who established the Church through his preaching and ministry, through his selection of the Apostles as the Church's first leaders, and, most especially, through the total gift of himself on the Cross.

© kram9 / Shutterstock.com

Just as everything a beautiful flowering plant needs in order to grow is contained in one tiny seed, God's plan for the Church was present from the very beginning of time.

Jesus Preaches the Good News

Jesus' preaching of the Good News of God's love and salvation established the Church. Jesus knew that he would not always be physically present in an ordinary manner with his followers. So, in accordance with God's plan, he focused his earthly ministry on establishing the Church that would continue his mission after his saving work had been fulfilled through his life, death, Resurrection, and Ascension—the Paschal Mystery. When we celebrate this Mystery in the Eucharist, Jesus is fully present to us, strengthening us as we continue his mission.

Jesus preached through both his words and his actions. He taught his followers how to live in peace with one another by loving their enemies (see Matthew 5:44), extending forgiveness freely (see Luke 6:37), and serving people who are hungry, homeless, sick, or in prison (see Matthew 25:35–26). In his preaching, Jesus particularly emphasized the **Reign (or Kingdom) of God**. He used **parables**, drawn from the everyday experiences of the people of his time, to teach about what the Reign of God is like. For example, he compared the Reign of God to a father who welcomes home a wayward son (see Luke 15:11–32), to a tiny seed that grows into a magnificent tree (see Mark 4:30–32), and to a small amount of yeast that makes a huge batch of dough rise (see Luke 13:20–21). In these and other powerful images, Jesus invited his listeners to share in his mission of making God's Reign a reality. He welcomed all people to participate in this mission by following him: rich and poor, women and men,

In what way do you think the Parable of the Prodigal Son is a parallel for the Kingdom of God?

Reign of God ➤ The reign or rule of God over the hearts of people and, as a consequence of that, the development of a new social order based on unconditional love. The fullness of God's Reign will not be realized until the end of time. Also called the Kingdom of God.

parable ➤ Generally a short story that uses everyday images to communicate religious messages. Jesus used parables frequently in his teaching as a way of presenting the Good News of salvation.

the sick and the well, the proud and the humble.

Jesus also preached through his actions, including his miracles. Whether healing people afflicted with leprosy, blindness, or paralysis (see Matthew 9:1–8, Mark 10:46–52, and Luke 17:11–19), raising the dead (see Matthew 9:18–26; Mark 5:21–43; Luke 7:11–15, 8:40–56; and John 11:1–44), feeding a crowd (see Matthew 14:15–21), or calming a storm (see Mark 4:35–41), Jesus demonstrated his care and concern, his authority, and his willingness to put his teachings into action. His miracles both proclaimed and began a time in which the ancient prophecy of Isaiah would be fulfilled:

> The spirit of the Lord GOD is upon me,
>> because the LORD has anointed me;
> He has sent me to bring Good News to the afflicted,
>> to bind up the brokenhearted,
> To proclaim liberty to the captives,
>> release to the prisoners,
> To announce a year of favor from the LORD.
>
> (Isaiah 61:1–2)

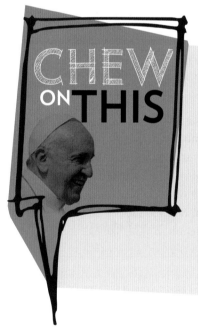

Today too, as always, the Lord needs you, young people, for his Church. My friends, the Lord needs you! Today too, he is calling each of you to follow him in his Church and to be missionaries. The Lord is calling you today! Not the masses, but you, and you, and you, each one of you. Listen to what he is saying to you in your heart. ("Apostolic Journey to Rio De Janeiro on the Occasion of the XXVIII World Youth Day," July 27, 2013)

Jesus Chooses the Apostles

Have you ever worked on a group project for class and been frustrated by a lack of leadership? Everyone might want to work to get a good grade on the project, but, without a leader, it can be hard to get the project organized. If one or two students in the group take on this leadership role, they can make a to-do list, figure out deadlines for each part of the project, and arrange times when the whole group can meet together. The result can be a much smoother, less frustrating process—and maybe even a better grade!

© wavebreakmedia / Shutterstock.com

When trying to work on a project or carry out a plan, good leadership is essential to success. What responsibilities did Jesus task the Apostles with?

Jesus knew that the Church he was establishing would need leadership, and, for that, he chose the Twelve Apostles. The word *apostle* comes from the Greek word *apostolos,* which means someone who is sent out, as a kind of ambassador, with a particular task, message, or mission. So when Jesus chose the Apostles, he sent them out with the power and authority to preach, teach, and heal in his name (see Matthew 10:1–15 and Mark 3:13–19).

The Apostles Jesus chose were ordinary people. Some, like Andrew, Peter, James, and John, were fishermen, which was a common occupation at that time. These were men whom ordinary people could relate to and trust. On the other hand, Matthew was a tax collector. Most people hated tax collectors because they worked for the Roman government, so Jesus' choice of Matthew to be an Apostle must have been very startling, to say the least. Yet, the idea that Jesus would choose someone whom others would find "unworthy" drew interest and curiosity.

The Twelve Apostles	Clues That the Apostles Were Ordinary People
Simon (Peter)	Peter was a fisherman. Known for being impulsive and emotional, he was also dearly loved by Christ. Though his faith in Jesus was deep, he also denied even knowing him during the time of Jesus' arrest.
Andrew	Andrew was Peter's brother and also a fisherman.
James	James, son of Zebedee, was probably a local fisherman when he met Jesus.
John	John, brother of James, was also a fisherman.
Philip	There isn't much information about Philip's background, but it is clear that he was one of the first followers of Jesus. He encouraged others, specifically Nathaniel, to do the same.
Bartholomew	Many people can relate to Bartholomew, who followed along after Philip without really knowing who Jesus was.
Thomas	Thomas was likely born in Galilee, which is mostly farming country. He most likely would have been a tradesman, craftsman, or farmer. He doubted Jesus' Resurrection until he saw and touched Christ's physical wounds.
James (sometimes referred to as James the Less)	We know very little about James. The fact that he is relatively obscure might be his most relatable characteristic. People can relate to him being a rather ordinary follower of Christ.
Matthew	Matthew was a tax collector for the Romans, and would have been looked down on for collaborating against the Jews with the Roman government.
Simon (the Zealot)	Simon was called "the Zealot." He was a member of a group known as political radicals, determined to overthrow the Romans.
Jude	Along with Simon the Zealot and James the less, Jude is among the least-known disciples. He has been characterized as a tenderhearted, gentle man.
Judas Iscariot	Judas was an outsider and stranger to all the other Apostles. Though he betrayed Jesus, we know he regretted his actions because he threw down the silver he had received for identifying Jesus, and committed suicide.

Although Jesus entrusted the Apostles with sharing in his mission and leading the Church, they were not perfect. For example, they sometimes failed to understand Jesus' most basic teachings. James and John, the sons of Zebedee, were overly concerned with rank and privilege (see Mark 10:35–40). Perhaps most notably, Peter, who was specifically chosen by Jesus to be the head of the Apostles, denied that he even knew Jesus at the time when Jesus needed him most: when he was facing death.

If the Apostles, despite their mistakes, imperfections, and even sinfulness, could be chosen by Jesus to serve as leaders of the Church and share in his mission, then so can all of us—so can you! Even if you feel like you have little or nothing to offer the Church, the example of the Apostles teaches us that God accepts and delights in *whatever* we offer. Are you a talented writer, singer, or visual artist? Do you have a gift for putting others at ease with a listening ear and a compassionate heart? Are you great at motivating and organizing people to accomplish something? God accepts each and all of our gifts, our talents, our best efforts, our time, and our very selves, and puts all of this at the service of his kingdom. ✳

HMMMMM. . . What gift or talent can you offer to serve and build up the Church?

Article 3

The Church Is Born: Jesus' Death and Resurrection

During Jesus' lifetime, his preaching and ministry planted the seeds of the Church, according to God's plan. However, the Church was born primarily out of the events that occurred near the *end* of Jesus' earthly life; that is, his total self-giving through his death on the cross and his Resurrection.

Jesus' Death

Jesus' death and Resurrection are the climactic events of the entire Paschal Mystery. By freely accepting his death on the cross, Jesus triumphed over death forever, redeemed us, and made it possible for us to share eternal life with him in Heaven.

All four Gospels tell the story of Jesus' Passion and death on the cross. However, the Gospel of John contains a unique detail that the other Gospels lack. When a Roman soldier puts a sword in Jesus' side, "blood and water flowed out" (John 19:34). This detail is not meant to be gruesome. Rather, its symbolism is meant to teach us something about the Church.

This detail tells us that the Church was born from the side of the crucified Christ. In other words, the Church came about because of the suffering that Jesus freely underwent on the cross for the sake of our salvation. Perhaps in your health or biology class, you have seen a video of a woman giving birth. The birth process is painful, and, when the baby is born, the blood and water that have kept him or her alive for nine months in the womb flow out of the woman's body. In and through this suffering, new life—a new human being—emerges. Similarly, in and through Christ's suffering on the cross, new life—the Church—begins.

© ANURAK PONGPATIMET / Shutterstock.com

How is the birth of a baby a symbol for the birth of the Church?

In all four Gospels, one woman is among those who first receive the Good News of Jesus' Resurrection: Saint Mary Magdalene (first century). Mary Magdalene has sometimes been confused with other Gospel women named Mary, such as Mary of Bethany (the sister of Martha and Lazarus). She has also been mistakenly identified as a prostitute. However, the Gospel witness is clear: Mary Magdalene was her own person. She was among the group of women disciples who accompanied Jesus during his ministry and who used her resources to help provide for him (see Luke 8:3). She was present with Jesus when he died, even though many of the other disciples had run away in fear (see Matthew 27:55–56). And, the Risen Jesus entrusts her with the task of proclaiming the resurrection to the Apostles (see John 20:17–18). For this reason, Saint Thomas Aquinas (1225–1274) gave Mary Magdalene the title "Apostle to the Apostles." Those who think that women have not been important in the life of the Church need look no farther than Mary Magdalene to correct this mistaken assumption. She is truly, in the words of Pope Francis, "the Apostle of the new and greatest hope" ("General Audience," May 17, 2017).

The reference to water and blood also symbolizes two of the sacraments. Water is meant to remind us of **Baptism**, and blood is meant to remind us of the **Eucharist**. Baptism is the sacrament by which we are reborn in Christ and become members of the Church. The Eucharist is the center of life in the Church, because sharing in it unites us with Christ and with the Christian community and reaffirms our commitment to live as Jesus' disciples. By symbolically referring to Baptism and the Eucharist in the account of Jesus' death on the cross, the Gospel of John portrays these sacraments as a sort of "parting gift" from Jesus. They allow us to share in the new, resurrected life that Jesus' death brought about.

Baptism ➤ The first of the Seven Sacraments and one of the three Sacraments of Christian Initiation (the others being Confirmation and the Eucharist) by which one becomes a member of the Church and a new creature in Christ.

Eucharist, the ➤ The celebration of the entire Mass. The term can also refer specifically to the consecrated bread and wine that have become the Body and Blood of Christ.

Jesus' Resurrection

You know from your study of the Gospels that Jesus' death on the cross is not the end of the story. Rather, the story continues with the discovery of the empty tomb, the appearances of the Risen Jesus, and the Apostles' growing faith in the Resurrection.

The Risen Jesus appears to the Apostles (and some other disciples) for forty days after his death. In some of these appearance stories, he shares a meal with them (see Luke 24:30 and John 21:10–13). In others, he teaches them what it means to believe in him (see John 20:24–29). These appearances help the Apostles to understand what being part of the Church involves: gathering to celebrate the Eucharist, recognizing the presence of the Risen Christ in one another, keeping faith even in difficult or confusing times, and sharing the Good News with others.

The appearance stories clarify that Jesus' Resurrection is what makes the Church possible. The presence of the Risen Jesus with the Apostles and disciples empowers them to take on the leadership of the Church. After Jesus ascends to the Father, they are responsible for sharing the Good News, with the reassurance that Jesus will be with them always, "until the end of the age" (Matthew 28:20).

Today, the Risen Christ continues to be present in and with the Church in the power of the Holy Spirit. It is Christ who meets us in Word and sacrament, Christ who unites through the Church's leaders and ministers, and Christ who guides us toward wisdom and holiness. ✳

© Romolo Tavani / iStock.com

A crucifix is a reminder of Christ's suffering and sacrifice for us. But the empty cross is also a powerful symbol, a reminder that Jesus' Resurrection is what makes the Church possible.

HMMMMM... In your own experience, how has suffering sometimes led to new life and hope?

UNIT 1

Article 4
Matthew's Message: Where Two or Three Are Gathered

Do you have a favorite Gospel? At this point, you probably have a good sense of how the four Gospels are similar to one another, as well as the ways in which each Gospel is unique. Those unique elements—the stories, people, and themes that no other Gospel has—sometimes cause people to have a favorite Gospel. For example, they may enjoy the parables of Luke (like the Parable of the Good Samaritan and the Parable of the Prodigal Son), the Christmas story as told by Matthew, or the symbolism and imagery of John (like the vine and the branches or the Good Shepherd).

The Gospel of the Church

Although this course will give you the opportunity to explore Scripture passages from both Testaments, the Gospel of Matthew will receive special emphasis because it is known as "The Gospel of the Church." You may be thinking that *all* four Gospels are Gospels of the Church. In one sense, that's true, because all the Gospels are proclaimed in the Church's liturgy and shape the Church's beliefs, practices, and teachings. However, Matthew is the only Gospel that actually uses the word *church*.

Can you think of two or three characteristics that make the Gospel of Matthew different from the other Gospels?

The Greek word that we translate into English as *church* is *ekklesia*, which means "an assembly or gathering of people." In the Greek translation of the Old Testament, *ekklesia* was used to refer to the assembly of the Chosen People: for example, when they gathered before God at Mount Sinai to receive the Law. The early Christians used this same word to refer to their own gatherings, except these gatherings were of those whom God had called to be Jesus' disciples. In Matthew's Gospel, the word *ekklesia* appears three times: once in chapter 16—in a passage that we'll look at in-depth later in this course—and twice in chapter 18.

Gathered in Christ's Name

In Matthew 18:15–20, Jesus emphasizes the communal nature of the Church. The Church can help us to live in harmony with one another, to resolve disputes, and to repent when we have sinned. The passage ends with a beautiful affirmation of the power of a praying community, as Jesus promises that "Where two or three are gathered in my name, there am I in the midst of them" (verse 20).

Perhaps you have felt Christ's presence in a huge cathedral packed with people, at an all-school liturgy, or at a youth rally with thousands in attendance. Although these can be amazing experiences, this passage assures us that the Church can exist on a smaller, quieter scale as well. All that is needed is two or three people, gathered in faith, and Jesus is there. ✳

© Freedom Studio / Shutterstock.com

The Gospel of Matthew is known as "The Gospel of the Church." Whether we are in a packed church or a small group, Jesus assures us he is there.

MAKE IT SO

Praying together with a friend or two can be a powerful experience that strengthens both our shared faith and our friendship. If you have a friend with whom you would like to pray, invite him or her to join you in your school's chapel one day a week, either in the morning before school or in the afternoon after the school day ends. Read a short Scripture passage together, voice your prayers aloud, and end with the Lord's Prayer or the Hail Mary. Eventually you may invite other friends to join you. Notice how praying together brings you closer to one another and to God. And remember Jesus' promise to be with you, whenever and wherever "two or three are gathered together in my name" (Matthew 18:20).

OVERVIEW of the Gospel of Matthew

- **Time period:** Probably written around AD 75–80.
- **Author:** An unknown Jewish Christian, traditionally the Apostle Matthew.
- **Intended audience:** A Jewish Christian community, likely in Antioch, Syria.
- **Themes:** Jesus as the fulfillment of Old Testament prophecies; Peter as a key leader in the early Church; Jesus commissions his followers to continue his teaching and ministry.
- **Reasons for writing:** It connects the life and teachings of Jesus to important leaders and events of the Old Testament. This Gospel also captures a picture of Jesus as the Son of God and Teacher of the New Law.

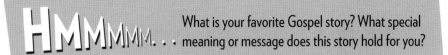

HMMMMM. . . What is your favorite Gospel story? What special meaning or message does this story hold for you?

1. Who established the Church according to God's divine purpose and mission?

2. What group of people served as the first leaders of the Church? Which person was foremost among these leaders?

3. Who founded the Catholic Worker movement? What does this movement do?

4. How did Jesus preach the Good News through both his words and actions?

5. How do we know that the Apostles were not perfect? What can we learn from that?

6. What unique detail about Jesus' death on the cross does the Gospel of John contain? What two things can we learn about the Church from this detail?

7. In all four Gospels, who is among those who first receive the Good News of Jesus' Resurrection? Why is this important?

8. What does the Greek word *ekklesia* mean? What is the significance of this word in Matthew's Gospel?

ART STUDY

THE CHURCH

1. How does this image represent the preaching and ministry of Jesus?
2. What is the significance of having so many people featured in this artwork?
3. Where do you think you might find yourself in this painting? Why?

CHAPTER 2

Animated by the Holy Spirit: The Church Grows and Flourishes

HOW HAS THE CHURCH KEPT GOING ALL THESE YEARS?

SNAPSHOT

Article 5   Page 31
The Holy Spirit Is Sent: Pentecost
• Pre-read: Acts of the Apostles 2:1–41

Article 6   Page 35
The Holy Spirit Sustains: The Early Church
• Pre-read: Acts of the Apostles 7:54–8:3, 9:1–22, and 15:1–35

Article 7   Page 40
The Holy Spirit Sanctifies: The Church Today
• Pre-read: Romans 8:22–27

Article 8   Page 43
Focus on Pope Francis: "The Joy of Love"
• Pre-read: "The Joy of Love," paragraphs 1–7, 86–88, and 325

Article 5
The Holy Spirit Is Sent: Pentecost

Do you have friends you trust 100 percent? Friends who are always available for you and who would do anything to help you? If you are lucky enough to have friends like these, you know that if they make you a promise, you can trust them to follow through and keep that promise. Faithful friends won't disappoint you.

During his earthly life and later when he appeared to the disciples after his Resurrection, Jesus promised to be with them always, and to send them the Holy Spirit. The Holy Spirit would be their "Advocate" (John 14:26), strengthening them to continue Jesus' mission and empowering them to witness to the Gospel, even "to the ends of the earth" (Acts 1:8). Like a good friend who always keep his word, Jesus is faithful to this promise, sending the Holy Spirit upon the disciples at **Pentecost**.

© Renata Sedmakova / Shutterstock.com

Pentecost

Fifty days after the first Easter Sunday, the Holy Spirit fully revealed the Church, which had been eternally planned by God the Father and established by Jesus Christ. The Acts of the Apostles uses two dramatic images to describe the descent of the Holy Spirit at Pentecost: wind and fire.

Advocate, Comforter, Helper, Paraclete . . . These are all names for the Holy Spirit, who was sent by Jesus to the Apostles on Pentecost to strengthen them and empower them to witness to the Gospel.

Pentecost ➤ The fiftieth day following Easter, which commemorates the descent of the Holy Spirit on the Apostles and disciples.

Think about wind for a moment. We cannot see it directly, but we can notice its effects. Whether a gentle breeze that refreshes us on a warm afternoon or a strong gust that makes us want to get inside as quickly as possible, wind leaves powerful effects in its path. This makes it a fitting image for the Holy Spirit. The "strong, driving wind" (Acts 2:2) that accompanied the outpouring of the Spirit reminds us of the Holy Spirit's power that sweeps away our sinfulness, stubbornness, and fear, giving us holiness, reverence, and courage.

Now, think about fire, which, like wind, is powerful. Fire provides warmth and comfort, causes change, and creates energy. Without it, we'd be stuck taking cold showers, eating raw food, and shivering all winter! Fire is also sometimes used as a metaphor. For example, when we say that someone is "on fire," we mean that he or she is passionate about that topic and committed to taking action. Similarly, the tongues of fire that came to rest on the disciples symbolize the Spirit's transformative energy. Once touched by and filled with that energy the disciples begin to speak in various languages. Therefore all those people from many nations who were gathered in Jerusalem heard the Gospel proclaimed to them in a way that they could understand. The global spread of the Gospel message, and of the Church, had truly begun!

Peter's Preaching

Some of those gathered in Jerusalem on that first Pentecost Sunday were amazed by what they heard and saw. Others were simply confused. Still others thought that the only possible explanation for all the commotion was that the disciples were drunk! In an effort to clarify what is happening, Peter addresses the crowd in an enthusiastic and powerful speech.

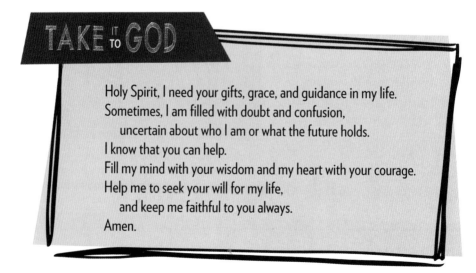

TAKE IT TO GOD

Holy Spirit, I need your gifts, grace, and guidance in my life.
Sometimes, I am filled with doubt and confusion,
    uncertain about who I am or what the future holds.
I know that you can help.
Fill my mind with your wisdom and my heart with your courage.
Help me to seek your will for my life,
    and keep me faithful to you always.
Amen.

What are some clues that the Apostles had experienced the transformative power of the Holy Spirit?

After declaring that the disciples cannot possibly be drunk, because it is only 9 a.m., Peter preaches about the Old Testament prophecies that have been fulfilled by Jesus' Paschal Mystery. He concludes with this compelling statement of Christian faith: "Therefore let the whole house of Israel know for certain that God has made him both Lord and Messiah, this Jesus whom you crucified" (Acts 2:36). The forcefulness of Peter's words convinces many people in the crowd, moving them to faith. In fact, three thousand people were baptized that very day!

Living in the Power of the Holy Spirit

Jasmine was assembling bagged lunches faster than she ever had in her life. Sandwich, apple, and candy bar into the brown bag. Sandwich, apple, candy bar. Over and over again. And the sandwiches just kept coming! When she signed up for this service project, it had sounded fun, but now she was getting a little tired of sandwiches, apples, and candy bars.

Finally, all the lunches were made. Her campus minister, Ms. Gomez, gathered the whole group together and led them in prayer before they went out to deliver lunches to people in need. As she stood in a circle with her classmates, listening to Ms. Gomez pray for the people they were about to meet, Jasmine had a moment to catch her breath and reflect. As she paused to pray, she felt the presence of the Holy Spirit in her heart and with the group. She was certainly proud of how she and her classmates were choosing to spend their Saturday morning. She believed, without a doubt, that it was the Holy Spirit who had given all of them the motivation and courage to actually show up and do this work. With the Holy Spirit's power and strength behind them, they were making a real difference for many poor and hungry people in her city.

As the prayer ended with a chorus of "Amen," Jasmine and her classmates each grabbed a box of lunches and headed out to the van. The promises that Jesus made to the Apostles and to his first disciples are the same promises that he makes to us: to be with us always, in and through the power of the Spirit. The next time you pray, serve those in need, or participate in the Sacraments of the Church, try to be aware of the Holy Spirit's presence with you, as Jasmine was, and resolve to open yourself more and more to the Spirit's gifts. ✳

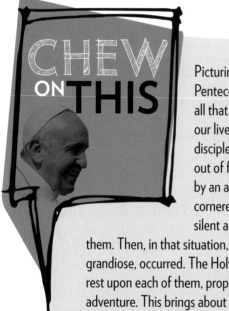

CHEW ON THIS

Picturing [the Apostles on the day of Pentecost] can help us come to appreciate all that God dreams of accomplishing in our lives, in us and with us. That day, the disciples were together behind locked doors, out of fear. They felt threatened, surrounded by an atmosphere of persecution that had cornered them in a little room and left them silent and paralyzed. Fear had taken hold of them. Then, in that situation, something spectacular, something grandiose, occurred. The Holy Spirit and tongues as of fire came to rest upon each of them, propelling them towards an undreamt-of adventure. This brings about a total change! ("Apostolic Journey of His Holiness Pope Francis to Poland on the Occasion of the XXXI World Youth Day," July 30, 2016)

HMMMM. . .

What image would you use to symbolize the Holy Spirit? Why?

Article 6
The Holy Spirit Sustains: The Early Church

When Franco was about to graduate from eighth grade, his parents shared some surprising news with him. Their family would be moving from their small town in upstate New York, where Franco had lived his entire life, to New York City, about six hours away by car. His mom had gotten a job teaching at a university there, so they would need to move over the summer. Franco would be going to high school without any of the friends he had known since kindergarten. He felt crushed.

As the family prepared for the move, there was so much for Franco to do. Pack up his belongings for the movers, give away things that he wasn't going to take with him, say goodbye to his friends, and find out about the new school he'd be attending. One day, in the midst of all this busyness, Franco realized that he was actually excited about all the changes that were about to happen. He was still sad and even a little angry, knowing that he would miss his friends and the place that had been home to him for so long. But he was also eager to see what it would be like to live in New York City. Perhaps he would grow and change in ways that he couldn't even imagine. When the day finally came to get in the car and leave his old life behind, he felt ready.

© Tupungato / Shutterstock.com

Have you ever experienced both excitement and uncertainty at the same time? How can these types of experiences help us to grow?

The Growth of the Early Church

In the months and years following Jesus' death and Resurrection, the early Church experienced a mix of excitement, growth, turmoil, and uncertainty similar to what Franco felt as he prepared for his move. Jesus' commissioning of the Apostles (see Matthew 28:16–18) is a public recognition that they will be continuing his mission. This event, called the Great Commission, recognizes the Church's mission to share the Good News of Christ with the whole world. Those who believe were to be baptized, adding to the numbers of those who profess their faith in Christ. Together with the sending of the Holy Spirit at Pentecost, the Great Commission inspired the Apostles' mission and sustained the Church as it grew and flourished.

Another key event in the early Church's expansion was the conversion of Saint Paul (d. c. 67). Paul had persecuted Christians with great determination, even to the point of supporting the execution of Saint Stephen (d. 33). Then he encountered the Risen Lord Jesus while traveling on the road from Jerusalem to Damascus. As a result, he was baptized and became one of the early Church's great Apostles. His missionary journeys throughout the Mediterranean world contributed greatly to the spread of the Gospel, especially to **Gentile** (non-Jewish) communities.

© Sergey Kohl / Shutterstock.com

After his dramatic conversion experience, Saint Paul spread the Gospel to many communities, especially Gentile communities. He is sometimes known as the Apostle to the Gentiles.

Gentile ➤ A non-Jewish person. In Sacred Scripture, the Gentiles were the uncircumcised, those who did not honor the God of the Torah. Saint Paul and other evangelists reached out to the Gentiles, baptizing them into the family of God.

UNIT 1

CATHOLICS **MAKING** A DIFFERENCE

Servant of God Fr. Augustine (Augustus) Tolton was born into slavery in 1854 in Missouri. After his father died serving in the Union Army during the Civil War, Tolton escaped from slavery with his mother and three siblings. The family made their way north to Illinois, settling in Quincy.

As a teen, he began to feel called to the priesthood, but there was just one problem: no seminary in the United States would accept an African American student. Tolton saved his money until he had earned enough to travel to Rome and enroll in the seminary there. After his ordination in 1866, Father Tolton returned to serve at St. Joseph Parish in his adopted hometown of Quincy. He was met with suspicion both from parishioners and from his brother priests and was frequently subjected to racial slurs and discrimination. Later, he moved to Chicago, where he ministered to that city's large African American community until his death in 1897. In 2010, the Archdiocese of Chicago officially opened the process to seek canonization for Augustine Tolton. The first African American priest could very well become the first African American saint.

Challenges and Conflicts

The Church also encountered many challenges and conflicts in its early years. Some of these challenges came from the Roman authorities, while others came from within the Jewish community.

One major challenge that the early Church faced was persecution. Because neither the Roman nor Jewish authorities fully accepted the Church, they often arrested those who professed belief in Jesus Christ. Of these, some became martyrs. These believers were so deeply committed to Jesus that they were willing to die rather than give up their faith in him. Saint James (d. first century), who was "killed by the sword" (Acts 12:2) on the orders of King Herod, is believed to have been the first of the Twelve Apostles to be martyred.

---

martyr ➤ A person who voluntarily suffers death because of his or her beliefs. The Church has canonized many martyrs as saints.

Saint Stephen is another important example of an early Church martyr. The Acts of the Apostles describes Saint Stephen as "filled with grace and power" and as capable of "working great wonders and signs among the people" (Acts 6:8). He was also a talented and captivating speaker, able to preach about God's faithful love with great power and conviction. When an angry crowd stoned him to death, his final words reflected his deep faith. First, he prayed, "Lord Jesus, receive my spirit" (Acts 7:59). Then, as Jesus did from the cross (see Luke 23:34), he forgave those who killed him: "Lord, do not hold this sin against them" (Acts 7:60).

Another challenge that the early Church confronted was how to manage the increasing numbers of Gentile males who were becoming part of the Church through Baptism. Recall from your study of the Old Testament that **circumcision** was the sign of God's covenant with the Jewish People. Some early Christians believed that Gentiles who wished to become Christian had to first be circumcised and *then* be baptized. You can imagine that Gentile men were not exactly thrilled by this idea! These same early Christians also thought that Gentile converts to Christianity should follow all the laws of the Old Testament, including the Jewish dietary laws.

Due in great part to the testimony of Paul and Barnabas at the Council of Jerusalem, it was determined that Gentiles would not have to be circumcised or follow the restrictive dietary laws of Judaism in order to become followers of Jesus.

Because there was disagreement on how to handle all these questions related to Gentile converts, Paul and Barnabas traveled to Jerusalem in order to consult the Apostles. At this meeting, which became known as the Council of Jerusalem, the Apostles determined that requiring circumcision and adherence to the Old Testament's dietary laws would be an unnecessary burden for Gentiles. In addition, they

---

circumcision ➤ The act, required by Jewish Law, of removing the foreskin of the penis. Since the time of Abraham, it has been a sign of God's covenant relationship with the Jewish People.

affirmed that God made no distinction between Jewish and Gentile converts to Christianity, for both had received the Holy Spirit and both had been "saved through the grace of the Lord Jesus" (Acts 15:11). So Gentiles wishing to convert to Christianity needed only to avoid **idolatry** and unlawful marriages. They didn't need to worry about circumcision or the dietary laws. The Apostles' authority in resolving this complex question reflects their essential role as recognized leaders in the early Church.

For a moment, imagine what it might have been like to be a Christian in the Church's early years. In some places, it would have been dangerous, with the risk of persecution and even martyrdom always looming as a possibility. It would have been challenging, with questions and problems arising that no one had ever thought about before. But, it also would have been exciting, as a group of people—initially small, but ever growing—committed themselves wholeheartedly to continuing the mission of Jesus, in the power of the Holy Spirit. Such passionate, faithful commitment has enabled the Church both to survive and to thrive for many centuries. ✳

OVERVIEW of the Acts of the Apostles

- **Time period:** Written around AD 80; describes events that occurred around AD 30–65.
- **Author:** Often identified as Luke, who also wrote the Gospel of Luke.
- **Intended audience:** Gentile Christians.
- **Themes and events:** Pentecost; the spread of the Gospel throughout the Mediterranean world to both Jews and Gentiles; the Jerusalem Council; Paul's conversion and missionary journeys.
- **Reasons for writing:** Acts of the Apostles is the second half of Luke's two-volume work. It was written to demonstrate how Christianity moved beyond Jewish circles, and how Christ became the light of the world for the Gentiles.

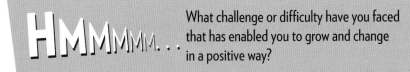

HMMMMM. . . What challenge or difficulty have you faced that has enabled you to grow and change in a positive way?

idolatry ➤ The worship of other beings, creatures, or material goods in a way that is fitting for God alone.

Article 7
The Holy Spirit Sanctifies: The Church Today

Today, the Holy Spirit continues to be present in and through the entire Church. Through the Holy Spirit, Christ **sanctifies**—that is, makes holy the Church. This does not mean that the members of the Church are perfect. If people had to be perfect to be part of the Church, the Church would be very small indeed! Rather, it means that through the Church, we are able to become holy by being fully united both with God and with all of our brothers and sisters in faith. We become more holy when we receive the Holy Spirit in the sacraments. The gifts or charisms of the Holy Spirit inspire us to live a moral life.

The Spirit's Gifts

One way the Holy Spirit sanctifies the Church is by imparting gifts that help the members of the Church to fulfill the mission of faithfully proclaiming the Gospel. You have probably learned about the Gifts of the Holy Spirit in other courses, especially if you have received (or are preparing to receive) the Sacrament of Confirmation. As a reminder, these gifts are Wisdom, Understanding, Knowledge, Counsel (Right Judgment), Fortitude (Courage), Piety (Reverence), and Fear of the Lord (Wonder and Awe). The Holy Spirit pours out these gifts upon the entire Church, in order to call us to greater holiness and to bind us together in unity.

In addition, the Holy Spirit gives special graces, or **charisms**, to individual Christians or groups to benefit and build up the entire Church. Charisms are one of the ways God continues to enter the world through our cooperation. When we use the charisms we are gifted with, they benefit other people. Members of **religious communities**, who commit themselves to a particular charism, are a great example of this. The Christian Brothers operate schools—often focused on serving poor and disadvantaged students—throughout the world. The Sisters of Mercy focus on direct service in the areas of health care, housing, and education, and on advocacy around issues of environmental justice and the empowerment of women. The Holy Spirit bestows on some people the charismatic gifts of exercising various ministerial and leadership

---

sanctify ➤ To purify or make holy.

charism ➤ A special grace of the Holy Spirit given to an individual Christian or community, for the benefit and building up of the entire Church.

religious communities ➤ A group of men or women religious who are joined by a common charism.

roles within the Church. All of these many and varied Gifts of the Holy Spirit work together to support the Church's mission of faithfully proclaiming the truth of the Gospel, for the salvation of the world.

The Christian Brothers were founded in France by a priest named John Baptist de La Salle (1651–1719). Over 99,000 young people are enrolled in Lasallian schools in the United States and Canada today.

MAKE IT SO

One of the seven Gifts of the Holy Spirit is Fortitude, also called Courage. Being courageous doesn't mean that we are not afraid! Rather, it means that we act with confidence and grace, doing what we know to be right *even if* we are afraid. What are some situations in your own life in which the Spirit's courage could come in handy?

- standing up for someone who is being bullied
- reaching out to a student who is having trouble making friends
- refusing to cheat on a test or copy homework
- serving at a homeless shelter in a neighborhood where you and your friends don't usually hang out

Ask the Holy Spirit to show you other ways in which you can try to cultivate the gift of courage. And know that your courageous words and actions enrich and build up the entire Church.

The Gifts of the Holy Spirit **Saint Thomas Aquinas** **(1225–1274)**	The Bible's Fruits of the Holy Spirit **Galatians** **5:22–23**	The Traditional Fruits of the Holy Spirit **2 Corinthians 6:6–7** **Ephesians 4:2, 5:9** **2 Peter 1:5–7**	Charisms or Spiritual Gifts **1 Corinthians 12:28**
Wisdom	Love	Charity	Apostle
Understanding	Joy	Joy	Prophet
Counsel	Peace	Peace	Teacher
Strength	Patience	Patience	Mighty Deeds / Miracles
Knowledge	Kindness	Kindness	Gifts of Healings
Fear of the Lord	Generosity	Goodness	Assistance
Piety	Faithfulness	Long Suffering	Administration
	Gentleness	Humility	Tongues

The Spirit Helps Us to Pray

Another way the Holy Spirit helps us grow in holiness is by assisting us in prayer. Have you ever tried to pray, but you just couldn't find the words? Maybe you were too sad or upset to think clearly, or maybe you felt like no words could capture what you were feeling inside. In Saint Paul's Letter to the Romans, he addresses this very problem. When we don't know how to pray, Saint Paul assures us that "the Spirit too comes to the aid of our weakness . . . the Spirit itself intercedes with inexpressible groanings" (Romans 8:26). In other words, the Holy Spirit sanctifies us by helping us to pray. The Holy Spirit gives us the words to reach out to God in our need, and the Holy Spirit opens our hearts so that we might listen attentively to God's voice.

The next time you are struggling to pray, remember Saint Paul's reassurance. Allow the Spirit to pray within you, strengthening your faith and leading you along the path of holiness. ✳

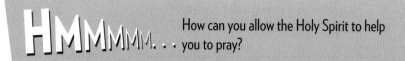

HMMMMM. . . How can you allow the Holy Spirit to help you to pray?

Article 8
Focus on Pope Francis: "The Joy of Love"

On March 13, 2013, white smoke poured from the chimney atop the Sistine Chapel in Vatican City. *Habemus Papam!* We have a pope! Soon after, the world learned that Cardinal Jorge Mario Bergoglio, then the archbishop of Buenos Aries, Argentina, had been elected as the 266th **Pope** and would take the name Francis in honor of Saint Francis of Assisi (c. 1181–1226). The new Pope greeted the tens of thou-sands of people gathered in Saint Peter's Square with a simple "good eve-ning" and with a request to pray both for him and for his predecessor, Pope Benedict XVI. With that, a new era in the Church's long history began.

Pope Francis teaches, leads, and proclaims the Gospel message in many ways, including apostolic exhortations.

The Pope serves as the **Bishop** of the **Diocese** of Rome. However, as the successor of the Apostle Peter, he has supreme authority and jurisdiction over the whole Church throughout the world. The Pope's ministry of teaching and leadership unites the Church, bearing witness to Jesus' desire that his followers "may all be one" (John 17:21).

Pope ➤ A title used by the Bishop of Rome, who is the successor of Saint Peter and shep-herd of the Universal Church.

bishop ➤ One who has received the fullness of the Sacrament of Holy Orders and is a successor to the Apostles.

diocese ➤ Also known as a "particular" or "local" Church, the regional community of believers, who commonly gather in parishes, under the leadership of a bishop. At times, a diocese is determined not on the basis of geography but on the basis of language or rite.

© neneo / Shutterstock.com

One of the ways the Pope teaches, leads, and proclaims the Gospel is by issuing documents and statements about various topics that he believes to be important for both the Church and the wider world. This book will give you the opportunity to explore five such documents that Pope Francis has issued during his time in this office. We'll begin with "The Joy of Love" (*"Amoris Laetitia"*), which Pope Francis published as an **apostolic exhortation** following two meetings (called **synods**) that he held with other bishops to discuss issues and topics related to family life.

"The Joy of Love"

We can learn a lot about this document simply from its title. The title emphasizes that God has intended our families to be loving and joyful communities. Think of the many ways in which the members of your own family show love for one another. Every family is different, but maybe your own list would include some or all of these expressions of love:

- listening patiently
- freely seeking and offering forgiveness
- preparing meals
- helping with household tasks
- supporting one another in difficult times
- welcoming new members to the family—perhaps a new baby, or perhaps a grandparent who has moved in
- putting others' needs before your own

What are some ways you can contribute to your family or community by being more loving and joyful?

apostolic exhortation ➤ One of several types of documents that are written by the Pope. Its purpose is not to define doctrine, but to encourage people in some aspect of living the faith.

synod ➤ A group of bishops from around the world who, at the Pope's invitation, gather in Rome to discuss with him matters of concern to the Universal Church.

Notice that Pope Francis didn't title this document the *burden* of love, or the *responsibility* of love, but, rather the *joy* of love. Loving one another, especially within the context of the family, should make us deeply and genuinely happy. The family is sometimes even called the "domestic Church," helping us to understand that what is true for the Church is also true for the family. Families should be a place in which we meet the love of God, through the love that family members show one another. And through their involvement in church, school, and community, families share the love of God with the world.

I DIDN'T KNOW THAT!

How does the Pope get to be Pope? When a pope passes away or retires from his ministry, all the members of the worldwide College of Cardinals—the group from whom the next pope will be chosen—gather at the Vatican, in Rome, for a special meeting called a conclave. During the conclave, all cardinals who are below the age of eighty meet together in the Sistine Chapel. Under the guidance of the Holy Spirit, they vote by secret ballot on who they believe the next pope should be. They must keep voting until one cardinal gets a two-thirds majority.

After each vote, the ballots are counted and then burned, in order to ensure that the voting remains secret. If no one has gotten a two-thirds majority, then black smoke comes out of the chimney atop the Sistine Chapel, and the cardinals continue voting. When the cardinals

finally succeed in their mission, white smoke comes out of the chimney (chemicals are added to the ballots to make the smoke white). This, along with the bells of Saint Peter's Basilica ringing, signals that a new pope has been elected.

The Complexity of Families

In tackling the topic of family life, Pope Francis not only affirms the Church's teachings on marriage and family but also offers practical advice for all those seeking to live faithfully as a spouse, a parent, a child, a sibling, a cousin, an in-law, and in all the other relationships that make up a family. He gives a lot of attention to Scripture, especially to the example of the Holy Family (Jesus, Mary, and Joseph) and to Saint Paul's famous meditation on love, found in First Corinthians 13:1–13.

Throughout the document, Pope Francis emphasizes the diverse and complex circumstances of family life today. For example, he acknowledges the ways in which poverty, unemployment, and violence can have an impact on families, causing stress and suffering. He recognizes the realities of divorce,

© Olivia Storch / Saint Mary's Press

Pope Francis does not shy away from difficult topics, such as the complexities of families. Acknowledging that poverty, violence, and lack of proper education have a negative impact on children is something no pope has done before.

single parenthood, and homosexuality. He denounces sexism and other forms of injustice that prevent each member of a family from reaching his or her full, God-given potential. In discussing the Church's role in serving and supporting families, particularly those touched by these and other struggles, Pope Francis states in "The Pastoral Challenges of the Family in the Context of Evangelization" that "the Church must accompany with attention and care the weakest of her children, who show signs of a wounded and troubled love, by restoring in them hope and confidence, like the beacon of a lighthouse in a port or a torch carried among the people to enlighten those who have lost their way or who are in the midst of a storm" (number 28).

Perhaps one of the most striking images in "The Joy of Love" is its description of the Church as a "family of families" (number 87). The Church is the family of God, made up of many families, each one unique and each one blessed. Pope Francis continues by reflecting that "the Church is good for the family, and the family is good for the Church" (number 87). The Church accompanies families with pastoral guidance and authentic teaching, while families build up the Church through generous service and self-sacrificial love. No family is perfect, but *every* family has some role to play in proclaiming the Good News of salvation in both word and deed. ✳

HMMMMM. . .

If you could ask Pope Francis one question about his ministry as the Pope, what would you ask, and why?

1. What happened to the Apostles on Pentecost?

2. What two symbols does the Acts of the Apostles use to describe the descent of the Holy Spirit?

3. What was the significance of Saint Paul's conversion to Christianity?

4. What was decided at the Council of Jerusalem regarding Gentile converts?

5. What challenge did Servant of God Fr. Augustine Tolton face in his effort to follow God's call to be a priest?

6. What three types of gifts does the Holy Spirit give to the Church?

7. What is the focus of the apostolic exhortation "The Joy of Love"? What important message is contained in this document's title?

8. What is a conclave?

SYMBOLS OF THE HOLY SPIRIT

1. What symbols of the Holy Spirit's presence do you see? What might these symbols mean?

2. Which of these symbols do you think best captures the Holy Spirit's power? Why?

3. Which of these symbols do you find to be most appealing or comforting? Why?

UNIT 1 HIGHLIGHTS

CHAPTER 1 Founded by Christ:
The Church Begins

The Development of the Family of God

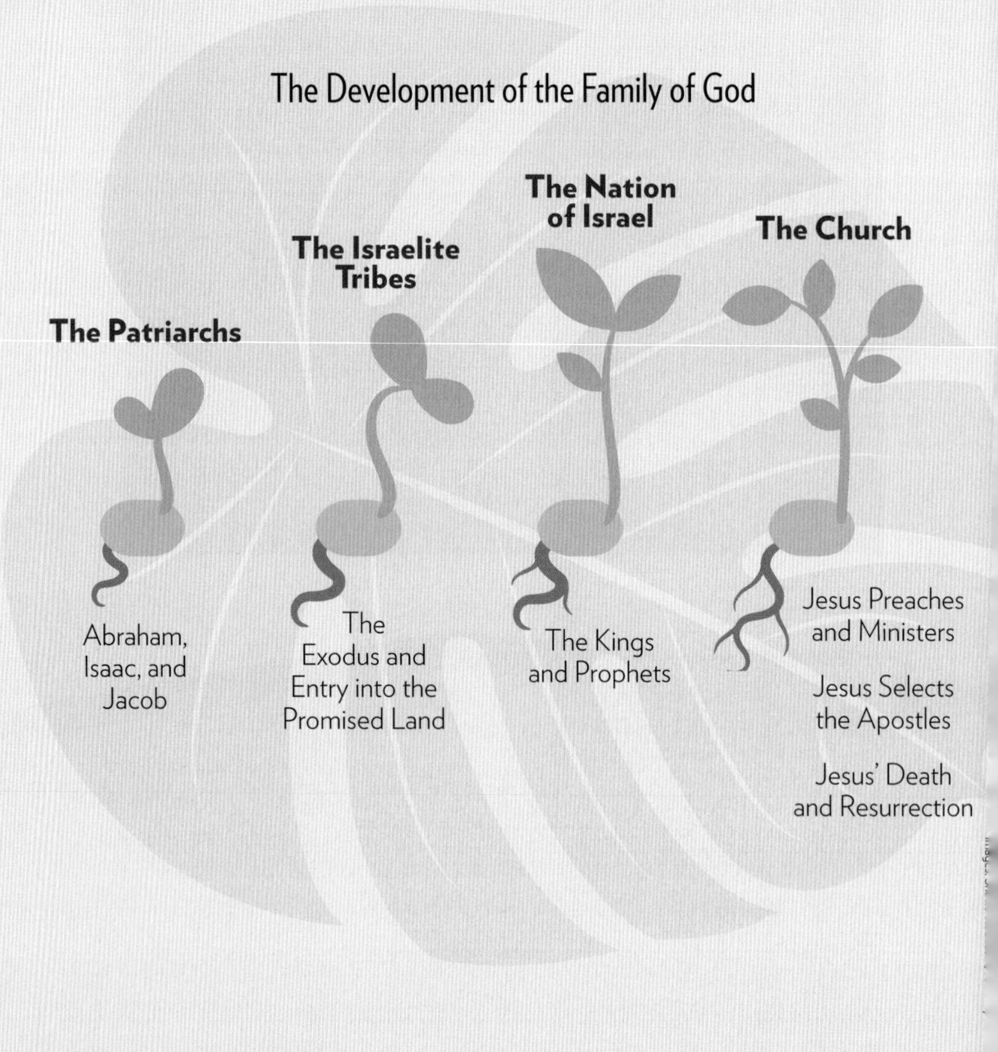

The Patriarchs

**The Israelite
Tribes**

**The Nation
of Israel**

The Church

Abraham,
Isaac, and
Jacob

The
Exodus and
Entry into the
Promised Land

The Kings
and Prophets

Jesus Preaches
and Ministers

Jesus Selects
the Apostles

Jesus' Death
and Resurrection

CHAPTER 2   Animated by the Holy Spirit:
The Church Grows and Flourishes

The Holy Spirit Sustains

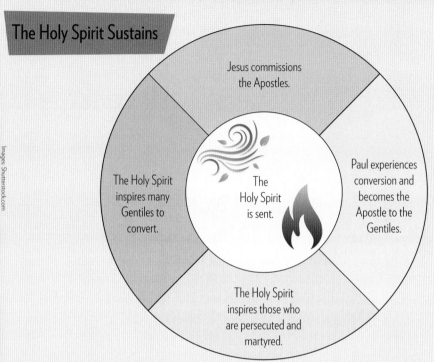

Jesus commissions
the Apostles.

The
Holy Spirit
is sent.

Paul experiences
conversion and
becomes the
Apostle to the
Gentiles.

The Holy Spirit
inspires many
Gentiles to
convert.

The Holy Spirit
inspires those who
are persecuted and
martyred.

Images: Shutterstock.com

Gifts of the Holy Spirit

Wisdom

Understanding

Knowledge

Counsel
(Right Judgment)

Fortitude
(Courage)

Piety
(Reverence)

Fear of the Lord
(Wonder and Awe)

Fruits of the Holy Spirit

Love

Joy

Peace

Patience

Kindness

Generosity

Faithfulness

Gentleness

Self-Control

Charisms (Spiritual Gifts)

Apostle

Prophet

Teacher

Mighty Deeds/
Miracles

Gifts of Healing

Assistance

Administration

Tongues

UNIT 1
BRING IT HOME

WHAT DOES THE CHURCH HAVE TO DO WITH GOD?

FOCUS QUESTIONS

CHAPTER 1   How did the Church get started?

CHAPTER 2   How has the Church kept going all these years?

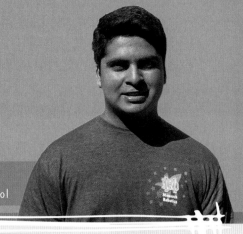

RICHARD
Mater Dei High School

After reading the unit, I think I stopped a little short. Jesus planted the seeds of the Church with the Apostles. They traveled far to spread the Good News of salvation. But the unit also focuses on part of the Gospel of Matthew where Jesus promieses that "where two or three are gathered in my name, there am I in the midst of them" (18:20). So, I really think that God also established the Church so people can be together, to worship and pray and to support one another.

REFLECT

Take some time to read and reflect on the unit and chapter focus questions listed on the facing page.

- What question or section did you identify most closely with?

- What did you find within the unit that was comforting or challenging?

UNIT 2
The Marks of the Church

WHY DOES THE CHURCH MATTER?

LOOKING AHEAD

CHAPTER 3 Page 56
The Church Is One

CHAPTER 4 Page 80
The Church Is Holy

CHAPTER 5 Page 102
The Church Is Catholic

CHAPTER 6 Page 120
The Church Is Apostolic

UNIT 2

I think the Church matters because it welcomes everyone, whether you have a lot of money to contribute or are at a low point in your life. I have a friend who went to Catholic school with me from third through eighth grade. He wasn't Catholic, but he had an "Aha!" moment in fourth grade, and he decided to convert. He has had such an affirming experience that he wants to share it with everyone he knows.

OLIVIA
New Smyrna Beach
High School

CHAPTER 3
The Church Is One

HOW CAN MEMBERS OF THE CHURCH BE UNITED ALL AROUND THE WORLD?

SNAPSHOT

Article 9 Page 57
The Church: Willed by God to Be One
- Pre-read: 1 Corinthians 12:1–13, Galatians 3:23–29, Ephesians 4:1–6

Article 10 Page 61
One in Faith

Article 11 Page 65
One in Worship

Article 12 Page 69
One in Leadership and Witness
- Pre-read: John 17:20–26

Article 13 Page 72
Divisions, Wounds, and Brokenness

Article 9
The Church: Willed by God to Be One

"I believe in one, holy, catholic, and apostolic Church." You have probably prayed these familiar words hundreds of times during the Nicene Creed at Mass. Have you ever paused to wonder what that part of the Creed means? Or why it's important enough even to be in the Creed?

One, Holy, Catholic, and Apostolic are known as the **Marks of the Church**—attributes or qualities that Jesus shares with the Church through the power of the Holy Spirit. When introducing yourself to new people, you may choose several traits from many that could describe you. You might say that you are shy, you like comedies, your favorite drink is lemonade, and that you post most often on Instagram. But the four Marks of the Church are not random characteristics; rather, they are essential, interconnected features of the Church and of her mission. Although the Church already possesses these marks, Jesus calls us, as members of the Church, to seek to live them out more fully and completely.

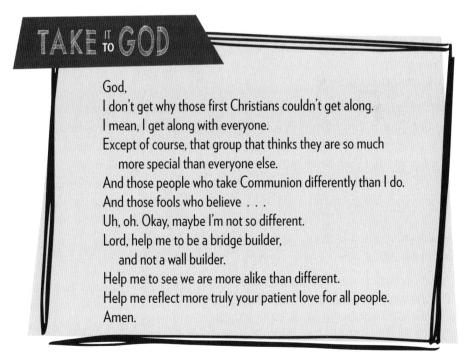

TAKE IT TO GOD

God,
I don't get why those first Christians couldn't get along.
I mean, I get along with everyone.
Except of course, that group that thinks they are so much
    more special than everyone else.
And those people who take Communion differently than I do.
And those fools who believe . . .
Uh, oh. Okay, maybe I'm not so different.
Lord, help me to be a bridge builder,
    and not a wall builder.
Help me to see we are more alike than different.
Help me reflect more truly your patient love for all people.
Amen.

Marks of the Church ➤ The four essential features or characteristics of the Church: One, Holy, Catholic (universal), and Apostolic.

UNIT 2

The foundation of all four marks is the Church's unity as one Body of Christ. We can begin by reflecting on how the Church's unity is rooted in the very nature of God.

Sources of the Church's Unity

First and foremost, the source of the Church's unity is the unity of the three Divine Persons of the **Blessed Trinity**, the one, eternal God who is Father, Son, and Holy Spirit.

Second, the Church is united because of the saving work of Jesus Christ. His life, death, and Resurrection restored the unity of all humanity that had once been lost by sin.

The Blessed Trinity is the primary source of the Church's unity.

Last, the Church is one in and through the power of the Holy Spirit, present in the hearts of all those who believe throughout the world. We can rightly say that the Church is united in Jesus Christ through the Holy Spirit, according to the eternal plan of God the Father.

Scripture and Unity

The writings of Saint Paul, found in the New Testament, give us many insights into the Church's unity. In the years following Jesus' death and Resurrection, Paul wrote letters to many early Christian communities. He taught them about God's desire that they be united as one. For example, the community in the city of Corinth (located in modern-day Greece) struggled with competition, division, and disagreement. They argued about who in the community was most important (see 1 Corinthians 1:11–12 and 3:5–7), and they had different opinions about how to pray and worship together (see 1 Corinthians 11:17–22 and 14:26–33).

Trinity (Blessed Trinity) ➤ Often referred to as the Blessed Trinity, the central Christian mystery and dogma that there is one God in three Persons: Father, Son, and Holy Spirit.

In response, Paul reminds them that "there are different kinds of spiritual gifts but the same Spirit; there are different forms of service but the same Lord; there are different workings but the same God who produces all of them in everyone" (1 Corinthians 12:4–6). Paul further tells them that the ultimate source of their unity is their Baptism. Whether they were originally Jews or Greeks (Gentiles), slaves or free people, the Corinthians are now united as one, through the Holy Spirit.

Paul had a unique message for each of the early Christian communities. He urged the Ephesians to look beyond their differences and to focus on their unified identity as God's holy people.

When the community at Ephesus (located in modern-day Turkey) encountered similar problems, Paul instructed them to strive "to preserve the unity of the spirit through the bond of peace: one body and one Spirit . . . one Lord, one faith, one baptism; one God and Father of all" (Ephesians 4:3–6). Paul is inviting the Ephesians to look beyond superficial differences, like how much money someone has, their family background, or their social status. Rather, they should focus on what really matters: their shared identity as God's holy people.

In another letter, Paul gets frustrated when the Galatian community cannot seem to understand and put into practice the message of Christian unity—so much so that he calls them "stupid Galatians!" (Galatians 3:1). Paul is like a parent or teacher whose children or students aren't getting along, and finally he just can't take it anymore! But he still loves the Galatians, and he won't give up on them. So he tries to teach them about the unity that they are called to share with one another and with Christians throughout the world. Again, he roots this unity in Baptism, affirming the equality not only of Jews and Greeks, and not only of slaves and free persons but also of women and men: "There is neither Jew nor Greek, there is neither slave nor free person, there is not male and female; for you are all one in Christ Jesus" (3:28).

Unity in Diversity

Fast-forward almost two thousand years. Today, the Church has spread far beyond the Mediterranean world in which Saint Paul first traveled and preached. The Church exists all over the globe—in nearly every nation and culture on Earth. In fact, the Catholic Church is one of the most culturally, ethnically, linguistically, and liturgically diverse organizations on the planet! Clearly, being "one" does not mean sameness or uniformity. How then, are we "one"? What are the ways in which we are visibly united in the world? The remainder of this chapter will explore three key ways in which the Church, throughout the world, is "one":

- We are one in our faith and belief.
- We are one in our prayer and worship.
- We are one in our leadership and witness.

The chapter will conclude by looking at the ways in which the Church's unity has been harmed at various points in the Church's history. ✳

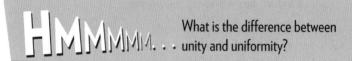

HMMMMMM. . . . What is the difference between unity and uniformity?

Article 10
One in Faith

The Church is united in the profession of one faith that has been passed down to us, over many centuries, from the Apostles. In other words, as members of the Church, we believe and profess the same truths. This unity in faith is perhaps most obvious when we profess the **creed** together at Mass.

The word *creed* comes from the Latin word *credo*, meaning "I believe." If you were to write a personal creed, or set of beliefs, it might include that you believe in being loyal to your friends, respecting all people, loving your family, and living your faith. When we talk about the Church's creed, we are talking about a Profession of Faith: a statement that summarizes the faith of Christians. In previous courses you have been studying these shared beliefs, truths that have been revealed by God through Sacred Scripture and Sacred Tradition. Over the years, the Church has developed many Professions of Faith to express these truths. Some creeds have arisen in response to the needs of a particular time or place, others as the result of an **Ecumenical Council**, and still others at the initiative of the Pope. Among all the creeds, two have a special place in the Church's life: the **Apostles' Creed** and the **Nicene Creed**.

A clear example of unity can be seen when all the members of the congregation profess the creed at Mass.

© Friedrich Stark / Alamy Stock Photo

UNIT 2

Apostles' Creed ➤ A profession of faith or statement of Christian belief; the Apostles' Creed developed from the baptismal creed of the ancient church of Rome and is considered to be a faithful summary of the faith of the Apostles.

creed ➤ An official profession of faith, usually prepared and presented by a council of the Church and used in the Church's liturgy. Based on the Latin *credo*, meaning "I believe."

Ecumenical Council ➤ A gathering of the Church's bishops from around the world convened by the Pope or approved by him to address pressing issues in the Church and in the world.

Nicene Creed ➤ The formal statement or profession of faith commonly recited during the Eucharist.

One Faith, Two Creeds

The Apostles' Creed	The Nicene Creed
Developed from the baptismal creed of the ancient Church of Rome, summarizes the faith of the Apostles.	Developed at the Church's first two Ecumenical Councils: the Council of Nicaea in 325 and the Council of Constantinople in 381.
I believe in God, the Father Almighty, Creator of heaven and earth, and in Jesus Christ, His only Son, our Lord, who was conceived by the Holy Spirit, born of the Virgin Mary, suffered under Pontius Pilate, was crucified, died and was buried; He descended into hell; on the third day He rose again from the dead; He ascended into heaven, and is seated at the right hand of God the Father Almighty; from there He will come to judge the living and the dead. I believe in the Holy Spirit, the Holy Catholic Church, the communion of Saints, the forgiveness of sins, the resurrection of the body, and life everlasting. Amen. (*Roman Missal,* page 547)	I believe in one God, the Father almighty, maker of heaven and earth, of all things visible and invisible. I believe in one Lord Jesus Christ, the Only Begotten Son of God, born of the Father before all ages. God from God, Light from Light, true God from true God, begotten, not made, consubstantial with the Father; through him all things were made. For us men and for our salvation he came down from heaven, and by the Holy Spirit was incarnate of the Virgin Mary, and became man. For our sake he was crucified under Pontius Pilate, he suffered death and was buried, and rose again on the third day in accordance with the Scriptures. He ascended into heaven and is seated at the right hand of the Father. He will come again in glory to judge the living and the dead and his kingdom will have no end. I believe in the Holy Spirit, the Lord, the giver of life, who proceeds from the Father and the Son, who with the Father and the Son is adored and glorified, who has spoken through the prophets. I believe in one, holy, catholic and apostolic Church. I confess one Baptism for the forgiveness of sins and I look forward to the resurrection of the dead and the life of the world to come. Amen. (*Roman Missal,* page 528)

Notice that both creeds contain basic truths about the Father, the Son, and the Holy Spirit, as well as other essential beliefs. Although the Nicene Creed is a bit more detailed than the Apostles' Creed, both summarize the faith that unites us as one Church throughout the world. Either creed can be professed at Mass, although many parishes use the Apostles' Creed during the Lent and Easter seasons, as well as at Masses at which large numbers of young children are present.

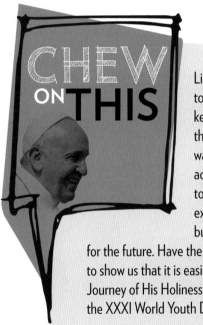

CHEW ON THIS

Life nowadays tells us that it is much easier to concentrate on what divides us, what keeps us apart. People try to make us believe that being closed in on ourselves is the best way to keep safe from harm. Today, we adults need you to teach us, as you are doing today, how to live in diversity, in dialogue, to experience multiculturalism not as a threat but an opportunity. You are an opportunity for the future. Have the courage to teach us, have the courage to show us that it is easier to build bridges than walls! ("Apostolic Journey of His Holiness Pope Francis to Poland on the Occasion of the XXXI World Youth Day," July 30, 2016)

The Power of a Shared Creed

It can be tempting to glide over the words of the creed during Mass. Perhaps sometimes you mumble the creed or say the words half-heartedly or just zone out for a few minutes and miss it entirely. As with any prayer that we pray over and over again, there can be a risk that we take that prayer for granted or that the powerful words have a lesser impact on us because they are so familiar.

The next time you are at Mass, resolve to pay attention to the creed. Speak the words slowly, prayerfully, and mindfully, remembering that you are saying aloud the very heart of our shared faith. Listen, as well, to the people around you saying the same words, and remember that those very words unite you with the more than *one billion* Catholics around the world who, like you, profess this one faith. ✳

The words we say in both the Apostles' Creed and the Nicene Creed are the very heart of what we believe in.

HMMMMM. . .

Why is it important to say aloud what we believe?

Article 11
One in Worship

Ellianna was so excited to be going to El Salvador over Christmas vacation to visit relatives from her father's side of the family. She had only been there once before, but she had been too little to remember anything. She was looking forward to being in a new place, getting to know cousins she had never met, and eating her grandmother's cooking that she had heard so much about.

While in El Salvador, the family attended midnight Mass on Christmas Eve. The Church was packed with people and beautifully decorated. Ellianna was amazed to realize that even though she only knew a few Spanish words, she knew *exactly* what was going on during the Mass. She'd never really thought about how Mass is the same all over the world. Even in a different language, the prayers, actions, and rituals were all very familiar. She felt completely at home and connected with all the people celebrating the Christmas liturgy together in that packed church.

Ellianna discovered that the prayers and rituals of the Mass are the same whether she attends at home or in El Salvador. Through the liturgy, we are connected to Catholics all over the world.

UNIT 2

© Flory / iStock.com

66   Chapter 3: The Church Is One

UNIT 2

Praying and Worshipping as One

Besides being united in our shared beliefs, the Church is united in the common celebration of divine worship, especially the sacraments. As Ellianna found on her trip to El Salvador, the Eucharistic liturgy, or Mass, unites us with Catholics around the globe. You could go to Mass anywhere in the world and be able to follow the actions of the liturgy, even if you do not understand the local language. Even the Scripture proclaimed would be the same readings that you would hear in your own home parish, because all Catholic parishes around the world use the same *Lectionary* that assigns the Scripture readings for both daily and Sunday liturgies.

All the sacraments—but especially the Eucharist—reflect our unity as one Church and, at the same time, strengthen and deepen that unity. This is because when we celebrate the sacraments, we encounter Christ, who nourishes us, heals us, forgives us, and unites us as one body. The power and presence of Christ, in the Holy Spirit, transcends any boundary of place, culture, or language.

In what way do you think the Eucharist reflects our unity as one Church?

Lectionary ➤ The official liturgical book containing the readings of the Mass, the Gospels, the Responsorial Psalms, and the Gospel Acclamations.

CATHOLICS **MAKING** A DIFFERENCE

The town of Taizé is in eastern France. This is where Br. Roger Schutz-Marsauche sheltered refugees who were fleeing the German-occupied part of France during World War II. After the war, Brother Roger, along with six of his companions, took vows of celibacy and community life as a way of continuing their ministry of welcoming guests and bearing witness to their Christian faith. Soon, others were attracted to the community. Today, more than a hundred brothers—some of whom are Catholic, and some Protestant—are a part of the Taizé community. Most live in Taizé, although some serve in Africa, Asia, and South America, ministering among people who are marginalized or oppressed. The Taize community has been a magnet for young people. While guests at Taize, young people can meet, pray, converse, and socialize with their peers from around the world.

Eastern Catholic Churches

Quick question for you: How many Catholic Churches are there? If you answered "one," you're correct. If you answered "twenty-two," you're also correct! What?

The **Roman Catholic Church**, sometimes also called the Latin Rite Church, is probably the Catholic Church that is most familiar to you. She is in communion with twenty-one other Catholic Churches: the **Eastern Catholic Churches**. These Eastern Catholic Churches include, for example, the Armenian Catholic Church, the Chaldean Catholic Church, the Coptic Catholic Church, and the Maronite Church. All twenty-two Catholic Churches, united as one, recognize the authority of the Pope.

The word *Eastern* refers to the Eastern half of the Roman Empire, which was based in Constantinople, but these Churches originated in a variety of locations, including Eastern Europe, the Middle East, North Africa, and India. Now, however, due to migration, members of these Churches can be found

Roman Catholic Church ➤ Refers to the Western Roman Rite Church that is based in Rome.

Eastern Catholic Churches ➤ The twenty-one Churches of the East, with their own liturgical and administrative traditions, which reflect the culture of Eastern Europe and the Middle East. Eastern Catholics are in union with the Universal Catholic Church and her head, the Bishop of Rome.

throughout the world, including in the United States. Because they developed in particular regions, these Churches have their own traditions of prayer and worship, which are different from the Roman Catholic liturgical tradition. So, if you attend a liturgy at an Eastern Catholic Church instead of a Roman Catholic Church, you will recognize some, but not all, of its components. The most obvious difference will be that the liturgy will be in another language, such as Ukrainian, Armenian, or Syriac, and the liturgy will incorporate elements that are similar to what is practiced in Roman Catholic Churches. The interior of the church building may look different as well. It may incorporate many **icons** of Mary and the saints. The altar may also be separated from the main part of the church by a large screen or partition called an **iconostasis**.

The liturgies of these Eastern Catholic Churches may look, sound, and feel very different from liturgies of the Roman rite. Yet, their underlying meaning and saving power, through the presence of Jesus Christ, are the same.

© blirow61 / iStock.com

In all Catholic liturgies, the Scripture is proclaimed, and bread and wine are consecrated to become the Body and Blood of Jesus Christ. Indeed, all of us—in both the East and the West—are united as one Catholic Church in and through these multiple, diverse liturgical traditions. ✳

In addition to the Roman Catholic Church, there are twenty-one Eastern Catholic Churches that reflect the culture and liturgical traditions of Eastern Europe and the Middle East.

In what ways can symbols and rituals be more powerful and memorable than spoken words alone?

icon ➤ From a Greek word meaning "likeness," a sacred image of Christ, Mary, or the saints, especially in the artwork of the Eastern Churches.

iconostasis ➤ A screen or partition with doors and tiers of icons that separates the bema, the raised part of the church with the altar, from the nave, the main part of the church, in Eastern Churches.

Article 12
One in Leadership and Witness

Think of a good leader you have seen in action or worked with. Maybe he or she is a team captain, a class president, a coach, or a scout leader. Think about the ways this person was effective in this leadership role. Good leaders unite us for a common purpose, get us excited and motivated to be our best selves, and push us toward accomplishing our goals with pride and integrity.

The Church's leadership—the Pope, in union with the bishops throughout the world—is the final way in which the Church is considered to be united as one. Our leaders' commitment to the Church helps us to bear witness to our faith with courage and authenticity.

One in Leadership

As you learned earlier in this course, Jesus entrusted the Church to Peter and to the other Apostles. Through the **Sacrament of Holy Orders**, the Apostles passed on that authority to their successors, and they to their successors, and

so on, all the way to the present day. In this way, today's bishops can be considered the direct "descendants" of the Apostles. This phenomenon, which unites us as one Church in both space and time—that is, throughout the world and throughout history—is known as **Apostolic Succession**.

The College of Bishops is an assembly of bishops, headed by the Pope, that holds the teaching authority and responsibility in the Church.

© Robert Hoetink / Shutterstock.com

Holy Orders, Sacrament of ➤ The sacrament by which baptized men are ordained for permanent ministry in the Church as bishops, priests, or deacons.

Apostolic Succession ➤ The uninterrupted passing on of apostolic preaching and authority from the Apostles directly to all bishops. It is accomplished through the laying on of hands when a bishop is ordained in the Sacrament of Holy Orders as instituted by Christ. The office of bishop is permanent, because at ordination a bishop is marked with an indelible, sacred character.

The Pope, the Bishop of Rome and head of the worldwide **College of Bishops,** is the leader who most visibly signifies the Church's unity. In fact, a key aspect of the **Petrine ministry** is the ministry of unity, especially strengthening unity wherever it has been weakened or forgotten. These may include places where Christians have been persecuted, where the Church has lost credibility due to the mistakes and sinfulness of her leaders, and where natural disasters, wars, and other tragedies have tested people's faith. In these and similar situations, the Pope is called to remind Catholics that we are united as one.

One in Witness

Lizzie's eyes were glued on Dominique as if her life depended on it. She hadn't really expected much from her ninth-grade retreat. She'd only been on a retreat once before, in eighth grade. It had been okay, but not anything like this. Dominique, a senior, was just finishing giving a witness talk about how her faith had grown during her years in high school. She talked about how much she got out of her religious studies classes, and how she loved being on the campus ministry retreat team. She said that faith isn't all sunshine, smiles, and flowers all the time. It can be hard. It was especially hard for Dominique to hold on to her faith when she went through a painful breakup during her

junior year. But, looking back, she said: "I know that God carried me through that time. I know that he loved me more than ever when I was hurting so much."

© CREATISTA / Shutterstock.com

Have you ever had a powerful experience on a retreat or at a concert? What was it about the experience that inspired you?

College of Bishops ➤ The assembly of bishops, headed by the Pope, that holds the teaching authority and responsibility in the Church.

Petrine ministry ➤ This term (an adjective form of Peter) refers to the ministry of the Pope as the successor of Saint Peter and the symbol of the unity and faith of all Christians.

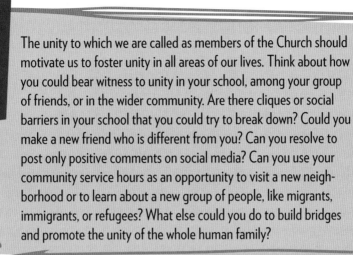

MAKE IT SO

The unity to which we are called as members of the Church should motivate us to foster unity in all areas of our lives. Think about how you could bear witness to unity in your school, among your group of friends, or in the wider community. Are there cliques or social barriers in your school that you could try to break down? Could you make a new friend who is different from you? Can you resolve to post only positive comments on social media? Can you use your community service hours as an opportunity to visit a new neighborhood or to learn about a new group of people, like migrants, immigrants, or refugees? What else could you do to build bridges and promote the unity of the whole human family?

Lizzie was amazed and inspired by Dominique's story. Right then and there, sitting on the floor at the retreat center, she knew that three years from now, she wanted to be on the retreat team. She wanted to be the one giving a talk and sharing her faith with the ninth graders.

In uniting us as one, the Church's leaders should inspire us to bear witness to our faith, in the way that Dominique inspired Lizzie. Their example should motivate us to share our faith through both our words and actions. The Church's members are called to be one in charity toward one another and toward the wider world, a world in which there is much suffering, discrimination, and oppression. This means that we must actively look out for one another, giving special attention and care to those who are poor, sick, lonely, or otherwise in great need.

Shortly before his death on the cross, Jesus prayed for the unity of all his followers: "That they may all be one, as you, Father, are in me and I in you" (John 17:21). Each of us, in union with Church leaders and through the grace and power of the Holy Spirit, has the potential to contribute to the Church's unity, so that this prayer and vision of Jesus may, someday, be fully realized. ✳

HMMMMM. . . What are some ways you have seen the Pope— or your own local bishop—foster unity among Catholics?

Article 13

Divisions, Wounds, and Brokenness

At this point, you might be thinking: "Well, all this talk of being united in faith, worship, leadership, and witness is great, but I see a lot of division in the Church. What about the fact that there are so many different churches that all claim the name of 'Christian'? Doesn't this mean that the Church is not really 'one' at all?"

These are good and valid questions! The reality of the Church's oneness and the reality of the Church's division are like two sides of the same coin. On the one side, the Church is really and truly one, according to the eternal will and plan of God the Father as expressed in the life and ministry of Jesus Christ. On the other side, the Church is still working to attain the *fullness* of the unity that God wills for all those who follow Jesus. Throughout history, the Church has been wounded, divided, and broken by various events, circumstances, and patterns of belief. These divisions are caused by misguided and sinful individuals within the Church, rather than by the Church itself. These have prevented the Church from truly and completely bearing witness as one, unified Body of Christ.

Heresies and Schisms

Some serious divisions within the Church are the result of heresies and schisms. A **heresy** is a teaching that rejects some aspect of Church **dogma** or **doctrine**. Heresies can arise at any time—including in the present day, in the form of various sects and cults, as well as **apostasy**. A sect or a cult is a group that breaks away from the Church, rejecting a true teaching of the Church or following a charismatic leader who is not in union with the Church. For example, some sects think that only the Extraordinary Form of the Roman Rite in Latin, the form of the Mass celebrated regularly before Vatican II, is fitting or even legitimate. Some of these sects consider themselves "true Catholics" even though they reject the authority of the Pope and bishops of the Church.

Heresies developed during the early centuries of the Church. These include Gnosticism, Arianism, Nestorianism, Monophysitism, and Apollinari-

---

heresy ➤ The conscious and deliberate rejection by a baptized person of a truth of faith that must be believed.

dogma ➤ Teachings recognized as central to Church teaching, defined by the Magisterium and considered definitive and authoritative.

doctrine ➤ An official, authoritative teaching of the Church based on the Revelation of God.

apostasy ➤ The act of renouncing one's faith.

Athanasius is a Father of the Church who vigorously defended Church teachings against the heretical ideology of Ariansim.

anism, heresies you probably studied in "Jesus Christ and the New Testament." As you recall, most of these belief systems promoted mistaken or misguided beliefs about Jesus Christ, which unfortunately still persist today. For example, some believed that Jesus was not fully divine, others that he was not fully human. Other heresies questioned Mary's role as the Mother of God and the fact that Christ made salvation possible for all people, not just a privileged few.

A **schism** is a definitive break, causing a division that is not easily healed. Some schisms have occurred in the Church when a community did not accept the teachings of an ecumenical council. For example, followers of Nestorianism were in schism following the Council of Ephesus (AD 431). The **theologian** Nestorius denied the doctrine of the Incarnation, and argued that in Jesus Christ there were actually two persons, one divine and one human. The Council of Ephesus condemned Nestorius as a heretic, and those who refused to accept this condemnation formed churches that were in schism. Fortunately, some of those churches later rejected Nestorianism and returned to union with the Catholic Church.

Just twenty years later, others rejected the Council of Chalcedon's (AD 451) teachings about the human and divine natures of Jesus Christ. These people embraced Monophysitism, which claimed that Jesus' divinity fully absorbed his humanity, leaving Jesus without a true human nature. The Council of Chalcedon rejected this heresy. Those who rejected the Council's teaching formed the oriental Orthodox Churches. They still exist in our time and continue to be in schism with the Catholic Church, though they have been in dialogue and believe that they have a faithful, not Monophysite, view of Christ.

---

schism ➤ A major break that causes division. A schism in the Church is caused by the refusal to submit to the Pope or to be in communion with the Church's members.

theologian ➤ One who engages in the academic discipline of theology, or "the study of God." A theologian engages in the pursuit of faith seeking understanding.

Historical events at this time probably contributed to these early divisions between the Western Church and some of the Eastern Churches. In the fourth century, the Roman Empire was divided into East and West, with the

The emperor Constantine moved the capital of the Roman Empire to Constantinople (modern-day Turkey) in AD 330.

Emperor Constantine's successors ruling the Greek-speaking eastern half from Constantinople (located in present-day Turkey), and other emperors ruling the Latin-speaking West from Rome. The distance and difficult travel conditions between the Churches in the East and the West made communication difficult. Remember that this was long before instant messaging and FaceTime—and also before airplanes, trains, the telephone, and even the postal service! These circumstances fostered miscommunication and disagreements for many centuries after the decline of the Roman Empire in the West, in the late fifth century.

Then, in 1054, Pope Saint Leo IX (1002–1054) sent a delegation from Rome to the Orthodox Patriarch Michael of Constantinople. After a series of disagreements, the Roman delegation excommunicated the patriarch. The patriarch, in turn, excommunicated the entire delegation and the Pope himself! This is why the current schism between Eastern Orthodox Christianity and the Catholic Church is often dated to 1054. However, later events, including the sacking and pillaging of Constantinople in 1204 by European crusaders, eventually led to a complete break in relations between the Eastern Orthodox Churches and the Catholic Church.

The Schism of 1054

Christians in Western Europe became the *Roman Catholic Church*

Christians in Eastern Europe became the *Eastern Orthodox Church*

This map shows the separation of the Eastern Orthodox Churches and the Roman Catholic Church, often called the East-West Schism, in 1054.

Despite ongoing differences, much progress has been made in recent years toward fostering full unity between the Catholic Church and the Orthodox Churches. For example, in February 2016, Pope Francis met with Patriarch Kirill, the head of the Russian Orthodox Church. This event was extraordinary and historic, because it was the first time that the Bishop of Rome and the Patriarch of Moscow (and all of Russia) had met in person since the schism of 1054. In a joint statement issued at the conclusion of their meeting, the two leaders said that they had spoken "heart to heart" about relations between the Churches and about the contributions that all people of faith can make to solving the many problems facing our world. They described Catholics and Orthodox Christians as "not competitors but brothers" ("Joint Declaration of Pope Francis and Patriarch Kirill of All Russia," signed in Havana, Cuba, February 12, 2016).

Pope Francis meets with H. H. Kirill, the Patriarch of Moscow and Russia, on February 12, 2016, to discuss the relationship between Orthodox Christians and Catholics.

The Protestant Reformation

You may be familiar with some of the key people who helped to launch the **Protestant Reformation** in the early sixteenth century. In a world history course, you may have learned, for example, about Martin Luther, a German monk and priest who criticized the Church's practice of selling indulgences. After he did not reach a resolution with the Church, he was excommunicated, and his followers formed a new ecclesial community known as Lutherans. You may also have studied King Henry VIII of England, who broke with the Catholic Church because he rejected papal authority concerning divorce. When the Pope would not allow this, Henry established the Church of England, declared himself the head of that Church, and granted himself permission to divorce and remarry. Other notable figures of the Protestant Reformation include John Calvin, John Knox, and John Wesley. Each of these gathered followers and formed ecclesial communities that broke with the Catholic Church.

The various leaders of the Protestant Reformation emphasized two key points known by their Latin terms: *sola scriptura* ("Scripture alone") and *sola gratia* ("grace alone"), both of which contradict the truth of Catholic teaching. *Sola scriptura* refers to the idea that only Scripture transmits Divine Revelation, denying that we need both Scripture and Tradition to understand God's saving plan. *Sola gratia* refers to the idea that salvation comes only through God's grace, not through any human effort. Although it is true that grace is God's gift to us, and the ultimate source of our salvation, we must freely choose either to cooperate with that gift or to reject it.

© Everett Historical / Shutterstock.com

Martin Luther posted his *Ninety-five Theses* to the door of the Wittenberg Castle church in 1517. His eventual excommunication would lead to the Protestant Reformation.

Protestant Reformation ➤ The movement that began in the early sixteenth century and sought changes to the Roman Catholic Church. This eventually led to the formation of separate Protestant ecclesial bodies.

UNIT 2

In October 1517, the German monk and priest Martin Luther published his *Ninety-five Theses,* a list of questions and topics regarding the Catholic Church that he wanted to discuss and debate. This event is widely considered to have launched the Protestant Reformation, which spread throughout Europe from Germany.

Nearly five hundred years later, in October 2016, Pope Francis traveled to Sweden to help kick off a yearlong commemoration of the five hundredth anniversary of the Protestant Reformation. Along with the president of the Lutheran World Federation, he attended a prayer service at the Lutheran cathedral in the city of Lund. The two leaders also signed a joint statement pledging their commitment to greater unity between Catholics and Lutherans.

A More Perfect Union

When Cameron and Mariela celebrated the Sacrament of Marriage twenty-seven years ago, they became truly *one,* united in Christ as husband and wife. Yet, in reflecting on their married life, they find that they have grown *more united* over the years. This greater unity has sometimes come through good times they have shared. But they have felt most closely and deeply united when they have struggled together through experiences of suffering, hurt, loss, and brokenness.

The experience of Cameron and Mariela can teach us something about the Church. From its earliest days, the Church has truly been one. And yet God calls the Church to acknowledge the ways in which this unity has been damaged and to seek to heal those wounds. In so doing, the Church will deepen the unity that is already present, becoming an ever more authentic sign of God's saving love. ✳

HMMMMM. . . Why do you think it has been so difficult for the Church to attain the full and complete unity that Christ desires?

UNIT 2

1. Briefly explain the meaning of the four Marks of the Church.

2. Describe the three sources of the Church's unity.

3. What are the two creeds we say most often?

4. How do the sacraments unite us as one Church?

5. How does the Taizé community help to promote Christian unity?

6. What is the relationship of the Eastern Catholic Churches to the Roman Catholic Church?

7. What was the source of the schism between the Roman Catholic Church and the Eastern Orthodox Churches?

8. How does the Pope promote the Church's unity?

9. What two main beliefs of the Protestant Reformation contradict the truth of Catholic teaching?

The Evolution of Protestant Denominations

THE EARLY CHRISTIAN CHURCH

THE ROMAN CATHOLIC CHURCH

Peter

ANGLICANISM

Anglicanism – 1534
King Henry VIII,
Founder

Episcopal Church (USA) 1607

Methodism – 1738
John Wesley,
Founder

Pentecostalism
Early 20th
Century

Charismatic/
Non-Denominational Churches
1960s

PROTESTANTISM

Lutheranism – 1521
Martin Luther, Founder

Reformed – 1520s
John Calvin and Ulrich Zwingli,
Founders

Presbyterianism – 1560s
John Knox, Founder

Baptist – 1609
John Smyth,
Founder

Images: Shutterstock.com

CHAPTER 4
The Church Is Holy

IF THE CHURCH'S MEMBERS ARE REGULAR, IMPERFECT PEOPLE, HOW CAN THE CHURCH BE HOLY?

SNAPSHOT

Article 14   Page 81
The Church: Both Human and Divine

Article 15   Page 85
Grace: A Gift and an Opportunity
• Pre-read: John 6:1–15

Article 16   Page 88
The Communion of Saints

Article 17   Page 92
Mary: Model of Holiness
• Pre-read: Luke 1:26–38

Article 18   Page 95
Focus on Pope Francis: "Rejoice and Be Glad"
• Pre-read: "Rejoice and Be Glad," numbers 1–2 and 110–157

Article 14
The Church: Both Human and Divine

Lying on his bed staring up at the ceiling, Matt tried not to think about the fight he'd just had with his mom. But he couldn't seem to get it out of his head. Couldn't she understand how angry he was at the Church? She saw the same news reports that he did, about how some of the Church's leaders and ministers had done terrible things. Some had even lied about it later, trying to cover up what happened. When Matt went to Mass, all he could think about was how the people he was supposed to trust the most had betrayed him.

There was a knock at the door. "Can I come in?"

"Sure—okay," Matt answered.

His mom sat on the edge of the bed hesitantly. "Matt, I'm sorry I wasn't listening to you very well. I do hear that you are angry and have questions about being part of a Church where such horrible things could happen. If I'm honest with you, I've wondered this too. But Matt, no one's perfect. Even people who are supposed to be role models and examples sin and make terrible mistakes. I know that's frustrating and disappointing. I'm upset about it too. But, I think there's so much good in the Church. Even though some people have really messed up, the Church is still the best way we have to experience God's presence. So, I just really hope that you won't give up on it. That's all I'm asking."

Matt was relieved that at least they weren't fighting anymore. "I'll think about it, Mom, okay? I'll think about it."

TAKE IT TO GOD

Dear God,
There's been so much bad news about the horrible crimes committed by
   leaders in the Church.
It makes me wonder about whether the Church is really what you want it to be.
Help me to remember that despite the sins of its members,
   you are ultimately in charge.
You will never let the Church fail in the saving work you have for it to do.
Alone, we may struggle to bring about change, but together, we can do
   great things.
Help the Church to be a place of acceptance and love for all,
   to strive for progress in becoming perfect as you are perfect.
Amen.

Sinless, Yet Made of Sinners

The Church has both divine and human dimensions. For example, as the Body of Christ, the Church is holy and sinless. Members of the Church share in this holiness. Yet because the members of the Church are human, they sin, as do all human beings. The **holiness** of the members of the Church is *real*, but it is *imperfect:* this is not a contradictory statement! But the Church is more than the imperfect members we can see. She has an invisible dimension as a bearer of divine life, a mystery we can see only with eyes of faith. This invisible mystery builds on the visible reality. Through the action of the Holy Spirit, the aspects of the Church we can see put us in touch with her divine dimension.

The Holy Spirit assures us that the Church is always carrying out Christ's mission, despite the sins and failures of its individual members. Through us, God is doing what we could never do on our own. Our work is participation in the real, but unseen, divine life of the Trinity. God is all-holy, the source of all holiness, and all human beings are called to live holy lives. This is why all members of the Church, including the Church's leaders and ministers,

are invited to continual **conversion**: to a renewal of mind and heart that turns us away from sin and toward God. The Church fosters this conversion, ongoing renewal, and purification in a variety of ways, most especially through the sacraments, including the **Sacrament of Penance and Reconciliation.**

© Oleksandr Dudryk / Shutterstock.com

It can be challenging to understand that the Church is perfect and holy although it is made up of individuals who are imperfect and sinful.

holiness ➤ The state of being holy. This means to be set apart for God's service, to live a morally good life, to be a person of prayer, and to reveal God's love to the world through acts of loving service.

conversion ➤ A profound change of heart, turning away from sin and toward God.

Penance and Reconciliation, Sacrament of ➤ One of the Seven Sacraments of the Church, the liturgical celebration of God's forgiveness of sin, through which the sinner is reconciled with both God and the Church.

In both his words and actions, Pope Francis provides an example of a Church leader who fully embraces this call to ongoing conversion and growth in holiness. In an interview that occurred early in his papacy, Fr. Antonio Spadaro asked Pope Francis: "Who is Jorge Mario Bergoglio?" (This is Pope Francis's baptismal name. When someone is elected Pope, he chooses a new name.) The Pope's frank response startled many people: "I do not know what might be the most fitting description. . . . I am a sinner. This is the most accurate definition. It is not a figure of speech. . . . I am a sinner" ("Interview with Pope Francis by Fr. Antonio Spadaro," September 2013). Likewise, when leading penitential services at St. Peter's Basilica, generally during Lent, Pope Francis makes sure that he is the first of those assembled to go to confession. In this way, he humbly acknowledges his own human sinfulness and his desire to grow in holiness, and, by his example, he encourages us to do the same. ✳

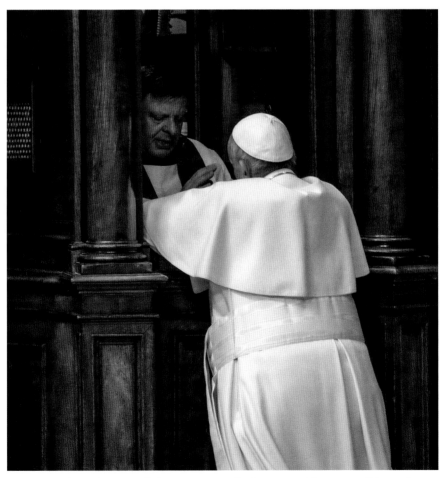

Even Pope Francis regularly participates in the Sacrament of Penance and Reconciliation in order to acknowledge his own sinfulness and his desire to grow in holiness.

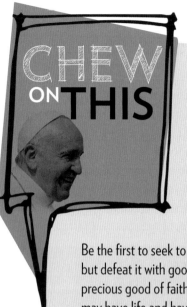

CHEW ON THIS

My dear young friends, you have a particular sensitivity towards injustice, but you are often disappointed by facts that speak of corruption on the part of people who put their own interests before the common good. To you and to all, I repeat: never yield to discouragement, do not lose trust, do not allow your hope to be extinguished. Situations can change, people can change. Be the first to seek to bring good, do not grow accustomed to evil, but defeat it with good. The Church is with you, bringing you the precious good of faith, bringing Jesus Christ, who "came that they may have life and have it abundantly" (John 10:10). ("Apostolic Journey to Rio De Janeiro on the Occasion of the XXVIII World Youth Day, Visit to the Community of Varginha," July 25, 2013)

HMMMMMM. . .

What does holiness mean to you? What words, attitudes, or actions do you think would indicate that a person is holy?

Article 15
Grace: A Gift and An Opportunity

Opening ourselves to God's gift of **grace** allows us the opportunity to grow in holiness. Grace empowers us to respond to God's call and to live as faithful disciples of Jesus.

Grace is a gift that God gives us freely and generously, with no strings attached. You are already experiencing the benefits of grace, even if you don't think about it or if you call it something else. Your ability to make choices, to make your life or the life of others better, is grace. When you experience the joy of love, given or received, it is grace. When you use your talents to make music or art, to solve a problem, or to play a sport, it is grace. Life itself is a gift from God; it is all grace!

We don't have to earn grace or convince God that we deserve it. It is simply offered to us. But, in order for us to receive the full benefits of his grace, we must actively cooperate with it. Otherwise, it's like a gift that we never unwrapped, or a gift card that we used once, stuck in our wallet, and forgot about. We still have it, but it's not doing us any good.

How Can We Cooperate with Grace?

When we cooperate with grace, our desire to grow in holiness makes us attentive to God's presence and open to God's call. There are three main ways in which we can cooperate with grace, and they're easy to remember, because they all begin with *s:* sacraments, Scripture, and service. Let's look at each one of these in more detail.

Regular reception of the sacraments is essential for members of the Church. Beginning with our Baptism, Christ enriches us through all the sacraments, which he entrusted to the Church for our salvation. The sacraments that we celebrate most often, as a regular part of our life of faith and holiness, are the Eucharist and Penance and Reconciliation. Our participation in the Eucharist—minimally, every Sunday (or Saturday evening) and every holy day of obligation—draws us into communion both with God and with our brothers and sisters in faith. Celebrating the Sacrament of Penance and Reconciliation

grace ➤ The free and undeserved gift that God gives us to empower us to respond to his call and to live as his adopted sons and daughters. Grace restores our loving communion with the Holy Trinity, lost through sin.

UNIT 2

How do you think receiving the Eucharist helps us to cooperate with God's grace?

allows us to humbly acknowledge our sins and failings, to receive God's mercy, and to have a fresh start.

In addition to the sacraments, Christ also entrusted his Word to the Church as a privileged means of encountering him and of growing in holiness. When we use our imagination to pray with Scripture, especially the Gospels, we immerse ourselves in the saving work of Jesus Christ as evidenced in his teachings, miracles, death, and Resurrection.

For example, think about the miracle of Jesus feeding a crowd of thousands of people with only five loaves of bread and two fish. It's probably a story that you know well—all four Gospel writers describe it. But if you read it slowly and prayerfully, you can try to imagine yourself in the scene. Picture yourself in that crowd, watching Jesus perform this miracle. What new insights do you get into the meaning of the story, and how it is calling you to holiness?

When you reflect on the account of Jesus feeding thousands with just several loaves of bread and a few fish, what deeper questions does it lead you to consider?

Maybe the Gospel story leads you to reflect on Jesus' power as the divine Son of God and to consider how you might be more open to his power in your own daily life. Or maybe it prompts you to think about issues of hunger and poverty. For so many of the world's people, including in the United States, the question of "Where can we buy enough food for them to eat?" (John 6:5) is not an abstract problem. It is a real, daily struggle. Or maybe the story inspires you to think about what you truly hunger for—not a physical hunger for lunch or a snack, but your deep longings. Do you hunger for acceptance and love? for comfort and security? for a sense of meaning and purpose? This Gospel story assures us that only Christ, present to us in and through the Church, can truly satisfy these hungers.

Engaging in works of service, charity, and justice is another means of cooperating with grace. A spirit of service can begin in your own home, if you, for example, do a household chore without complaining, or help a younger sibling with homework. From there, the possibilities are endless. You could volunteer at a shelter for people who are homeless, organize a canned food drive at your school, or write letters to legislators to advocate for the human rights of immigrants. Giving our time, talent, and energy for the good of someone else is a beautiful, meaningful way to respond to, and cooperate with, the grace that God first gave us.

What opportunities have you had to cooperate with God's grace through works of service, charity, or justice?

If you feel drawn to the sacraments, to Scripture, or to service, recognize that it is God's grace, alive within you, that is nudging you toward these practices that will help you to mature in holiness. God loves us first, and the very gift of that love and divine grace empowers us to respond to it courageously and generously. And if participating in the sacraments, praying with Scripture, or serving others gives you a feeling of joy, satisfaction, or peace, that too is God's gift to you. It's God's way of saying: "Awesome job! Keep up the good work!" ✳

UNIT 2

HMMMMM. . .
What is a specific step that you could take to cooperate with grace more fully?

Article 16
The Communion of Saints

When you think of the word **saint**, what comes to your mind? Perhaps you think of saints from the New Testament, like Saint Peter, Saint Paul, or Saint Mary Magdalene. Perhaps you think of the saint whose name you chose as a Confirmation name or the saint who is the patron of your parish or school. Or perhaps you recall a saint whose life you have studied, researched, and maybe even admired. These are all valid responses but, you could just as accurately, and easily, have thought of yourself!

The word *saint* comes from the Latin word *sanctus*, which means "holy." *All* of us are called to be holy; therefore, *all* of us are called to be saints. That is, we are called to be open to the grace of God, to be transformed by our saving belief in Jesus Christ, and to bear witness, through our words and actions, to the power and presence of the Holy Spirit. All people who faithfully live out this call will, one day, be fully united with God in Heaven.

Why Do the Saints Matter?

Canonized saints are essential for our own journey of holiness because they are both guides and intercessors. As guides, the saints are models of holiness. Their example of faithfulness to the Gospel should encourage and inspire our own choices. It's important to remember that the saints were holy, but not without their sins and flaws. They did not follow some unattainable path to God that the rest of don't have access to. Rather, they were real human beings who tried their best, with God's grace, to be faithful within the circumstances of their own lives, even as they struggled with temptation, sin, fear, and failure. Yes, they were extraordinarily faithful to God's call, but not in any way beyond our own ability to do!

---

saint ➤ Someone who has been transformed by the grace of Christ and who resides in full union with God in Heaven.

canonize ➤ The act by which the Church officially recognizes a deceased Catholic as a saint.

For example, before Saint Augustine of Hippo (354–430) was baptized, he followed a heresy called Manicheanism. He also fathered a child without being married. Yet, he became one of Christianity's most influential theologians. When Saint Oscar Romero (1917–1980) was appointed as the archbishop of San Salvador, he at first supported El Salvador's wealthy, powerful people. Yet, within months, he became an ally of the country's poor, who were oppressed by injustice and violence. He was seen as such a threat to the political and religious establishment that he was martyred on March 24, 1980, while presiding at the Eucharist.

Saint Augustine of Hippo (354–430) converted from a life of heresy, sin, and excess to pursuing a life of holiness and working for those suffering injustices. He is an example for our own pursuit of holiness.

UNIT 2

I DIDN'T KNOW THAT!

How far would you go to grow in holiness? Would you walk 500 miles? That's how far people travel—on foot, or sometimes by bike—on the ancient route of the Camino de Santiago pilgrimage, which stretches from the French-Spanish border all the way across northern Spain. A pilgrimage is a journey undertaken for a spiritual purpose. It is a kind of retreat-in-motion, an opportunity to grow closer to God through the act of traveling to a sacred place.

In recent years, the Camino de Santiago has surged in popularity, including among college students and young adults. People usually take forty days to walk the whole Camino. The most popular time to undertake the Camino is in the summer, in order to complete the pilgrimage on Saint James' feast day, July 25. They celebrate a special Mass to welcome pilgrims. Afterwards, the entire city honors their patron saint with festive music, food, and fireworks.

As intercessors, the saints, who dwell with God in Heaven, are able to join us in our prayer to God, interceding with God on our behalf. Many people mistakenly think that Catholics pray *to* the saints, but this isn't true. Catholics pray to God the Father, in the name of Jesus Christ, in the power of the Holy Spirit. However, we invite the saints to pray *with us*. In this way, we on Earth are united with those in Heaven. Together, we bring our needs, concerns, and hopes to God, in faith.

The Solemnity of All Saints

The **Solemnity** of All Saints occurs each year on November 1. On this day, the Church commemorates all canonized saints as well as all holy women and men who, throughout the ages, have faithfully carried out God's will. Many of these saints are not famous. No books have been published about them, and you wouldn't find much information about their faith and good works on the internet. And yet, on November 1, the Church celebrates all of these people, whose holiness may be known only to God. In doing so, the Church recognizes that all good and holy people, both living and dead, are part of the great "cloud of witnesses" (see Hebrews 12:1) whose example may nourish and inspire our own journey toward holiness. ✳

© el lobo / Shutterstock.com

The Solemnity of All Saints celebrates all canonized saints and holy men and women who have lived their lives as faithful servants to God.

---

solemnity ➤ An important holy day in the Catholic liturgical calendar, such as Christmas, Easter, Pentecost, and All Saints' Day.

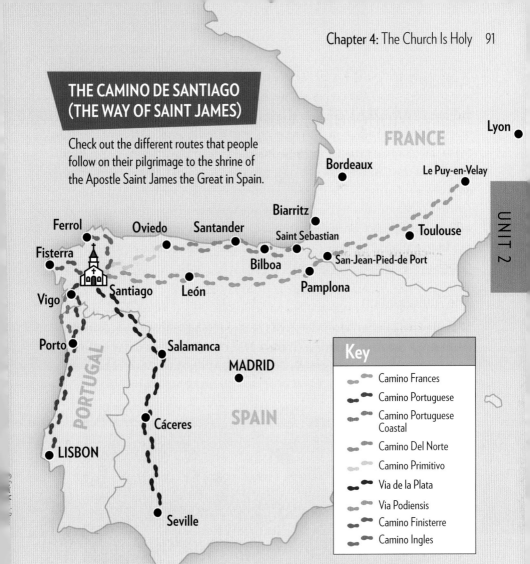

THE CAMINO DE SANTIAGO (THE WAY OF SAINT JAMES)

Check out the different routes that people follow on their pilgrimage to the shrine of the Apostle Saint James the Great in Spain.

FRANCE

Lyon

Bordeaux

Le Puy-en-Velay

Biarritz

Ferrol

Oviedo

Santander

Saint Sebastian

Toulouse

Fisterra

Bilboa

San-Jean-Pied-de-Port

Santiago

León

Pamplona

Vigo

Porto

Salamanca

MADRID

PORTUGAL

SPAIN

Cáceres

LISBON

Seville

UNIT 2

Key

- Camino Frances
- Camino Portuguese
- Camino Portuguese Coastal
- Camino Del Norte
- Camino Primitivo
- Via de la Plata
- Via Podiensis
- Camino Finisterre
- Camino Ingles

HMMMMM. . .

Who is a saint with whom you feel some special connection? What do you think is the most important thing you could learn from this person's life?

Article 17
Mary: Model of Holiness

Preeminent among the saints is the Blessed Virgin Mary, Mother of God, Mother of the Church, and our own Mother. Mary is a uniquely perfect model of holiness, charity, and faith, because she embraced God's will and Jesus Christ's redemptive work, and because she was attentive to the promptings of the Holy Spirit. Conceived without **Original Sin** through the miracle of the **Immaculate Conception**, Mary illustrates what is possible when we give ourselves completely to God's will.

The Annunciation

To understand better what Mary's life of discipleship can teach us, consider the story of the **Annunciation** (Luke 1:26–38), in which the angel Gabriel appears to her in her hometown of Nazareth. At the time, Mary is betrothed in marriage to Joseph.

The Annunciation refers to the visit of the angel Gabriel to the Virgin Mary to announce that she had been chosen to bear the Son of God.

Original Sin ➤ The sin by which the first humans disobeyed God and thereby lost their original holiness and became subject to death. Original Sin is transmitted to every person born into the world, except Jesus and Mary.

Immaculate Conception ➤ The Catholic dogma that the Blessed Virgin Mary was free from sin from the first moment of her conception.

Annunciation ➤ The biblical event that includes the angel Gabriel's visit to the Virgin Mary to announce that she is to be the Mother of the Savior.

In this story, Mary does not simply passively receive a message and accept it without question. Rather, she interacts with and converses with the angel Gabriel. For example, the text tells us that she is "greatly troubled" (Luke 1:29) by Gabriel's greeting. Maybe she is confused about what is happening, or she might be afraid or anxious. Any of these reactions would be perfectly understandable for someone encountering an angel!

The story continues by telling us that Mary "pondered what sort of greeting this might be" (Luke 1:29). Mary is clearly thinking, wondering, and trying to make sense of the extraordinary event that she is experiencing. Gabriel seems to sense her state of mind and urges her not to be afraid. He assures her that she has "found favor with God" (1:30). Then Gabriel announces the big news! Mary is to conceive a child, bearing a son named Jesus, who "will rule over the house of Jacob forever" (1:33). Mary responds to this announcement by asking a very practical question. How can this possibly happen, when she is unmarried, never having had sexual relations? Her willingness to question the angel Gabriel demonstrates her desire to try and understand the meaning of his message about God's plan for her life.

UNIT 2

CATHOLICS MAKING A DIFFERENCE

An African slave. An immigrant. A convert to Catholicism. A religious sister for more than five decades. All of these phrases describe the extraordinary life of Saint Josephine Bakhita (1868–1947).

Born in 1869, in the Darfur region of what is now Sudan, Saint Bakhita was kidnapped by slave raiders when she was about nine years old. After being bought and sold multiple times, she was eventually sold to the Italian consul in Khartoum, who took her with him to Italy. She eventually came to a Catholic boarding school with the daughter of her owner. It was here that she first encountered the Church and the story of Jesus Christ. She was baptized in 1890. Bakhita won her freedom and entered religious life as a member of the Daughters of Charity of Canossa (the Canossian Sisters), professing her vows three years later. She remained a Sister for fifty-one years, until her death in 1947. Saint Bakhita's feast day has been designated as the International Day of Prayer and Awareness Against Human Trafficking.

At the very end of this story, after Gabriel answers her question, Mary says "yes" to God. She does not have all the answers that she may have wanted. She cannot possibly know all that lies ahead of her and all that will be asked of her, including watching her only son be tortured and executed. Yet without seeing the entire road before her, she declares, "Let it be done to me according to your word" (1:38).

Theologians and historians believe that Mary was quite young when the angel Gabriel visited her—probably about the age that you are now. Somehow, even as a teen, Mary found the courage, strength, faith, generosity, and determination to choose to follow God's will. Her example can and should inspire each of us to try to do the same: to say "yes" to God's call.

Mary remained perpetually both virgin and mother throughout her life. At the time of her death, her body and soul were taken into Heaven, an event the Church celebrates on August 15, the Solemnity of the **Assumption** of the Blessed Virgin Mary. On this day, and on other Marian feasts and solemnities that occur throughout the year (such as the Solemnity of Mary, the Mother of God on January 1 and the Solemnity of the Immaculate Conception on December 8), the Church invites us to give thanks for Mary's witness. Together we pray for the grace to grow in holiness, with the help of her guidance and intercession. ✳

© Bill Perry / Shutterstock.com

The Feast of the Assumption celebrates Mary's assumption, body and soul, into Heaven. Mary did not have to suffer an earthly death due to her immediate and complete "yes" to God's plan for her.

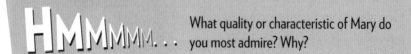

HMMMMMM. . .
What quality or characteristic of Mary do you most admire? Why?

Assumption ➤ The dogma that recognizes that the body of the Blessed Virgin Mary was taken directly to Heaven after her life on Earth had ended.

Article 18

Focus on Pope Francis: "Rejoice and Be Glad"

On March 19, 2018, Pope Francis released the apostolic exhortation "Rejoice and Be Glad" *("Gaudete et Exsultate")*. A church document is generally known by its first few words—in this case, "Rejoice and Be Glad," a quote from the **Beatitudes** (Matthew 5:12). Much like "The Joy of Love" *("Amoris Laetitia")*, the title of this exhortation starts on a positive note. It indicates that seeking to grow in holiness does not mean that our lives will be sad, somber, or boring. Rather, holiness can lead us to the deep and lasting joy that comes from cultivating a close relationship with God. This joy allows us to trust in God's love and mercy, even when we encounter setbacks or struggles.

Pope Francis wrote this document in order to provide practical help and advice for living out the call to holiness. He reminds us that this call is not restricted to certain members of the Church; instead, it is universal: "To be holy does not require being a bishop, a priest, or a religious. We are frequently tempted to think that holiness is only for those who can withdraw from ordinary affairs to spend much time in prayer. This is not the case" ("Rejoice and Be Glad," number 14). Of course, prayer is still important. In fact, prayer and action—particularly

Actions of charity and justice, in addition to prayer, are part of our calling to serve those who are poor, hungry, displaced, and homeless.

UNIT 2

Beatitudes ➤ The teachings of Jesus that begin the Sermon on the Mount and that summarize the New Law of Christ. The Beatitudes describe the actions and attitudes by which one can discover genuine happiness, and they teach us the final end to which God calls us: full communion with him in the Kingdom of Heaven.

acts of service to help people who are hungry, homeless, suffering, or in any kind of need—must go hand-in-hand. Pope Francis reminds us that the Beatitudes (see Matthew 5:1–12) and the **Corporal Works of Mercy** (see Matthew 25:31–46) can inspire us and direct us as we carry out these acts of service.

Signs of Holiness in Today's World

Within the Gospel framework of the Beatitudes and the Corporal Works of Mercy, Pope Francis draws our attention to five "signs or spiritual attitudes" ("Rejoice and Be Glad," number 110) that he believes are particularly important to cultivate on our journey toward holiness, particularly "in the light of certain dangers and limitations present in today's culture" (number 111). First, he urges us to develop a sense of *perseverance, patience, and meekness* in all our interactions with others, both in person and online. He mentions the "networks of verbal violence" (number 115) that exist on the internet, because people post things online that they would never say in person. If you have experienced or witnessed this type of cyberbullying, you know that it is cruel, hurtful, and inconsistent with the Gospel message and the example of Jesus.

© fizkes / Shutterstock.com

Do you think your text messages and social media interactions can impact your journey toward holiness?

Corporal Works of Mercy ➤ Charitable actions that respond to people's physical needs and show respect for human dignity. The traditional list of seven works includes feeding the hungry, giving drink to the thirsty, clothing the naked, sheltering the homeless, visiting the sick, visiting prisoners, and burying the dead.

Second, this document advocates *joy and a sense of humor* as a mark of a holy person. Pope Francis invokes his patron, Saint Francis of Assisi (c. 1181–1226), as an example of someone who took complete delight in life's simple pleasures: "He could be overwhelmed with gratitude before a piece of hard bread, or joyfully praise God simply for the breeze that caressed his face" ("Rejoice and Be Glad," number 127). To be clear, this joy is not the superficial happiness that we might experience when we get a new phone or video game. That happiness is only temporary, fading away along with our initial excitement.

In contrast, the joy that Pope Francis is referring to never fades, even in times of suffering, and the more we share it with others, the more it grows. If you can remember a time when you were truly happy—maybe you nailed a difficult piece you'd been practicing on the piano for weeks, or maybe you bonded with one of your siblings in a really deep conversation—then you have experienced the kind of joy that Pope Francis hopes for all of us.

Next, Pope Francis invites us to serve others with *boldness and passion,* going out to people on the "fringes" ("Rejoice and Be Glad," number 135) of our society whose suffering may otherwise be overlooked or neglected. He also emphasizes that this work should not be undertaken alone, but, instead, with others *in community* who can strengthen and encourage us. Think, for example, about the difference between completing community service hours by yourself, or with a group of your friends. By yourself, you may be anxious about going to an unfamiliar place and working alongside people you have never met. With friends, you may be much more relaxed, and you may have fun! This is the power of a community of faith and service.

What is the benefit of serving others in community rather than serving alone?

UNIT 2

© Monster Ztudio / Shutterstock.com

Last, Pope Francis reaffirms the centrality of *prayer* for a life of holiness, stating that "I do not believe in holiness without prayer" ("Rejoice and Be Glad," number 147). However, our prayer does not have to be long or difficult. We simply must develop the habit of being aware of God's presence, and of setting aside "some moments" to spend "alone with God" (number 149).

The Holiness of Daily Life

Take a moment to think of the small details of your everyday life, what Pope Francis refers to as "the little details of love" ("Rejoice and Be Glad," number 145). These could include the laughter of a family member, your best friend's loyalty, a parent's compassionate concern, or your favorite teacher's enthusiasm. You could also think of more tangible things, like food, clothes, shelter, and education. We can easily overlook these details in the rush of daily living. If we can be attentive to these small, daily blessings, we become more aware of God's goodness, and we grow in holiness.

MAKE IT SO

Remember that Pope Francis invoked Saint Francis of Assisi as an example of someone who took delight in life's simple pleasures. He reminds us that Saint Francis could be overwhelmed with gratitude before a piece of hard bread or praising God for the breeze that caressed his face. How can we experience this deep joy rather than superficial happiness? Have you considered writing in a gratitude journal? Identifying the things we are grateful for helps to make us more positive people, deepen our relationship with God, and make us holy. There are many ways to focus on gratitude in our daily lives: journals, planners, and even gratitude apps! The more we share gratitude and joy with others, the more it grows, as does our holiness in the sight of God.

Echoing Pope Francis's advice to make holiness part of our everyday life, we can try to incorporate daily prayer. Saint Ignatius of Loyola (1491–1556), founder of the Society of Jesus, or Jesuits, developed a format for daily prayer called the Examen. Praying the Examen at the end of your day can help you to cultivate an awareness of God's presence in your daily life and to grow in holiness. If you'd like to try praying the Examen, here are the basic steps:

- Find a quiet, comfortable place where you can be undisturbed for a few minutes. Open your heart to the Holy Spirit, and ask God to be with you.
- Bring to mind two or three things that you are grateful for. Take a moment to praise and thank God for these blessings.
- Go over your day and look for signs of God's presence in your activities, your decisions, and all the people you interacted with. Notice, in particular, how you responded to God's presence.
- Express sorrow to God for any sins you committed this day, or any words or actions that you regret.
- Ask God for the wisdom and grace to recognize, and respond to, his loving presence in your life tomorrow.
- Conclude your time of prayer in one or more of the following ways:
  - Record some thoughts or insights in your journal.
  - Pray the Our Father.
  - Simply sit in silence for a moment, as you rest in God's holy presence. ✻

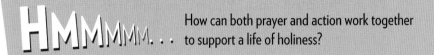

HMMMMM. . . How can both prayer and action work together to support a life of holiness?

UNIT 2

1. What does it mean when we say that the Church has both divine and human dimensions?

2. Why are all members of the Church called to continual conversion?

3. What are three ways in which we can cooperate with grace?

4. Why are canonized saints important for our life of faith?

5. What is a pilgrimage?

6. How does the story of the Annunciation help us to understand the Blessed Virgin Mary's life of discipleship?

7. What is the significance of Saint Josephine Bakhita's feast day?

8. What are the five signs of holiness in today's world that Pope Francis identified in "Rejoice and Be Glad"?

Canonized Saints

Although we are all called to be saints, the Church officially recognizes and proclaims some deceased Catholics to be saints through a process called canonization. This process is generally quite lengthy and can begin only after a person has died.

CONGRATULATIONS! YOU'VE BEEN CANONIZED!

START →

1 Earthly death

Did you sacrifice your life in order to save someone else's life?

Did you die for your faith as a martyr?

7  HELLO my name is Saint

"It's a miracle!—Part II." A second miracle must be attributed to the person's intercession.

The Pope can waive this requirement.

2 Five-year waiting period after the person's death.

6 HELLO my name is Blessed

A miracle is found to be associated with the candidate. The person receives the title "Blessed" in a special ceremony called a beatification.

A bishop opens an investigation.

- Examines the person's writings
- Interviews those who knew the person
- Submits a report to a Vatican office called the Congregation for the Causes of Saints

 **3**

4  HELLO my name is Servant of God

If the Vatican approves the report, it declares the person "Servant of God."

5 HELLO my name is Venerable

The Vatican investigates the person's virtue. If the investigation is successful, the Pope declares the person "Venerable."

CHAPTER 5
The Church Is Catholic

HOW DOES THE CHURCH INTERACT WITH DIFFERENT PEOPLE AND CULTURES?

SNAPSHOT

Article 19   Page 103
Breaking Boundaries, Cultivating Connections

Article 20   Page 107
Evangelization: The Gospel Reaching Far and Wide

Article 21   Page 112
Inculturation: The Gospel Taking Root

Article 19
Breaking Boundaries, Cultivating Connections

On April 1, 2014, bishops from Guatemala, Mexico, and the United States journeyed to the city of Nogales, which sits exactly on the U.S.–Mexico border: half of the city is in Arizona, and half is in the state of Sonora, Mexico. On the U.S. side of the 30-foot-tall border fence, the bishops celebrated a bilingual Eucharistic Liturgy. They prayed for justice for migrants and immigrants and to remember all those people from Central America and Mexico who have died on the dangerous journey north to the United States. One of the most moving parts of the liturgy came during Holy Communion. The bishops ministered the Eucharist not only to those gathered with them on the U.S. side of the border but also to those on the Mexican side. People reached their hands through the iron slats in the fence to receive the Precious Body of the Lord. Nearly two years later, on February 17, 2016, Pope Francis did something similar during his apostolic journey to Mexico. He celebrated a liturgy in Ciudad Juarez, just 300 feet from the Rio Grande and the U.S. city of El Paso, Texas.

© AP Photo / Matt York

Catholic bishops ministered the Eucharist to Catholics on both the American and Mexican sides of the border wall during a bilingual Eucharistic Liturgy.

UNIT 2

TAKE IT TO GOD

God, sometimes when people look differently than I do,
    or speak a language that I can't understand,
    or dress or eat or act in a way that I don't recognize,
I am afraid and anxious.
Give me your eyes, God, so that I can see your image and your
    presence in all people.
When I feel insecure, gently remind me that the Good News was meant
    for everyone, not just for people who look and act like me.
Amen.

Catholic Means Universal

Liturgies like these, celebrated at the intersection of two countries and cultures, help to highlight the meaning of the word **Catholic**. From the Greek word *katholikos*, *Catholic* means "universal." The Church is Catholic—the third mark of the Church—in two senses. First, the Church is Catholic because Christ is present in her. In the Church, we find the fullness of Christ's body, from whom the Church receives the fullness of the means of salvation. Second, the Church is Catholic because Christ has sent the Church out on a mission to the whole world.

As you learned in chapter 3, the Church is sent to the whole world and exists worldwide. Called by Christ to serve all people, to proclaim to them the Good News, and to be for them the means of salvation, the Church exists for *everyone*, including those who are members of the Church and those who are not. In fact, because of God's will that all people be saved, salvation comes from the Church, even for those who are not Church members. How exactly this happens—how all people potentially could be saved by God, even those who do not belong to the Church—is beyond our limited human understanding.

Catholic ➤ Along with One, Holy, and Apostolic, Catholic is one of the four Marks of the Church. *Catholic* means "universal." The Church is Catholic in two senses. She is Catholic because Christ is present in her and has given her the fullness of the means of salvation and also because she reaches throughout the world to all people.

As Catholics, we know and believe that the absolute best and most complete way to connect with God is through the Sacraments of the Church, especially the Eucharist. However, we also know and believe that no one is beyond the reach of God's saving love. God embraces the whole world—those who believe in him and those who do not—with infinite mercy and boundless compassion.

What do you think it means to say that the Church is called to an inclusive message of salvation that can help us to rediscover our unity as one human family?

Because the Church is called to minister to the whole human race—without exception—her global, inclusive message of salvation can help us to rediscover our unity as one human family. The Eucharistic Liturgies celebrated on the U.S.–Mexico border bear witness to this reality. Indeed, no border or boundary, no wall or fence, can contain or restrict the grace of the Holy Spirit, who draws us all together, in faith, as one community. ✳

UNIT 2

CATHOLICS **MAKING** A **DIFFERENCE**

Founded in 2007 by Gabe Huck and Theresa Kubasak, the Iraqi and Syrian Student Project (ISSP) offers educational support and scholarships to North American colleges to refugees displaced by war in Iraq and Syria. ISSP helps these students to navigate the college application process and visa requirements, and to gain greater proficiency in English. For young refugees forced to flee the violence in their homelands, going to college in the United States or Canada represents a chance to realize their full potential in a place of safety. To date, ISSP has assisted more than eighty young people, many of whom hope to return to Iraq or Syria one day to help with rebuilding and renewal.

© d13 / Shutterstock.com

HMMMMM. . .

In what ways does your parish or school serve the needs of the whole human family? How could you support these efforts?

Article 20
Evangelization:
The Gospel Reaching Far and Wide

Jake burst through the front door so quickly that his sister Kayla nearly jumped off the couch. "What's the matter with you?" she asked, annoyed by the interruption to her Netflix-and-popcorn night. "It's soooooo good! You HAVE to see it!" said Jake. Rolling her eyes, Kayla said, "You know I couldn't care less —" but Jake interrupted her. "I *know* you're not a Star Wars person. I know. But this latest one is so awesome. Good action. Cool characters. You'd really love it. Or," he corrected himself, "at least like it." "Whatever," Kayla said, turning back to the screen, as Jake pulled out his phone. He wanted to tell *everyone* about this movie.

When something good happens—whether you've seen a great movie, aced a test, or landed a summer job—your natural instinct is probably to share that good news with your friends, family, and anyone else who might listen to you. Your excitement may bubble up so much that you find it hard to stop talking about it—even if the people you are talking *to* are less than enthused!

Scoring a game-winning goal, acing a test, getting into our college of choice . . . We feel compelled to share our excitement and good news with everyone around us!

The Good News: Meant to Be Shared

At the core of the Church's mission is **evangelization**: sharing the Good News of Jesus Christ through both words and actions. This mission to evangelize is rooted in God's loving desire that all people be saved and know the truth that will unite them with him. Jesus entrusted this mission to the Apostles, who entrusted it to their successors, and they to their successors, and so on, to the present day. Yet, evangelization is not only the responsibility of the Church's leadership. Rather, it is the responsibility of every believer. Imagine if all of us were as energized about our faith as Jake is about the latest Star Wars movie. Think of the powerful impact we could have!

Recognizing that the Church needed to renew and deepen its efforts to share the Gospel message, Pope Saint John Paul II called for a **new evangelization**. Pope Benedict the XVI built on this call and challenged Catholics to find new ways to share the Gospel message with people who have become discouraged or disillusioned with traditional religion. These popes

Christ calls all members of the Church to share the Gospel of salvation through the witness of both our words and actions. Evangelizing with words can mean talking with others about your faith in Jesus; using social media with truth, kindness, and wisdom; and speaking up on behalf of the rights of immigrants, people who are incarcerated, the unborn, and other marginalized groups. Evangelizing with actions can mean respecting your parents and teachers, helping a classmate who is struggling, volunteering to be a lector at your school or parish, or serving meals at a shelter or soup kitchen. What other ways can you think of to share the Good News of God's redeeming love?

---

evangelization ➤ The proclamation of the Gospel of Jesus Christ through word and witness.

new evangelization ➤ A renewed effort, called forth by Pope Saint John Paul II, to bring the Gospel of Christ to individual believers, especially to those who, though baptized, have never fully heard or accepted the Christian message.

recognized that even Christians are affected by religious doubts and discouragement and that we first need to renew our own spiritual lives before we can share our faith with others. In the spirit of the new evangelization, the Church invites all of us to deepen our faith, to renew our commitment to Christ, and to bear witness to the Gospel with courage, creativity, and enthusiasm.

In carrying out the work of evangelization, the Church dialogues respectfully with those who have never heard the Gospel, as well as with those who have rejected it or never seriously considered it. The Holy Spirit guides these missionary efforts, which must never involve force or coercion. Instead, they must be characterized by patience, humility, charity, and a deep trust in the ways in which God is at work in the life of every human being.

UNIT 2

Inviting a friend to pray before or after school is a gentle gesture. What are some other ways you can evangelize that aren't forceful or coercive?

For example, let's say that you decide to invite a friend who doesn't usually go to Sunday Mass to join you and your family at church this weekend. This is a powerful act of evangelization. If she says yes, great! Do all you can to make her feel welcome and to encourage her to come back. However, if she says no, don't get upset, or angry, or make her feel guilty. Whether her response is a yes or a no, God is at work in her life, and you have planted an idea in her mind and heart. Maybe she *will* go to Sunday Mass at some point—even if it's not with you.

UNIT 2

Tuning In and Logging On

The Church adapts her evangelizing strategies in order to communicate the Gospel in ways that are meaningful and relevant for people. For example, in the 1930s, a new medium—thought by many to be very exciting and cutting-edge—was finding its way into more and more people's homes: the radio. Fr. Fulton J. Sheen saw the radio's potential for evangelization.

Father Sheen reasoned that if most people had radios in their homes, why not make use of them as a means of sharing the Good News? So, for twenty years, he hosted a weekly radio program called *The Catholic Hour*. In the 1950s, when television started to become more popular than radio

© Everett Collection Historical / Alamy Stock Photo

With so many more forms of communication now, who do you think might be the Father Sheen of today?

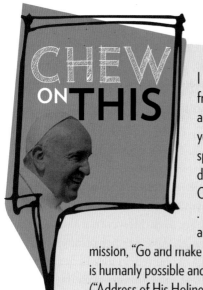

CHEW ON THIS

I am here to meet young people coming from all over the world, drawn to the open arms of Christ the Redeemer. . . . These young people are from every continent, they speak many languages, they bring with them different cultures, and yet they also find in Christ the answer to their highest aspirations. . . . Christ has confidence in young people and entrusts them with the very future of his mission, "Go and make disciples." Go beyond the confines of what is humanly possible and create a world of brothers and sisters! ("Address of His Holiness Pope Francis on the occasion of World Youth Day," July 22, 2013)

in household entertainment, Bishop Sheen adapted, creating and hosting two TV programs, *Life is Worth Living* and *The Fulton J. Sheen Show*. At its peak, his show attracted an audience of thirty million people. He even won two Emmy awards for Most Outstanding Television Personality! Archbishop Sheen died in 1979 and has been declared venerable by the Catholic Church in the process towards canonization.

Today the new frontier of evangelization is not radio or TV, but social media. Is your phone always buzzing with updates and notifications from your social networking accounts? If so, you know that the Church has to use the internet and social media in order to evangelize effectively. Most Catholic dioceses and parishes now maintain websites, and many have a presence on social media. Even Pope Francis regularly tweets @pontifex and posts to Instagram @franciscus! In sharing the saving message of Jesus Christ, the Church tries to connect with people right where they are. Increasingly, in today's world, where people "are" is online. ✳

© ViewApart / iStock.com

Did you know that the Pope has both a Twitter and Instagram account? Check them out!

HMMMMM. . . How could you use social media to promote justice, charity, peace, the sanctity of human life, and other Gospel values?

Article 21
Inculturation: The Gospel Taking Root

In Latin American countries and communities, the nine days prior to Christmas are especially busy and festive. Each night, beginning on December 16, neighborhoods stage a candlelight procession that reenacts Mary and Joseph's search for shelter in Bethlehem. Moving house to house, singing all the while, the procession ends at a different home each night, with the host family providing food and drink for everyone to share. This Advent tradition, called *Las Posadas*, is an expression of Catholic faith that is deeply rooted in Latin American culture. It illustrates what happens when the Catholic Church encounters a new culture. Both the Church and the culture are changed.

National Park Service

This is a traditional Advent procession called *Las Posadas*. Groups of friends and neighbors travel from house to house, singing and then dining at a different family's house for nine days prior to Christmas.

Because the Church is a truly Catholic, global body, she exists in a variety of cultures and societies. In each of these diverse circumstances, the Gospel must take root in ways that are culturally appropriate and meaningful. This process is called **inculturation**.

---

inculturation ➤ The process whereby the Gospel becomes incarnate or cultivated within a particular culture. Each culture influences the way the Gospel is understood and practiced.

Inculturation involves a mutual encounter and respectful dialogue between the Christian faith and a specific culture. It is a two-way process that must always respect cultural identity and practices without betraying, altering, or watering down the truth of the Gospel. In fact, with some creative thinking, certain elements of a given culture can be understood as essential preparation for receiving the Gospel. For example, Pope Saint John Paul II (1920–2005) suggested that traditional African ancestor worship paves the way for African people to understand and accept the Christian belief in the Communion of the Saints. This practice of venerating the ancestors makes it easier for Africans to become Christian, because they are already very open to the idea of the Church as one united Body of Christ, made up of both living and deceased members. Similarly, Black Elk, a Lakota Catholic, saw traditional Lakota ceremonies as a preparation for Christianity. In particular, he thought that the Sun Dance—a ceremony in which participants voluntarily endure suffering for the benefit of others—helped the Lakota people to understand Christ's sacrifice on the cross.

UNIT 2

I DIDN'T KNOW THAT!

World Youth Day is not actually a day! Rather, it's a weeklong celebration that includes numerous opportunities for young people—both teens and young adults—to study, pray, engage in service, and meet peers from all over the world who are trying to deepen and enliven their own faith. Since Pope Saint John Paul II initiated this tradition in 1986, World Youth Day has been held every two to three years at different locations throughout Europe, North America, South America, and Australia.

By the way, did you notice that all the "Chew on This" quotes in this book are from Pope Francis's speeches and homilies at past World Youth Days? Think of his words as directed not only to World Youth Day participants but to all young people—including you!

Cultural Expressions of Faith

Expressions of faith that are rooted *both* in the values and traditions of a particular culture *and* in the life of the Church are a powerful means of evangelizing because they strengthen people's connection to both their culture and their faith. For example, as Latin Americans celebrate *Las Posadas*, the celebration of *Simbang Gabi* draws Filipino communities together in the final days of Advent for a series of nine pre-dawn Masses. In Spain, during Holy Week, cities and towns organize dramatic penitential processions that wind through the streets accompanied by *pasos:* enormous floats decorated with life-sized wooden statues of Jesus, Mary, and other biblical figures. In Ethiopia, the liturgy incorporates an ancient, traditional form of chanting called *zema* that goes back all the way to the sixth century and uses a unique form of musical notation that is native to Africa.

© Cal Vornberger / Alamy Stock Photo

Similar to *Las Posadas, Simbang Gabi* brings Filipino communities together during the nine days before Christmas.

Las Posadas	An Advent tradition rooted in Latin American culture, Las Posadas is a candlelight procession from house to house re-enacting Mary and Joseph's search for shelter in Bethlehem.
Sun Dance	A Lakota ceremony in which participants voluntarily endure suffering for the benefit of others, the Sun Dance helps the Lakota people understand Christ's sacrifice on the cross.
Simbang Gabi	Filipino communities gather together in the final days of Advent for a series of nine pre-dawn Masses.
Pasos	In Spain, cities and towns organize processions during Holy Week that feature life-size statues of Jesus, Mary, and other biblical figures.
Zema	An Ethiopian traditional form of chanting, Zema uses unique musical notation in the liturgy.

UNIT 2

Many cultures incorporate devotion to Mary by promoting a particular Marian image that has been significant in their history. Polish people venerate Our Lady of Czestochowa, while many Mexicans are dedicated to Our Lady of Guadalupe. Our Lady of Fatima, Our Lady of Lourdes, and Our Lady of Montserrat are popular devotions in Portugal, France, and Spain, respectively.

Marian Images

Our Lady of Czestochowa

Our Lady of Guadalupe

Our Lady of Fatima

Our Lady of Lourdes

Our Lady of Montserrat

Black Madonna from Haiti

South Korean depiction of Mary and Jesus

The Church and Culture: It's Win-Win

Imagine for a moment if you were on a softball team in which everyone was an excellent pitcher, but no one could play third base. Or imagine being cast in a musical in which everyone could sing perfectly on key, but no one could dance. It's hard to think of being able to win a softball game, or produce a show, with everyone bringing the same skills to the effort. What is needed, instead, is a diversity of individual skills and talents, which work together to enrich the whole.

The encounter of the Church with various cultures is a little bit like this. Each culture brings unique gifts, perspectives, values, and traditions to the Church. African Catholics have infused the Church's liturgy with a lively, vibrant style, often incorporating dance, drumming, and clapping. Latino Catholics have brought customs like the Quincenara, the celebration of a young woman's fifteenth birthday with a Mass and a party. Asian Catholics have contributed their rich tradition of honoring their ancestors. For example, at a Vietnamese Catholic wedding, the couple may offer incense or place flowers at a small altar that holds photos of their deceased relatives.

Add to practices like these the rich diversity of languages, music, cultural dress, visual art, architecture, and food, and you have a Church that truly and beautifully reflects the fullness of Christ's body.

Cultural traditions like these enrich the Church, making her better able to fulfill her mission of serving the whole human family. Likewise, the Church brings to each culture the saving truth of the Gospel message. The Gospel enriches and transforms the culture, allowing it to grow in fidelity to Jesus and to the compassion, justice, and mercy he proclaimed. ✳

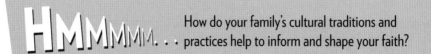

HMMMMMM. . . How do your family's cultural traditions and practices help to inform and shape your faith?

UNIT 2

1. What does the word *Catholic* mean?

2. What are the two ways in which the Church is Catholic?

3. What is the mission of the Iraqi and Syrian Student Project?

4. What is evangelization?

5. In what ways has the Church tried to adapt her evangelizing efforts to meet the needs of a changing world?

6. What does inculturation involve?

7. List several examples of cultural expressions of Catholic faith.

A REAL JESUS

1. What aspects of this image do you find to be unusual or thought-provoking? Why?

2. How is this image an example of inculturation?

3. In what ways could this image, and others like it, support the Church's mission of evangelization?

UNIT 2

CHAPTER 6
The Church Is Apostolic

HOW CAN WE BE A PART OF THE CHURCH'S MISSION TO SHARE THE GOOD NEWS?

SNAPSHOT

Article 22 Page 121
The Apostolic Tradition
• Pre-read: John 20:19–22

Article 23 Page 126
Sent Forth by Jesus
• Luke 9:1–6, 10:1–11

Article 24 Page 130
The Apostolate of the Laity

Article 25 Page 134
Matthew's Message: The Great Commission
• Pre-read: Matthew 28:16–20

Article 22

The Apostolic Tradition

Have you ever been asked or invited to do something and thought, "Who, me?" Maybe you thought something like, "I'm not good enough in Spanish to tutor someone," or "I can't run fast enough to make the varsity cross-country team," or "I'm just one person—I can't do anything about homelessness."

When Jesus invited the **Apostles** to share in his mission of proclaiming the Reign of God, they likely had similar thoughts. As you learned in unit 1, the Apostles were not superheroes. Rather, they were ordinary people, with jobs, lives, and families, whom Jesus called to be part of something extraordinary and life-changing. Their courageous response to this call helped to make possible the Church we know today as One, Holy, Catholic, and **Apostolic**.

TAKE IT TO GOD

Lord, I am ready. Send me.
Send me to the student who desperately needs a friend.
Send me to the teen who is pregnant and can't see a way forward.
Send me to the poor, the forgotten, and the homeless.
Send me to the migrant, the immigrant, and the refugee.
Send me to all who suffer.
In your Holy Wisdom, give me words that heal, hands that serve,
    and a heart that loves.
I know that you call me, Lord, and that you do not leave me alone.
I am ready. Send me.
Amen.

Apostles ➤ The general term *apostle* means "one who is sent" and can be used in reference to any missionary of the Church during the New Testament period. In reference to the twelve companions chosen by Jesus, also known as "the Twelve," the term refers to those special witnesses of Jesus on whose ministry the early Church was built and whose successors are the bishops.

apostolic ➤ To be founded on the Twelve Apostles.

How Is the Church Apostolic?

We can consider the Church to be Apostolic—the fourth mark of the Church—in three ways. First and most obviously, the Church is built and founded upon the Apostles, those who were chosen and sent out on a mission by Christ himself. As Jesus was sent on his divine mission of salvation by God the Father, the Apostles were sent by Jesus, to preach and to heal in his name, both during his earthly lifetime and after his death, Resurrection, and Ascension. In the Gospel of John's account of the Last Supper, Jesus makes clear that their mission from him and his mission from God are one and the same. He says, "Whoever receives the one I send receives me, and whoever receives me receives the one who sent me" (John 13:20).

© ZU_09 / iStock.com

Jesus was very intentional about who he chose as his Apostles. He had every confidence in them as he sent them out to spread the Good News.

Do you know one of the easiest, and yet most important, ways to share in the Church's apostolic mission? By voting! Involvement in the political process allows you to play a role in shaping local, state, and federal laws and policies to make them more consistent with Gospel values. Yet voter turnout in the United States, even for presidential elections, is typically only 50–60 percent of eligible voters.

Set a reminder on your phone: register to vote as soon as you are old enough! When election day comes, inform yourself about the candidates, especially where they stand on issues of human life and dignity. And then make your voice heard by voting!

Second, the Church is Apostolic because, with the help of the Holy Spirit, she preserves and hands on the teaching that Jesus entrusted to the Apostles. In this way, the Church ensures that Jesus' divine mission of salvation continues, until the end of time. As part of this mission, both **Sacred Scripture** and **Sacred Tradition** are passed on, communicating Divine Revelation to us. Together, they form the "single sacred deposit of the Word of God" (*Dei Verbum*, number 10, quoted in *Catechism of the Catholic Church*, number 97). Remember, the Word of God finds its full expression in the saving work of Christ. And the Apostles had the only firsthand experience of all of Christ's life, teaching, and mission. The Church carefully safeguards this deposit of faith, ensuring that future generations of believers will continue to have access to Jesus' authentic teaching.

Sacred Scripture ➤ The sacred writings of the Old and New Testaments, which contain the truth of God's Revelation and were composed by human authors inspired by the Holy Spirit.

Sacred Tradition ➤ *Tradition* comes from the Latin *tradere*, meaning "to hand on." Sacred Tradition refers to the living process of passing on the Gospel message and the Gospel handed on. It began with the oral communication of the Gospel by the Apostles, was written down in Sacred Scripture, and is interpreted by the Magisterium under the guidance of the Holy Spirit. Both Sacred Tradition and Sacred Scripture have their common source in the revelation of Jesus Christ and must be equally honored.

Last, the Church is Apostolic because she continues to be guided and taught by the Apostles in the form of their successors, the bishops. This apostolic tradition of preaching, teaching, and authority has been passed down through the Sacrament of Holy Orders, from bishop to bishop, through generations of leadership, all the way to the present day.

The successors of the Apostles are today's bishops. What are some ways you think bishops carry on the apostolic tradition of preaching, teaching, and authority?

Plugged In and Charged Up

When Jesus calls someone to a mission, he gives them not only the mission but also the power, through the Holy Spirit, to carry out that mission. Otherwise, what good would the mission be? About as good as a cell phone with a low battery and no charger! Consider the story of the appearance of the Risen Lord Jesus to the disciples gathered in the upper room after his death and Resurrection. To this frightened, confused group—so scared that they are huddled behind locked doors—Jesus entrusts a mission: "As the Father has sent me, so I send you" (John 20:21). But he doesn't stop there. He continues, "And when he had said this, he breathed on them and said to them, 'Receive the holy Spirit'" (verse 22).

The Holy Spirit provides the strength, grace, and wisdom that transforms this group into courageous witnesses of the Gospel message. After Pentecost, they share their faith with boldness, even at great risk to their own safety. Some of them travel great distances to other countries and regions, so that everyone can have the opportunity to hear the Good News.

UNIT 2

The Holy Spirit is often symbolized as fire, wind, or a dove. How do these images represent the strength, grace, courage, and wisdom that transformed the Apostles at Pentecost?

As the Spirit once did for those gathered in the upper room, so too the Spirit can and will do for us. The Spirit will turn our fear into courage, our reluctance into eagerness, and our apathy into passion. You might keep that in mind the next time someone invites you to consider doing something you think you can't do! ✳

What is one mission that you think Jesus may be inviting you to undertake, either now or in your future?

Article 23
Sent Forth by Jesus

In chapter 1, you learned that the word *apostle*, from the Greek *apostolos*, refers to someone who is sent out, as a kind of ambassador. In all four Gospels, Jesus chooses and sends forth the Twelve Apostles as sharers in his divine mission. In the Gospel of Luke, however, Jesus sends forth not only the Twelve, but also a larger group of seventy-two. Considering both of these passages from Luke's Gospel can give us further insight into how the Church is Apostolic.

The Sending Out of the Twelve

In chapter 8 of Luke's Gospel, Jesus heals a man possessed by demons, heals a woman suffering from a hemorrhage, and raises a twelve-year-old girl to life. Immediately following these miracles, Jesus gathers the Twelve Apostles and gives them authority over demons and the power to cure disease. In other words, he enables them to share in his own divine ministry. Like him, they will be able to travel to cities and towns, proclaiming the Reign of God by offering healing and mercy to those who are suffering.

Jesus gave the Apostles authority over demons and the power to cure disease. He enabled them to proclaim the Good News to Jews and Gentiles alike, offering healing and mercy.

In sending out the Twelve, Jesus offers specific directions regarding their journey. He instructs them to travel with nothing: no food, no bag, and no money. This may sound foolish to us: Who would go on a trip with no money and no luggage? But, Jesus wants them to rely completely on the grace of God, and the generosity and hospitality of others. He knows that not everyone will welcome them, and he urges them not to stress about that. Rather, they are simply to put it behind them—to "shake the dust" (9:5) from their feet—and move on.

The Sending Out of the Seventy-Two

One chapter later, Jesus appoints seventy-two people from among his **disciples** (Luke 10:1–11). He sends them out in pairs to the towns he intends to visit as a sort of advance team, to prepare the people there for his eventual arrival. As he did with the Twelve in Luke, chapter 9, Jesus also trusts this group to share in his mission of proclaiming the Reign of God and healing the sick. They are also to travel light and to recognize that not every town will roll out the welcome mat. In fact, some towns will actively reject both them and the message they preach. For this reason, Jesus emphasizes the potential danger of the mission they are undertaking: "I am sending you like lambs among wolves" (10:3).

UNIT 2

© Tycson1 / Shutterstock.com

Jesus also sent out seventy-two disciples in pairs of two. They faced dangerous conditions, reliance on the hospitality of strangers, and possible rejection. Why do you think the disciples came back rejoicing?

disciple ➤ Follower of Jesus.

The Gospel of Luke does not tell us much about the adventures of the Twelve or of the seventy-two, only stating that they "returned rejoicing" (Luke 10:17). We don't know how long they stayed on the road, how many places they visited, who they met, or what hardships they encountered. And we can't follow them on social media to find out! But, we can certainly conclude that the journey would have been a transformative opportunity for them to deepen their own faith as they shared the Good News with others.

A Circle Ever Wider

Jesus founded the Church on the unshakeable foundation of the ministry of the Twelve Apostles. Think of these Twelve as Jesus' inner circle—his closest friends and most trusted companions. Yet, Jesus also drew a much wider group around him than just the Twelve. He sent seventy-two disciples out on a special mission. Beyond them, many other women and men were drawn to his message and became his disciples. We don't know how many there were, but Saint Paul mentions Jesus appearing to over five hundred believers after his Resurrection (see 1 Corinthians 15:6). These disciples played crucial roles in helping to ensure the continued proclamation of God's Reign, both during his life and after his death and Resurrection.

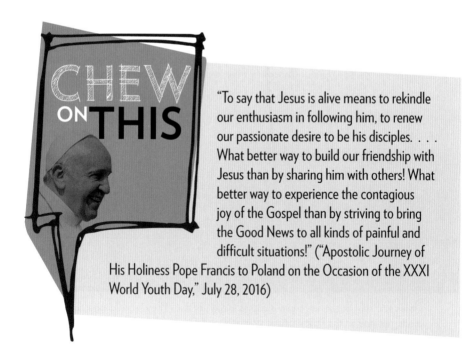

CHEW ON THIS

"To say that Jesus is alive means to rekindle our enthusiasm in following him, to renew our passionate desire to be his disciples. . . . What better way to build our friendship with Jesus than by sharing him with others! What better way to experience the contagious joy of the Gospel than by striving to bring the Good News to all kinds of painful and difficult situations!" ("Apostolic Journey of His Holiness Pope Francis to Poland on the Occasion of the XXXI World Youth Day," July 28, 2016)

Today, these crucial roles are ours to fill. We are the ones whom Jesus calls and sends out to share the Good News, to extend mercy to those who are suffering, to serve those in need, and to be "laborers for his harvest" (Luke 10:2). The circle around Jesus is no longer only twelve or even only seventy-two. That circle has grown wider and wider, and it includes you. Are you up to that challenge? ✳

OVERVIEW OF THE GOSPEL OF LUKE

- **Time period:** Possibly written around AD 80–85.
- **Author:** An unknown Gentile Christian, traditionally Luke, the physician and traveling companion of Saint Paul.
- **Audience:** Written to Theophilus (a Greek name meaning "lover of God"), who possibly represents any Christian.
- **Themes:** Jesus as a compassionate, merciful Messiah who heals divisions among people (including divisions of race, gender, and class); Jesus' followers are called to have special concern for the poor and marginalized.
- **Reason for writing:** To organize the teachings of Jesus and the events of his life, Passion, death, Resurrection, and Ascension "in an orderly sequence" for someone called Theophilus.

HMMMMM. . .   Why do you think that Jesus sent out the seventy-two in pairs, rather than alone or in small groups?

Article 24
The Apostolate of the Laity

All members of the Church—including you—are called to share in the Church's apostolic mission of sharing the Good News of Jesus Christ with the whole world. Each person shares in this mission in a unique way through an apostolate. An apostolate is a means of extending God's reign into the entire world. An individual's **apostolate** will vary, depending upon his or her **vocation**. For people who are called to the lay vocations of marriage or single life, the lay apostolate provides an opportunity to live out the values of the Gospel in every aspect of daily life: at home, at school, at work, and in many other settings.

You can live out your lay apostolate through your words and actions towards your friends and classmates at school, at your after-school job, and with your posts on social media.

---

apostolate ➤ The Christian person's activity that fulfills the apostolic nature of the whole Church when he or she works to extend the Kingdom of Christ to the entire world. If your school shares the wisdom of its founder, its namesake, or the charism of the religious order that founded it, it is important to learn about this person or order and his or her charism, because as a graduate you will likely want to incorporate this charism into your own apostolate.

vocation ➤ A call from God to all members of the Church to embrace a life of holiness. Specifically, it refers to a call to live the holy life as an ordained minister, as a vowed religious (sister or brother), or in a Christian marriage. Single life that involves a personal consecration or commitment to a permanent, celibate gift of self to God and one's neighbor is also a vocational state.

As a young person, you are part of the **laity**; that is, all people who are not ordained. The laity's unique, essential vocation is to evangelize and sanctify the world within their normal, everyday lives. This vocation is rooted in **Baptism**, the sacrament by which we became members of Christ's own body, the Church.

Adult members of the laity bring the Christian message into their offices or workplaces, their homes, and many other venues. As a young member of the laity, you may bring the Gospel message into your school, social media, the coffee shop, and any other place you hang out. The goal of the lay apostolate is to allow the Gospel to influence and guide every interaction you have with others and every decision you make.

UNIT 2

Lay Vocations

Most of the people with whom you interact on a daily basis—like your family members, your teachers and coaches, and your neighbors—are probably members of the laity. So, you know that the laity live in the world in various states of life, including marriage and single life.

Many laypeople are called to the vocation of marriage and family life. They meet another person, they fall in love, and, in the Sacrament of Matrimony, they are united with that person forever. Through their love for one another, God calls them to be parents, and to raise their children in a way that respects each child's vocation to follow Jesus. Married couples who are unable to conceive children on their own also foster new life through adoption or their support for other families.

© LightField Studios / Shutterstock.com

How do you think people discern their call to single life or the vocation of marriage and family?

laity (laypeople) ➤ All members of the Church with the exception of those who are ordained as bishops, priests, or deacons. The laity share in Christ's role as priest, prophet, and king, witnessing to God's love and power in the world.

Baptism ➤ The first of the Seven Sacraments and one of the three Sacraments of Christian Initiation (the others being Confirmation and the Eucharist) by which one becomes a member of the Church and a new creature in Christ.

UNIT 2

Other laypeople are called, either transitionally or permanently, to the single life. A transitionally single person does not plan to remain single; rather, he or she intends, at some point in the future, to follow a call to the vocations of marriage, religious life, or ordination. In contrast, a person who is permanently committed to the single life has made a personal consecration or commitment that takes on a lifelong, celibate gift of self to God and neighbor. Committed single people often have greater flexibility than married people to engage in charity and justice work, to care for ill or elderly family members, and to serve their parish or civic community.

I DIDN'T KNOW THAT!

The Vatican's Pontifical Council for the Laity has formally recognized 122 lay ecclesial movements: associations of Catholics who work together to live out their lay apostolate more authentically and to bring the Gospel message into all areas of society.

One such lay association is the Community of Sant'Egidio. Founded in 1968 by high school students in Rome, the leadership of these young people eventually gave rise to an international organization currently numbering more than fifty thousand laypeople, all of whom live in the world with regular jobs and families. Members of the community gather regularly for prayer; engage in direct service among those who are elderly, poor, or homeless; advocate around issues of justice, particularly for the abolition of the death penalty; and engage in international peacemaking efforts around the globe.

© Courtesy of Community of Sant'Egidio

Christmas Lunch in the Basilica of Santa Maria in Trastevere, Rome, has been organized since 1982 by the Community of Sant'Egidio (*www.santegidio.org*).

Your Apostolate

Your lay apostolate doesn't begin when you turn eighteen or when you graduate from college or when you make some major life decision. It has already begun. It began the moment you were baptized. It is both your right and your responsibility to spread the divine message of salvation through your words and your actions. Think for a moment about how you might do this:

- **At school:** Could you be patient and encouraging toward your teammates on the field or on the court? Could you invite an often-overlooked student to work on a group project with you? Could you introduce yourself to a new teacher and make him/her feel welcome at your school?
- **With friends:** Could you share your belief in God and how it impacts your choices? Could you offer to pray for or with a friend who is going through a difficult time?

- **At home:** Could you take a younger sibling to a game or other school event? Could you help more with cleaning, cooking, yard work, or other household chores? Could you offer to lead the prayer before a family meal?
- **At work:** Do you have a part-time job? If so, could you resolve to be kind, helpful, and courteous to

How do you think helping around the house, encouraging a teammate, or setting aside some of your money for those who are poor is a witness to your faith in Jesus?

your coworkers and supervisor? Could you set aside a small percentage of your wages to share with those who are poor?

In what other places and situations could your words and actions bear witness to your faith in Jesus? ✳

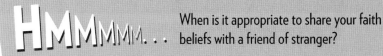
HMMMMM. . . When is it appropriate to share your faith beliefs with a friend of stranger?

UNIT 2

© kate_sept2004 / iStock.com

Article 25

Matthew's Message: The Great Commission

At the very end of the Gospel of Matthew—which, as you learned in chapter 1, is often called "The Gospel of the Church"—the Risen Lord Jesus appears to the disciples with some final instructions and a very compelling promise. This powerful passage appears only at the end of Matthew (see 28:16–20), and it deserves our close attention.

The Setup

It is after Jesus' death and Resurrection. The Risen Jesus has already appeared to "Mary Magdalene and the other Mary" (Matthew 28:1), after they had seen the empty tomb and heard the news that he had been raised. Jesus had given the women these directions: "Do not be afraid. Go tell my brothers to go to Galilee, and there they will see me" (28:10).

And so, the eleven disciples (that is, the Twelve Apostles minus Judas Iscariot) go to Galilee, "to the mountain to which Jesus had ordered them" (Matthew 28:16). There, they have an extraordinary encounter with the Risen Lord.

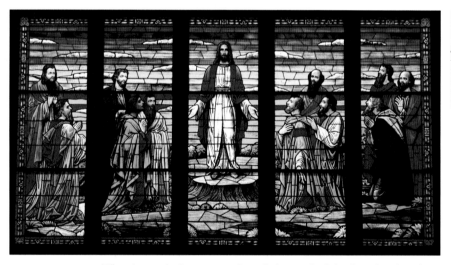

What do you think was going through the minds of the Apostles when the Risen Christ appeared to them? What words would you use to describe their reactions—*afraid, doubtful, in awe, confused, comforted?*

Worshipping and Doubting

Matthew tells us that when the eleven disciples see Jesus, "They worshipped, but they doubted" (28:17). Think about the two verbs in that sentence: worship and doubt. Of course, the disciples, seeing the Risen Lord Jesus for the first time, are moved to worship him. They are likely amazed and astounded by the miracle of his Resurrection. And yet, even as they worship, they doubt. Matthew doesn't specify what they doubt. Do they doubt what their eyes are seeing? Do they doubt that Jesus is really alive, and not a ghost? Do they think that this is simply too good to be true? Are they afraid of how Jesus' Resurrection might change their whole way of thinking and believing? Matthew gives us none of these details. However, he is clear that the disciples' doubt does not get in the way of their worship. They worship *even as* they doubt.

Like the eleven disciples gathered on the mountain with the Risen Jesus, you too may have doubts and questions about your faith. Eventually, you may resolve some of the difficulties that you ponder, but others may not have easy, clear, or straightforward answers. Doubting is normal for anyone, but perhaps especially for young people, as you wonder and try to understand fully what you believe. Matthew's Gospel assures you that your questions and doubts do not exclude you from the Church. Even as you doubt, you can still pray, worship, and participate in the life of the Church. You don't have to wait until you have it all figured out!

We can still go to school, spend time with friends, pray, and participate in our family life while we work through troublesome times.

The Commissioning

The Risen Jesus' short speech to the disciples has two parts: a commission and a promise. First Jesus acknowledges the power that he has received from his Heavenly Father. Then, he **commissions**, or sends forth, the eleven disciples, charging them to "make disciples of all nations" (Matthew 28:19), baptizing in the name of the Blessed Trinity and teaching everyone to obey his teachings.

---

commission ➤ To commission someone is to send him or her on a mission. Jesus commissioned the Apostles to carry out his mission to the world.

The disciples have no spoken lines in this passage, so we don't know their reaction to this commission. However, it's reasonable to think that they would have been at least a little bit intimidated. Make disciples of all nations? How were they supposed to do that? Jesus doesn't give them a road map, a to-do list, a game plan, a time frame—just a mission that he trusts them to carry out.

Jesus gives this commission not only to the eleven disciples, but also to us, his contemporary disciples. For us it can also seem like a tall order! You probably haven't baptized anyone, or traveled to other nations to share Jesus' teachings. Yet, if we are attentive to the needs of others in our midst, there are many ways to fulfill this commission. Perhaps your parish needs volunteers for the children's religious education program. Maybe your diocesan Catholic Charities offers opportunities to support or sponsor a refugee family. Or your school's Campus Ministry may need student leaders for liturgies, retreats, and service projects. When you say "yes" to invitations like these—instead of assuming that someone else will do it—you are responding with faith and courage to Jesus' commission.

Jesus commissioned the Apostles with the task of making disciples of all nations. You are called too. Perhaps you are called to volunteer with religious education, to support a charity, or to participate in service projects.

CATHOLICS MAKING A DIFFERENCE

In 1964, a single Catholic layperson named Jean Vanier made an extraordinary and life-changing decision. Troubled by the confinement and institutionalization of many people with intellectual disabilities, he invited two developmentally disabled young men to live with him in his home in Trosly-Breuil, France. From this initial act of generosity and courage, the global movement of L'Arche—"the Ark"—was born. L'Arche is an international network of small, home-based communities in which people with and without intellectual disabilities live together in a spirit of inclusion, faith, and friendship. Today L'Arche thrives in 152 communities in thirty-seven countries, including France. Jean Vanier shared his home with people with developmental disabilities until he died on May 7, 2019, at the age of 90.

Promising

This passage, and the entire Gospel of Matthew, ends with an extraordinary promise that Jesus extends to the disciples: he pledges to be with them always, "until the end of the age" (28:20). Hopefully, this promise reassures the disciples: Although Jesus has given them a huge mission, he will not leave them alone to accomplish it. Rather, his very presence with them will empower them to carry out all that he has asked.

One way Jesus is present with us is in the Sacrament of the Eucharist.

Like the commission, this promise is made not only to the eleven disciples but also to us. Jesus' promise to be with us "always" is fulfilled in the Church, where we encounter him in the sacraments, most especially and most intimately in the Eucharist. Receiving the Precious Body and Blood of the Lord brings us as close to Jesus Christ as we can possibly be in our earthly lives. When we are truly open to it, that closeness transforms us, from the inside out. The faithful presence of Jesus helps us to overcome our doubts and to joyfully carry out the mission that he has entrusted to us. ✳

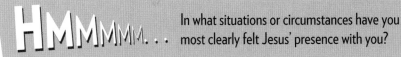

HMMMMM. . . In what situations or circumstances have you most clearly felt Jesus' presence with you?

1. What are the three ways in which we can consider the Church to be apostolic?

2. What is the relationship between Sacred Scripture and Sacred Tradition?

3. Why does Jesus instruct the Twelve Apostles and the seventy-two disciples to travel without a bag, money, or food?

4. What is the unique vocation of the laity?

5. What are lay ecclesial movements? What is one example?

6. At the end of the Gospel of Matthew, what commission does Jesus give to the eleven disciples? What promise does he make to them?

7. Who founded the L'Arche movement? What does this movement do?

ART STUDY

THE RISEN LORD

This painting by Chinese artist He Qi is titled *The Risen Lord*. He Qi illustrates Christian themes with the simple and beautiful art style used in rural China.

1. What strikes you about the way Jesus is portrayed in this painting?

2. Who might be the people in the four corners? What might be significant about their facial expressions and bodily gestures?

UNIT 2 HIGHLIGHTS

CHAPTER 3 The Church Is One

The Four Marks of the Church

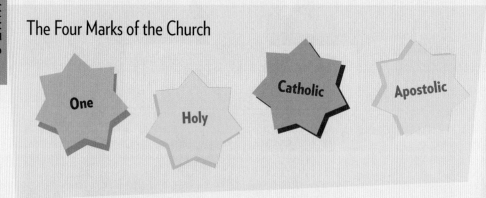

One

Holy

Catholic

Apostolic

The First Mark

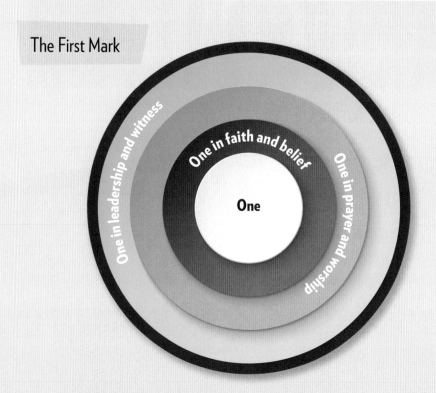

One in leadership and witness

One in faith and belief

One in prayer and worship

One

CHAPTER 4 ▪ The Church Is Holy

The Second Mark

The Church is holy because Christ is holy.

The Church is holy even though we, as individual members, are sinners.

Images: Shutterstock.com

Who Is Called to Be Holy?

The word *saint* comes from a Latin word that means "holy."

All the members of the Church are called to be holy; *all* of us are called to be saints.

Some saints are canonized and help us on our journey to holiness as guides and intercessors.

Holiness and Grace

Grace allows us to grow in holiness.

Grace is freely given to us by God.

GRACE

How do we cooperate with grace?

- We participate in the sacraments.
- We pray with Scripture.
- We engage in service, charity, and justice.

CHAPTER 5   The Church Is Catholic

The Third Mark

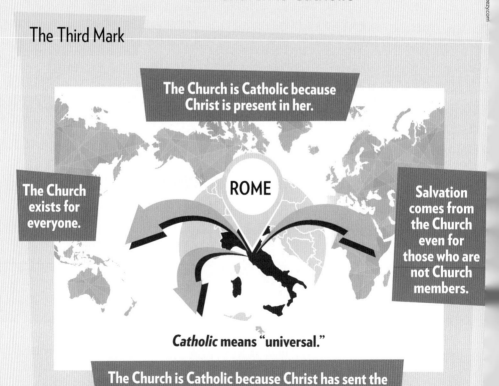

The Church is Catholic because Christ is present in her.

ROME

The Church exists for everyone.

Salvation comes from the Church even for those who are not Church members.

Catholic means "universal."

The Church is Catholic because Christ has sent the Church out on a mission to the whole world.

Inculturation

The Church can successfully evangelize by respecting cultural identity and practices without watering down the Gospel.

The Church uses appropriate cultural stories and symbols to communicate the Gospel message.

Images: Shutterstock.com

CHAPTER 6   The Church Is Apostolic

The Fourth Mark

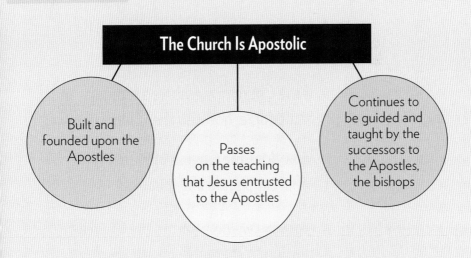

The Church Is Apostolic

Built and founded upon the Apostles

Passes on the teaching that Jesus entrusted to the Apostles

Continues to be guided and taught by the successors to the Apostles, the bishops

UNIT 2
BRING IT HOME

WHY DOES THE CHURCH MATTER?

FOCUS QUESTIONS

CHAPTER 3	How can members of the Church be united all around the world?
CHAPTER 4	If the Church's members are regular, imperfect people, how can the Church be holy?
CHAPTER 5	How does the Church interact with different people and cultures?
CHAPTER 6	How can we be a part of the Church's mission to share the Good News?

OLIVIA
New Smyrna Beach High School

After reading this unit, I feel even more strongly that the Church matters because the community of the Church supports people. The Church is a whole community of people whose arms are open wide. That's what the Church should be. It provides people with love and security, especially when they most need it. And the Church is so much more than Mass on Sunday. Living the way that Jesus lived—serving others—gives us a sense of purpose and belonging

REFLECT

Take some time to read and reflect on the unit and chapter focus questions listed on the facing page.

- What question or section did you identify most closely with?

- What did you find within the unit that was comforting or challenging?

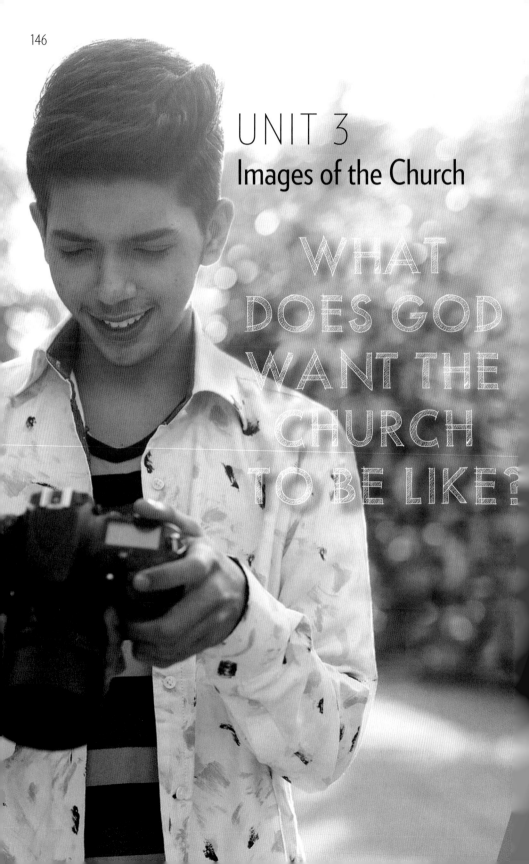

UNIT 3
Images of the Church

WHAT
DOES GOD
WANT THE
CHURCH
TO BE LIKE?

LOOKING AHEAD

CHAPTER 7   Page 148
The Church in Scripture

CHAPTER 8   Page 170
Traditional and Contemporary
Images of the Church

CHAPTER 9   Page 190
The Church and Other Religions

UNIT 3

When I first tried to answer this question, I thought, "How would I know what God wants the Church to be like?" But actually, God does reveal what he wants through Jesus, the Apostles, and the Bible. God wants the Church to be Heaven on Earth. The Church should be the source of good when there is evil in the world. The Church should be a place where people serve one another and help the less fortunate. And I think God would want us to do this work modestly, not letting everyone know what we are doing.

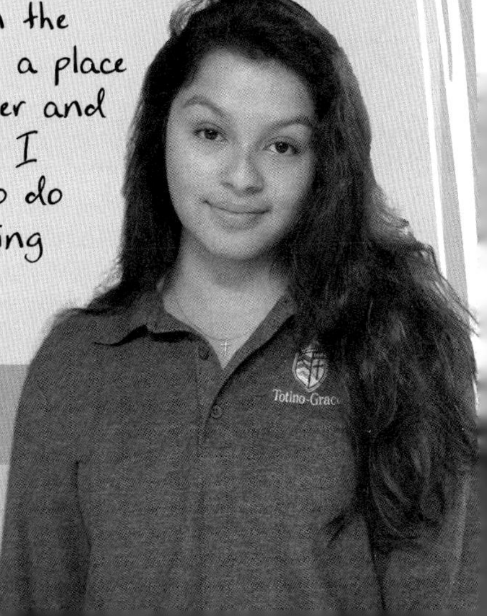

ROSA
Totino-Grace High School

CHAPTER 7
The Church in Scripture

UNIT 3

WHAT IMAGES FROM SCRIPTURE CAN HELP US UNDERSTAND THE CHURCH?

SNAPSHOT

Article 26   Page 149
Old Testament Images
- Pre-read: Genesis 7:6–9:17, 12:1–9, 15:1–6; Exodus 19:1–8; Zephaniah 3:12–20

Article 27   Page 157
New Testament Images: The Gospels
- John 10:1–15, 15:1–8

Article 28   Page 162
New Testament Images: The Epistles
- Pre-read: 1 Corinthians 12:4–31

Article 26
Old Testament Images

Nia's hands shook as she logged on to the online portal that would reveal her entire future. Well, not her *entire* future, but pretty close. She had applied early decision to her dream school, and she was about to find out if all her hard work and planning had paid off. She entered her password and then paused. "Okay," she thought. "Here we go." She tapped *submit*. Nothing happened. "Everyone's checking today—the server must be overloaded," she thought. Then, after what seemed like an eternity, the screen burst into green and gold—the school colors—and "Congratulations!" flashed across her laptop.

Nia screamed, then shouted, then started laughing. Soon tears of relief were streaming down her cheeks. She wanted to share her good news, but, for the first time in her life, she was completely speechless. She couldn't even get her thoughts organized enough to send a text. She told her-

We can share our emotions and feelings by using literal language, but sometimes that just doesn't seem enough. Metaphors, symbols, and images can get across what a simple description sometimes lacks.

UNIT 3

self to just type the simple words "I got in," but she knew that that couldn't do justice to her excitement and happiness. What was it Ms. Hauser always said in sophomore English class? "When literal language just won't do, use metaphors, symbols, and images too!" Who knew that silly little rhyme would ever actually come in handy? Nia thought for a moment and then started texting her message.

TAKE IT TO GOD

"They devoted themselves to the teaching of the apostles and to the communal life, to the breaking of the bread and to the prayers" (Acts 2:42).

God,
As the earliest followers of Christ were given clear instructions, increase my faith when I study your word in the Bible.
Help me bring others to you by sharing my faith in little and big ways.
Empower me to be part of Christ's saving mission when I participate in the Mass with my faith community.
Help me always show my Christian identity through my actions.
Amen.

Literal Versus Figurative

When we encounter a truly amazing and exciting experience, literal language just won't do. We need images, **symbols**, **metaphors**, and other types of **figurative language** to fully capture our thoughts and emotions. This is certainly true of the Church. The *Catechism* describes the Church as an "inexhaustible mystery" (number 753), meaning that literal language alone isn't adequate to describe the Church's reality. Literal language can scratch the surface, but to understand the Church more deeply, we need figurative language too. This is the language often used in the Bible.

In this unit, you will explore many images of the Church, beginning with those that appear in the Old and New Testaments and continuing with those that are rooted in Scripture but further developed in Tradition. Together, all of these images give us profound insight into the Church's immense, salvific mystery and her relationship to other religions.

---

symbol ➤ An object or action that points to another reality and leads us to look beyond our senses to consider a deeper mystery.

metaphor ➤ A figure of speech in which a word or phrase that ordinarily designates one thing is used to designate another, making an implied comparison.

figurative language ➤ A literary form that uses symbolic images, stories, and names to point to a deeper truth.

Recall that Jesus Christ founded the Church during his earthly ministry. So, during Old Testament times the Church on Earth did not yet exist. Yet, because the Church was part of God's eternal plan for the salvation of the world, we find hints in the Old Testament that **foreshadow** the Church that will come to be. Let's look at three key Old Testament stories or themes that prefigure the Church in this way.

Old Testament	Church Foreshadowing
Noah's Ark • The ark saves the faithful from the Flood. • The people and the animals pass through the waters of the Flood and come to physical salvation. • The Flood frees the Earth of wickedness, so Noah and his family can begin again. • God promises to never unleash such devastation again.	**The Church** • The Church saves her members through Christ's saving work. • Members of the Church pass through the waters of Baptism and come to spiritual salvation. • The Church, through the sacraments, saves us from sin. • God's saving love is fully and completely manifested in the Church.
Abraham • God forms his Chosen People starting with one faithful family: Abraham, Sarah, and Isaac. • The Israelites greatly increase in numbers and eventually spread throughout the known world. • The Israelites enter into the Mosaic Covenant with God marked by sacrificial blood. • God called Abraham—and, later, the whole nation of Israel—to be his Chosen People as part of his plan of salvation.	**The Church** • The Church begins when God calls one faithful family: Joseph, Mary, and Jesus. • The Church quickly grows in numbers and spreads throughout the entire world. • The members of the Church are part of the New Covenant marked by the sacrificial Blood of Christ. • God call us, and chooses to save us, in and through the Church.

UNIT 3

foreshadow ➤ To represent or prefigure a person before his or her life or an event before it occurs.

Old Testament	Church Foreshadowing
The Faithful Remnant • The "remnant" is the people of Israel who remain dedicated to God even after enduring great suffering, trials, and catastrophe. They are described as humble, honest, trustworthy, and willing to rely completely on God. • Through Zephaniah, God promises that all faithful people have a place among the remnant, even those who might otherwise be ignored or overlooked. • A faithful group of Jews return from Babylon to rebuild the city of Jerusalem and the Temple.	**The Church** • Saint Paul says, "So also at the present time there is a remnant, chosen by grace" (Romans 11:5). Paul is describing the first Christians who were empowered by the Holy Spirit and stayed faithful and joyful even in the face of disbelief and persecution. • The great assembling of all God's holy ones that Zephaniah foretold is fulfilled in the Church. • The first Christians became the foundation upon which God built the Church.

The story of Noah's ark from the Old Testament foreshadows the Church. What do you think the ark itself stands for?

Noah's Ark

You are likely familiar with the story of Noah's ark. You may have studied it in a prior course, or perhaps you have seen the story depicted in children's books or in popular entertainment. Who can forget the animals filing into the ark, two by two, ahead of the dramatic, forty-day rainstorm? The story's ending, in which God forms a covenant with all creation, symbolized by the rainbow, is also beautiful and memorable.

The ark can be understood to be a symbol that foreshadows the Church. Just as the ark saved all those in it from the Great Flood, so too the Church saves her members from sin through Christ's redeeming presence in the sacraments. To take this symbolism one step further, consider this. The people and animals in the ark passed *through* the waters of the Flood and came to *physical* salvation; that is, they survived the Flood. Similarly, members of the Church pass *through* the waters of Baptism to *spiritual* salvation, in and through Jesus Christ.

The ark also symbolizes salvation from the effects of sin. In the story of the Flood, Noah's family escapes from "the great wickedness of human beings . . . on earth" (Genesis 6:5). The Flood freed the Earth from the effects of this wickedness, so Noah's family could begin again. The Church, through the sacraments, saves us from sin. Through the Sacraments of Baptism and Penance and Reconciliation, we are freed from sin and experience God's forgiveness. We have a fresh start in living the life God calls us to.

Finally, in the covenant God formed with Noah, his family, and all creation, God pledged that "never again shall all creatures be destroyed by the waters of a flood" (Genesis 9:11). This sacred promise is evidence of God's saving love, a love that will be fully and completely manifested in the Church.

Abraham and the People of God

Just a few chapters after the Noah story in the Book of Genesis, God calls a man named Abram (who will later be known as Abraham) to journey to a new land. God promises Abram that He will make of him a great nation, in whom "all the families of the earth will find blessing" (Genesis 12:3). Abram responds to this call by simply following God's command—no questions asked! God says "Go," and seventy-five-year-old Abram goes, along with his wife Sarai (who will later be known as Sarah), his nephew Lot, and their entire household. They set out for the land of Canaan, which God pledges to give to Abram's descendants.

UNIT 3

Later, in Genesis 15:1–6, Abram does have some questions for God. He fears that he will die childless and that, as a result, his only heir will be his servant rather than a flesh-and-blood descendant. God replies by reiterating the divine promise: Abram will indeed have offspring who will be his heirs. To drive home this point, God invites Abram to consider the stars in the sky. Just as the stars are too numerous ever to count so too, will his descendants be. Abram responds with renewed faith in God (see Genesis 15:6). Although he is elderly and childless, he confidently trusts that God will really give him descendants who will become a great nation. (Later Sarai has some doubts and asks Abram to have a child with her maidservant, Hagar. But that's another story.)

God's promise to Abraham has come true! Abraham trusted in God, and God fulfilled the covenant by making Abraham's descendants as numerous as the stars.

The great nation that arises from Abraham and Sarah is the nation of Israel, God's own Chosen People. When the people of Israel gather at Mount Sinai, God enters a covenant with them, through Moses, and declares, "You will be my treasured possession among all peoples" (Exodus 19:5). When Moses shares this news with the Israelites, they declare without hesitation, "Everything the LORD has said, we will do" (19:8).

These Old Testament accounts help us to understand that the community of Israel foreshadowed the Church. In the Old Testament, God forms his Chosen People by starting with one faithful family: Abraham, Sarah, and Isaac. In the New Testament, the Church also begins when God calls one faithful family: Joseph, Mary, and Jesus. Just as the Israelites greatly increase in numbers and eventually spread throughout the known world, the Church quickly grows in numbers and spreads throughout the entire world. Just as the Israelites enter into the Mosaic Covenant with God marked by sacrificial blood (see Genesis 24:6–8), the members of the Church are part of the New Covenant marked by the sacrificial Blood of Christ. So just as God called Abraham—and, later, the whole nation of Israel—to be his Chosen People as part of his plan of salvation, so, too, does God call us, and choose to save us, in and through the Church.

UNIT 3

MAKE IT SO

The covenant that God first made with Abraham, Sarah, and their descendants continues in the life and faith of contemporary Jewish people. They revere their Scripture (which is similar to the Christian Old Testament) as God's Holy Word and follow the Law revealed to Moses at Mount Sinai. Although Jesus, Mary, Joseph, and the Apostles were all Jewish, there have been tensions, misunderstandings, and even violence between Jews and Christians throughout history. Here are some simple choices you can make to help bridge this gap with mutual understanding and dialogue.

- Make an effort to get to know Jewish young people in your school or neighborhood.
- Find out about educational or cultural events at your local Jewish Community Center or synagogue that are open to the public.
- Learn all you can about anti-Semitism and violence against Jewish people, especially the Holocaust.
- Make the Book of Psalms a regular part of your prayer, remembering that Jesus would have spoken those very same prayers in Hebrew, the religious language of his people.

The Faithful Remnant

A final Old Testament image that prefigures the Church is found in the writings of the prophets. Many of the prophets, including Isaiah (see 10:20–22 and 11:11–16), Jeremiah (see 23:1–4), and Micah (see 2:12 and 4:6–8), wrote about a faithful **remnant** of the people of Israel who would remain dedicated to God even after enduring great suffering, trials, and catastrophe. The prophet Zephaniah (see 3:12–20) describes this holy remnant as humble, honest, trustworthy, and willing to rely completely on God, rejoicing in his presence even in times of misfortune. Through Zephaniah, God promises that all faithful people have a place among the remnant, even those who might otherwise be ignored or overlooked: "I will save the lame, and assemble the outcasts; I will give them praise and renown" (Zephaniah 3:19).

The Jewish People see this prophecy fulfilled at the end of the Babylonian Exile. A faithful group of Jews return from Babylon to rebuild the city of Jerusalem and the Temple. The New Testament sees the prophecy also fulfilled in the start of the Church. In his Letter to the Romans, Saint Paul says, "So also at the present time there is a remnant, chosen by grace" (11:5). Paul is talking about those first Christians who were empowered by the Holy Spirit and stayed faithful and joyful even in the face of disbelief and persecution. They became the foundation upon which God built the Church. Thus, the great assembling of all God's holy ones, which Zephaniah foretold, is fulfilled in the Church.

What do we learn from these Old Testament accounts and their foreshadowing of the Church? We learn that the Church should be our refuge, protecting us from the evils present in the world. We learn that the Church is meant to be a large family, the children of God Jesus gathers together from every nation, language, culture, and way of life. And we learn that God can work through a remnant, a small faithful group, to accomplish his will and accomplish his saving plan. ✳

In what ways are images, symbols, and metaphors more powerful than literal language?

---

remnant ➤ A prophetic term for the small portion of people who will be saved because of their faithfulness to God.

Article 27
New Testament Images: The Gospels

During his earthly life and ministry, Jesus Christ began to put into action God the Father's plan for the Church. You learned in chapter 1 that Jesus proclaimed the Reign of God, or Kingdom of God, in both word and deed. Like the tiny mustard seed that gives rise to a magnificent tree (see Luke 13:18–19), the Church is the seed and beginning of the Kingdom. That seed will continue to grow and blossom until the Kingdom of God is fully realized when Christ comes again in glory.

Our primary source for learning about how Jesus proclaimed the Kingdom and established the Church is the four Gospels. As you have learned in previous courses, the Gospels are the written accounts of Jesus' life and teachings. These accounts were first passed on through the oral tradition—the Apostles' preaching and teaching—before being written down. Because the Gospels are exclusively focused on Jesus Christ and are based on the Apostles' accounts of his life and ministry, they are truly "the heart of all the Scriptures" (*Catechism of the Catholic Church*, number 125).

UNIT 3

© Shay Levy / Alamy Stock Photo

I DIDN'T KNOW THAT!

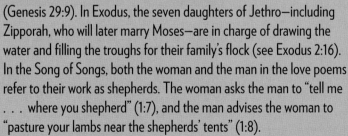

Female shepherds in the Bible? It's true! In the Book of Genesis, Rachel brings her father Laban's sheep to the well, "for she was the one who tended them" (Genesis 29:9). In Exodus, the seven daughters of Jethro—including Zipporah, who will later marry Moses—are in charge of drawing the water and filling the troughs for their family's flock (see Exodus 2:16). In the Song of Songs, both the woman and the man in the love poems refer to their work as shepherds. The woman asks the man to "tell me . . . where you shepherd" (1:7), and the man advises the woman to "pasture your lambs near the shepherds' tents" (1:8).

Today, among the nomadic Bedouin people who live in the desert areas of the Middle East, it is common for women and girls to care for the goats and sheep that are so essential for the family's survival. How does picturing a woman as a shepherd help to expand or enhance your understanding of Jesus as the "Good Shepherd"?

We can learn a great deal about the Church from images, symbols, and metaphors that appear in the Gospels. Two images that provide particularly rich material for study, prayer, and reflection are the Church as the flock gathered around Jesus, the Good Shepherd, and the Church as the branches growing from Jesus, the True Vine. Both of these images would be familiar to the people Jesus was speaking to. They would have been very familiar both with raising sheep and with tending grapevines.

The Good Shepherd: Knowing the Master's Voice

If you have ever had a dog as a pet, or spent time around dogs, you know the strong bond that dogs form with their human caregivers. Many dogs will run excitedly to the door when their people come home from work or school, but they may bark or growl at the mail carrier, a delivery person, or other stranger who comes knocking. Dogs know their caregivers, and they don't always trust someone who smells, sounds, or looks unfamiliar.

The image of Jesus as the Good Shepherd was one that many people of that time, and in that region, could relate to.

Similarly, shepherds and sheep spend a lot of time together—every hour of every day while the sheep are grazing! This closeness makes the sheep very familiar with the shepherd's voice. This is why the "sheep" gathered around Jesus, the Good Shepherd, know his voice and will not obey a stranger. Jesus emphasized this reality: "I know mine and mine know me" (John 10:14).

As members of Jesus' flock, we are called to spend time with Jesus. As members of the Church, we are called to be attentive to Jesus' voice, to follow his example, and to nurture a close relationship with him. We do this by reading and reflecting on his Word, by participating in the sacraments, and by serving others in his name. As we do this, we become so familiar with his "voice" that we recognize his presence in all of these experiences. Christ, in turn, nourishes us, provides for us, and guides us.

Jesus describes himself not only as the Good Shepherd but also as the "gate for the sheep" (John 10:7). At first this might seem confusing: How can a person be a gate? But, it makes sense if you know that shepherds brought the sheep into a structure called a sheepfold at night: a low, stone wall surrounding an open space. The sheepfold had an opening or gate in the wall so that the sheep could get in at night and get out in the morning. The shepherd slept in this opening. In this way, the shepherd would know if any thieves, lions, wolves, or other predators were trying to get in to steal or harm the sheep. His very own body would protect them. Jesus compares the shepherd's willingness to put his life on the line for the sheep to his own willingness to give his life for our salvation: "I will lay down my life for the sheep" (10:15).

UNIT 3

This is an actual sheepfold. Visualize the shepherd sleeping in the opening to protect the sheep from thieves or predators. Jesus is our Shepherd, who laid down his life for us.

Jesus' willingness, as the Good Shepherd, to give his life for his sheep reminds us that we too are called to give our lives for others. We may not necessarily be called to die for others. But we are called to serve others in a spirit of generosity and self-sacrifice. Like Jesus, we too can protect those who are poor and vulnerable from those who would harm them. We can give up some of our own comfort and security so that others may dwell in peace and safety. We can make a sacred commitment to use our gifts and talents to love and serve all members of the "flock" of the Lord.

The True Vine: Drawing Life from Jesus

In the Gospel of John's account of the Last Supper, after Jesus washes the disciples' feet, he offers them some final instructions and reflections. This sort of farewell speech includes a beautiful and thought-provoking extended metaphor. In it, Jesus describes God the Father as the vine grower, himself as the "true vine" (John 15:1), and us, the members of the Church, as the branches of this vine. If you've gardened or taken care of a houseplant, you know that if you cut a leaf or branch from a plant or tree, it withers and decays. It can't sustain itself on its own—it needs to be connected to the whole plant. Jesus is saying that we can't sustain ourselves without him. Jesus, through the Church, gives us life, wholeness, unity with God and with one another, and salvation.

Remaining closely united with and in Jesus enables us to "bear fruit" (John 15:4). A grapevine bears grapes that can be eaten or crushed to make juice or wine. When we remain in Jesus, we bear the spiritual fruits of holiness, charity, justice, peace, and compassion.

© assieteit / iStock.com

By tutoring, participating in food and clothing drives, feeding the homeless, drafting petitions against unethical practices, and more, young people "bear the fruit" of compassion, service, and justice.

UNIT 3

Close Bonds

Both the image of the flock gathering around the Good Shepherd and the image of the branches growing in the vine portray an incredibly close relationship. The sheep know the shepherd's voice and dwell with him day and night. The branches cannot truly be separated from the vine, for together they form one plant, one living entity. Thus, both images invite us into an intimate communion with Jesus the Lord: a close, personal bond that will lead us to a new and more abundant life.

To understand better what this close, personal bond might look like in practice, you might think about your relationship with your very close friends. With good and trusted friends, you can be 100 percent yourself. You don't need to pretend to be perfectly smart or flawlessly attractive. You can just be who you are. You may not always get to see your friends in person, but you probably connect often through texts, calls, or social media. If you have a problem, your close friends might be the first people you ask for help. Really good friends might even sense that something is wrong *before* you ask, because they know you so well. In all of these ways, our close friends help us to be our best and most authentic selves.

Our relationship with Jesus can be similar to these close friendships. Jesus invites us to be our true selves in his presence, to connect with him through prayer and the sacraments, and to ask him for help and guidance. When we nurture this close relationship with Jesus, we grow and flourish as our best selves and as faithful disciples. ✳

OVERVIEW OF THE GOSPEL OF JOHN

- **Time period:** Written around AD 90–110.
- **Author:** The Beloved Disciple, the Apostle John, or a follower/disciple of John.
- **Intended audience:** A community of Jews, Gentiles, and Samaritans in Ephesus (modern-day Turkey).
- **Themes:** Jesus as the Divine Son of God and the *Logos,* the Word of God Made Flesh; Salvation is available for those who believe in Jesus and commit their lives to him.
- **Reasons for writing:** In John's Gospel, the spotlight is on Jesus' divinity from beginning to end.

HMMMMM. . . What images from our everyday lives do you think Jesus would use to teach us about the Church today?

UNIT 3

Article 28
New Testament Images: The Epistles

Like Jesus, Saint Paul used images drawn from people's everyday lives in order to help them to understand the great mystery and gift of the Church. In his **epistles,** he portrays the Church as the Body of Christ, as the Temple of the Holy Spirit, and as the Bride of Christ. The image of the Body of Christ emphasizes the Church's unity and oneness. The image of the Temple of the Holy Spirit draws our attention to the Church's sacred identity as the dwelling place of the Holy Spirit. And the image of the Bride of Christ puts the focus on love: Christ's great love for the Church, a love stronger even than death.

Truly United: The Body of Christ

In the early decades of the first century AD, the Christian community in the city of Corinth was struggling. There were divisions, cliques, and fighting among people with differing priorities and beliefs. They could not agree on even the most basic decisions, like how to pray and celebrate the Eucharist together. Some Christians were still worshipping **idols** and engaging in immoral sexual practices. Tensions ran high between the rich and those who were poor, and some people thought they were better than everyone else. In order to address these problems that threatened to tear the community apart, Saint Paul uses an ingenious metaphor. He teaches the Corinthians—and us—that the Church is one Body of Christ. Christ is the head of the Body (see Colossians 1:18) and the members of the Church, through the power and presence of the Holy Spirit, together form all the Body's parts. Thus, the members are united both with Christ and with one another.

   As he elaborates on this metaphor, Paul explains that each part of the physical body has some distinctive contribution to make to the whole. For example, he asks: "If the whole body were an eye, where would the hearing be? If the whole body were hearing, where would the sense of smell be?" (1 Corinthians 12:17). Likewise, each member of the Body of Christ is called to offer his or her unique gifts to the Church. When this happens—when each person's gifts are welcomed, valued, and respected—then the unity of the one Body overcomes all other divisions, and the diversity of the Body comes to be seen not as a burden, but as a great blessing.

---

epistle ➤ Another name for a New Testament letter.

idol ➤ A false god.

© Production Perig / Shutterstock.com

Each of us is one out of many people. But each of us is part of the Body of Christ. When any part of the Body of Christ is suffering, we are called to respond.

Our unity as one Body of Christ means that we must not neglect those members of Christ's Body who are suffering. Think about this: If your nose were congested and runny, you wouldn't say, "That's just my nose—who cares?" You'd take some cold medicine. Or if you sprained your ankle playing field hockey, you wouldn't think: "Oh well, I have two ankles. I'm not going to worry about this one." You would ice it and wrap it until you felt better. When one part of our body suffers, we give it special attention.

Similarly, when one member of the Body of Christ suffers, we are called to respond. Whether that member is suffering prejudice, discrimination, poverty, hunger, or some other form of injustice, we should not be able to ignore that person any more than we could ignore our own runny nose! Rather, we must respond with practical help and healing, compassionate love.

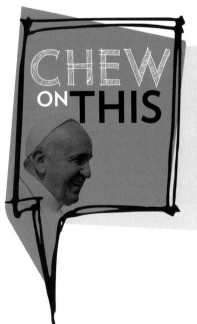

CHEW ON THIS

In every suffering brother and sister that we embrace, we embrace the suffering Body of Christ. ("Apostolic Journey to Rio De Janeiro on the Occasion of the XXVIII World Youth Day, Visit of Saint Francis of Assisi to the Providence of God Hospital—V.O.T.," July 24, 2013)

Truly Sacred: The Temple of the Holy Spirit

If the Church is the Body of Christ, the Holy Spirit is the Church's soul. The Holy Spirit dwells in and with the Church, giving her life, guiding her in all wisdom, and empowering us, her members. The Holy Spirit is the source of the many charisms given to both individuals and communities that benefit and build up the entire Church. For this reason, Paul refers to the Christian community as the Temple of the Holy Spirit. In his First Letter to the Corinthians, he invites them to consider this question: "Do you not know that you [plural] are the temple of God, and that the Spirit of God dwells in you?" (3:16). In his Second Letter to the Corinthians, he boldly asserts, "We are the temple of the living God" (6:16).

In the Old Testament as well as in Jesus' time, the Temple was the building in which God was present to the people of Israel in a unique way. Though the Israelites certainly believed that God was present throughout all creation, they believed God was uniquely present in the Temple. Paul is saying that the Holy Spirit is similarly present in a unique way in the People of God, the Church, and he is reminding the Corinthians that their actions should reflect this reality. Jesus is present in all of us as a community of disciples of Jesus. Paul's teachings help us understand how important it is to have unity within our Church. But also, it should encourage us to revere one another, respect one another, and reach out in love to one another, because in one another, we find the very presence of Jesus.

The Israelites believed that God was uniquely present in the Temple. Paul used this same imagery to help the early Christians understand how the Holy Spirit is present in the Church.

Truly Loved: The Bride of Christ

Paul uses the familiar image of a husband and wife to help early Christian communities understand the relationship between Christ and the Church.

UNIT 3

Paul uses an image drawn from marriage and family life in order to describe the Church. In many ways, marriage is the most intimate relationship that two people can share. In it, a man and a woman are united in an everlasting covenant. They become truly one, both in the physical act of sexual intercourse and in every other area of their lives. For this reason, Paul views marriage as a fitting metaphor for the relationship between Christ and the Church. As a husband and wife give themselves completely to each other in a gift of faithful love, so too did Christ love the Church, giving his life in order to redeem and sanctify her (see Ephesians 5:25–26).

Think of it this way: Marriage is a mystery because in a similar way to the parables, it conceals a truth about Christ and the Church. The divine reality hidden in the metaphor of marriage is that God ordained a permanent union between his Son and the Church. Human marriage is the earthly image of this divine plan. As Christ and the Church are to become one body, marriage reflects this pattern—husband and wife become one flesh. Human marriage gives us the image and language to understand Christ's relationship to the Church.

CATHOLICS **MAKING** A **DIFFERENCE**

© Sylvie Bouchard / Shutterstock.com

Many men and women religious have served the Body of Christ through the ministry of education, especially by educating students who would otherwise be overlooked or neglected. Saint Marie de L'Incarnation, OSU (1599–1672), traveled from France to Quebec in 1639 in order to bring Catholicism to the New World. Although many Europeans did not yet recognize the full humanity of Native North Americans, Saint Marie founded a school which educated French and Native American girls together. She even mastered the Algonquin, Huron, and Iroquois languages, so that she could communicate the Gospel more effectively.

Her courageous decision to educate people relegated to the margins of society reminds us that all members of the Body of Christ are equal in dignity, equally worthy of our care and concern, and equally loved and cherished by God.

In Ephesians 5:22–33, Paul compares in detail the relationship between Christ and the Church to husband and wife. The language from Ephesians can ruffle some feathers in light of today's modern culture. However, if read in the light that Paul truly intended, the analogy is actually beautiful and focuses on the love Christ had for the Church as the model for the love a husband and wife should have for each other. In Ephesians 5:21–25, Paul writes:

> Be subordinate to one another out of reverence for Christ. Wives should be subordinate to their husbands as to the LORD. For the husband is head of his wife just as Christ is head of the church, he himself the savior of the body. As the church is subordinate to Christ, so wives should be subordinate to their husbands. . . . Husbands, love your wives even as Christ loved the church.

This isn't about one person being less than another. To be subordinate means to put the other person's needs before your own. Husbands and wives should do this for each other, out of love and respect. As members of the Church, we are also called to do this for one another and to serve the needs of the world with respect.

The Church is God's gift to us. Although no image, symbol, or metaphor can fully capture the Church's reality, the numerous images of the Church that appear in both the Old and New Testaments can inspire us with vital insights. Whether they are from the Old Testament, from the Gospels, or from the Epistles, these images can nurture our faith, give us a sense of connection to the Church, and remind us that we have a unique contribution to make to the Church that no one else can. Each of us—no matter how unimportant or unworthy we may feel—truly belongs "in the household of God, which is the church of the living God, the pillar and foundation of truth" (1 Timothy 3:15). Each of us has both the responsibility and the power to help the Church live up to the beautiful vision these images express. ✳

UNIT 3

HMMMMM. . . Which of Paul's images of the Church—the Body of Christ, the Temple of the Holy Spirit, or the Bride of Christ—do you find to be the most interesting, helpful, or appealing? Why?

1. How does the story of Noah's ark foreshadow the Church?

2. How does the community of Israel foreshadow the Church?

3. What was the faithful remnant that was described by many of the Old Testament prophets? How was it fulfilled?

4. Why is Jesus both the "Good Shepherd" and the "gate for the sheep"?

5. What do the images of Jesus as the Good Shepherd and Jesus as the True Vine have in common?

6. What are three images of the Church that are found in Saint Paul's epistles?

7. What problems was the early Christian community in the city of Corinth experiencing? How did Saint Paul respond to these problems?

8. What was Saint Marie de L'Incarnation's primary ministry, and what can we learn from it?

What did we go over in class today?

Well, Mr. Tobin said the Church is a boat, a flock of sheep, a body, and branches.

Seriously?  That's what I need to study for the test?

LOL. Basically.

Not helpful! What did he mean?

 The Church is a boat that shelters and saves us.

 The Church is a flock of sheep called to follow Jesus.

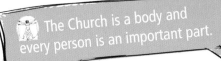 The Church is a body and every person is an important part.

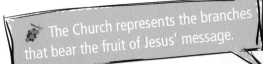 The Church represents the branches that bear the fruit of Jesus' message.

How is he going to test on that?

He said to think about which of the images helps us understand the Church. We probably have to write about it. If you want, I can go over my notes with you.

IMAGES OF THE CHURCH
TEXT EXCHANGE

CHAPTER 8

Traditional and Contemporary Images of the Church

HOW DO DIFFERENT IMAGES OF THE CHURCH HELP US TO UNDERSTAND WHAT THE CHURCH REALLY IS?

SNAPSHOT

Article 29   Page 171
Marian Images
• Pre-read: Luke 1:46–55, John 19:25–27

Article 30   Page 177
Vatican II Images

Article 31   Page 182
Pope Francis: The Church in the Heart of the Action

Article 29

Marian Images

As you learned in chapter 4, the Blessed Virgin Mary played a unique, essential role in salvation history by being the mother of Jesus, the Savior. Think about it: Mary knew Jesus before anyone else on Earth did! For this reason, her life provides us with several key images of the Church. These images, rooted in Scripture, have been further developed and refined in Tradition. Two Scripture passages in particular can help us to explore these Marian images: one from the very beginning of Jesus' earthly life and one from the very end.

Mary's Prayer: *The Magnificat*

When Mary discovers she is pregnant, she is filled with joy. Mary then gives voice to that joy through a prayer called the *Magnificat* (Luke 1:46–55). The words of this prayer make clear that Mary is already a model of faithful discipleship, even though Jesus has not even been born yet. And as the prayer of a faithful disciple, the *Magnificat* gives us several insights into what the Church is and how the Church is called to be in the world.

First, the *Magnificat* is a prayer of praise. It begins with the line, "My soul proclaims the greatness of the Lord" (Luke 1:46). That's like a more formal way of saying "Yay, God!" Praise is basically recognizing something with gratitude in our heart. So, to praise God is to recognize with gratitude something God is or that God does. The *Magnificat's* focus on praise teaches us that the Church is called to always give praise to God. We are to remember God's power, grace, and mercy, especially the saving work of Jesus Christ.

The *Magnificat* is the Blessed Virgin Mary's hymn of praise to the Lord. Mary travels to see her cousin Elizabeth, who is also pregnant. It is then that Mary expresses her joy.

Magnificat ➤ This is the first Latin word (from *magnus*, meaning "great," and *facere*, meaning "to make") and the title of the prayer of Mary in response to the Annunciation of the birth of Jesus in the Gospel of Luke (see Luke 1:46–55).

UNIT 3

Praising God seems easy when good things are happening. But the *Magnificat* reminds us to pray even when we are struggling and uncertain.

Praising God *always* might seem like a lot to ask. What about when you get a bad grade on a test, or fail miserably at volleyball tryouts? What about when *really* bad stuff happens, like serious illness, money problems, divorce, or the death of a loved one? Mary teaches us, through the *Magnificat*, to praise God even amid suffering and struggle. After all, at the moment of her prayer, she is facing tremendous uncertainty. She is an unmarried, pregnant teenager.

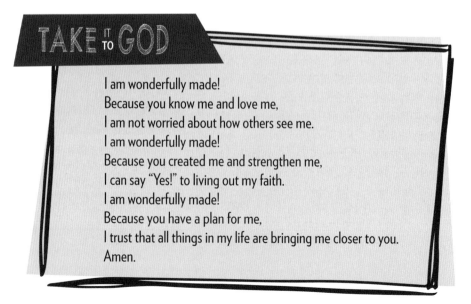

TAKE IT TO GOD

I am wonderfully made!
Because you know me and love me,
I am not worried about how others see me.
I am wonderfully made!
Because you created me and strengthen me,
I can say "Yes!" to living out my faith.
I am wonderfully made!
Because you have a plan for me,
I trust that all things in my life are bringing me closer to you.
Amen.

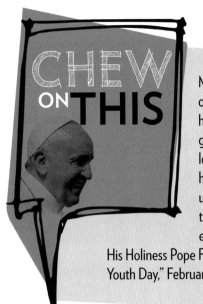

CHEW ON THIS

Mary's is a revolutionary prayer, the song of a faith-filled young woman conscious of her limits, yet confident in God's mercy. She gives thanks to God for looking upon her lowliness and for the work of salvation that he has brought about. . . . Her song helps us to understand the mercy of the Lord as the driving force of history, the history of each of us and of all humanity. ("Address of His Holiness Pope Francis on the Occasion of the XXXII World Youth Day," February 27, 2017)

UNIT 3

She may not even have yet told her fiancé, Joseph, that she is pregnant! In addition, she is Jewish, living in a territory occupied by the forces of the Roman Empire. Her entire people are facing a time of great unrest and insecurity. And yet, without completely knowing how her life will unfold, she praises God with great devotion and enthusiasm.

The *Magnificat* also gives us an image of the Church in service to the world. Mary praises God's concern for people who are in great need, especially those who are lowly and hungry. The Church, following this divine example, is called to renounce arrogance and privilege and to serve others in a spirit of true holiness, humility, and compassion.

Mary's prayer reminds us that the Church will endure forever, until the Reign of God is fully and perfectly realized at the end of time. "His mercy is from age to age" (Luke 1:50), she prays, according to the promise made "to Abraham and to his descendants forever" (1:55). Recall that Abraham and his wife, Sarah, lived almost two thousand years before Mary. By concluding the *Magnificat* with a reference to Abraham, Mary draws our attention to God's constant presence with his people through countless generations. That presence sustained Mary and all the disciples who followed Jesus in his earthly life, and it continues to sustain and guide all members of the Church today.

Mother of the Church: Words from the Cross

Fast-forward about thirty-three years. Jesus is being crucified, and he is very near to drawing his final breath. Mary is near the cross, gathered with her sister (who may or may not be Mary, the wife of Clopas), Mary Magdalene, and the **Beloved Disciple**. Jesus speaks directly to his mother and to the Beloved Disciple. To Mary, he says, "Woman, behold, your son" (John 19:26), and to the Beloved Disciple he says, "Behold, your mother" (John 19:27). With these words, he calls them into a new relationship with one another. He invites them to form a new family, a new community: the Church.

As Jesus is being crucified, he speaks directly to Mary and the Beloved Disciple, drawing them into a new relationship with each other.

Obviously we were not present there at the cross while Jesus was dying. But in a way, the Beloved Disciple symbolizes all disciples, including us. Jesus entrusts Mary to all his disciples as their mother and entrusts all his disciples to Mary as her children. In other words, Mary is the mother not only of Jesus, and not only of the Beloved Disciple, but of the entire Church. In this way, Mary also reminds us that the Church herself is like a mother. As Mary physically gave birth to Jesus, so too does the Church, through preaching the Word and celebrating the sacraments, give birth spiritually to new sons and daughters of God.

Beloved Disciple ➤ In the Gospel of John, an unnamed disciple who may have been the Apostle John.

Mary has been honored as the Mother of the Church since the Church's very beginnings. However, Pope Francis reenergized this devotion by establishing a new feast day that honors Mary with this title. The Memorial of the Blessed Virgin Mary, Mother of the Church is now celebrated throughout the world on the Monday after Pentecost Sunday. In highlighting Mary's presence

Pope Francis established a new feast day that honors Mary, The Memorial of the Blessed Virgin Mary, Mother of the Church, on the Monday after Pentecost Sunday.

UNIT 3

at Pentecost (see Acts 1:14), Pope Francis reminds us that her life of faithful discipleship and her openness to the outpouring of the Holy Spirit can guide our own path toward holiness. Like Mary, we are called to be people of prayer, who praise God in all circumstances. We are called to be completely open to the Divine Will, trusting God even as our lives unfold in surprising, unexpected ways. And we are called to offer our gifts and talents in generous, humble service to all those in need. ✳

Marian Images in the *Magnificat*	These Images Lived in the Church
The *Magnificat* is a prayer of praise. • Praise is recognizing something with gratitude in our hearts. • Praising God is recognizing with gratitude something God is or that God does.	The Church is called to always give praise to God. • We offer God praise at every Mass and other liturgies.
The *Magnificat* gives us an image of service. • Mary praises God's concern for people who are in great need, especially those who are lowly and hungry.	The Church must be a servant to the world. • We are called to renounce arrogance and privilege and to serve others in a spirit of true holiness, humility, and compassion.
Mary as Mother of the Church • As Jesus is crucified he speaks to his mother and to the Beloved Disciple. He calls them into a new relationship with one another. • Jesus entrusts Mary to all his disciples as their mother, and entrusts all his disciples to Mary as her children. • Mary physically gave birth to Jesus. • Mary led a life of faithful discipleship, and openness to the outpouring of the Holy Spirit led her to holiness.	Implications for the Church • This call to new relationship is an invitation for them to form a new family, a new community: the Church. • Mary is not only the mother of Jesus and of the Beloved Disciple, but of the entire Church. • The Church, through the sacraments and preaching of the Word, gives birth spiritually to new sons and daughters of God. • We are called to be people of prayer, open to the Divine Will, trusting God as our lives unfold in surprising and unexpected ways

 **HMMMMMM...** What word or phrase from the *Magnificat* most stands out to you or speaks to your heart? Why?

Article 30
Vatican II Images

The photos coming out of Rome in October 1962 were dramatic and eye-catching. They portrayed more than two thousand bishops from all over the globe gathered in Saint Peter's Basilica for the start of the Second Vatican Council, also known as **Vatican Council II**. Never before in the Church's history had that many Church leaders gathered together in one place. Over the next three years, the Council Fathers would meet four times, discussing various issues, topics, and questions about the Church, especially her relationship to the modern world. These Council sessions brought renewed attention to two important, scripturally based images of the Church: the **People of God** and a **pilgrim church**.

Vatican Council II was the largest gathering of Church leaders in one place, with over 2,500 official members in attendance.

Vatican Council II ➤ The Ecumenical or general Council of the Catholic Church that Pope Saint John XXIII convened as Pope in 1962 and that continued under Pope Saint Paul VI until 1965.

People of God ➤ An image of the Church, based on the Chosen People of the Old Testament and used in the documents of Vatican Council II, to describe the Church as a community of believers chosen by God.

pilgrim church ➤ An expression that came into common use at the time of Vatican Council II as a way of expressing the idea that all Christians are on a pilgrimage toward eternal life, just as the Chosen People were on a pilgrimage to the Promised Land.

UNIT 3

The People of God

As the People of God, the Church is the entire, worldwide community of baptized disciples. In other words, the Church is not only those who hold a particular title, office, or leadership role, like being a priest or a religious sister or brother. Rather, the Church is *all* of us: young and old, women and men, lay and ordained, gay and straight, rich and poor. Just as God once claimed the Israelites as his own chosen people and entered into a covenant with them, so too has God entered into a New Covenant with us. This New Covenant, established through the life, death, and Resurrection of Jesus and in the power of the Holy Spirit, unites us all with God and one another.

© DGLimages / Shutterstock.com

What groups do you belong to that give you a sense of belonging and community?

Think about the different groups that you belong to. There's your family, of course, and your classes at school. You may also belong to a sports team, a scout troop, a parish youth group, and school organizations like the yearbook staff, choir, 4-H, or the French club. Like these groups, the Church can give us a sense of meaning, belonging, and community. The Church can also help us to grow and flourish as our very best selves. However, it's important to understand that the Church is not simply one more group, club, or organization that you can list on your college applications. The Church is different in several key ways.

First, to belong to the Church, you don't just sign up, attend a meeting, put your name on an email list, or "like" the Church on Facebook. You become a member of the People of God through Baptism. Baptism requires faith in Christ, either our faith or the faith of our parents if we were baptized as infants. Through our shared faith, baptized Christians have a unique dignity and freedom as believers in God's own Son.

Second, the head of the People of God is not a team captain or president, but, rather, Jesus Christ, the Son of God and Messiah. Christ acts in and through the Church's earthly leaders and ministers to guide the Church and direct us toward greater holiness and fidelity.

Last, every group has some particular goal or purpose. The yearbook staff has to produce the yearbook by the end of the school year. Your soccer team may work toward advancing to the playoffs. Your scout troop may focus on raising money for a big summer camping trip. The Church's goal or purpose is much bigger and more crucial than any of these. The Church is the way to salvation, "an instrument for the redemption of all" *(Dogmatic Constitution on the Church [Lumen Gentium, 1964] number 9)*. Her ultimate destiny is the Kingdom of God. Christ began this Kingdom of God on Earth, and, through the Church, he will bring it to fullness and perfection at the end of time. As the People of God, we share in this Kingdom, both during our earthly lives and when we are united with God eternally in Heaven.

UNIT 3

A Pilgrim People

When you hear the word *pilgrim*, you might think of the people on the Mayflower who established the first of the thirteen English colonies. Maybe you even remember making pilgrim hats for Thanksgiving when you were in elementary school. However, a pilgrim is anyone who is on a journey for a sacred, religious purpose. So the people who landed in Massachusetts in 1620 certainly were pilgrims. But, when we talk about the Church as a pilgrim people, we are not talking specifically about Plymouth Rock and funny hats. We are talking about a much larger concept. All of us who are members of the Church are pilgrims. We are on a spiritual journey toward the Kingdom of God and a heavenly home.

The Camino de Santiago can be a physical challenge, but most who travel the journey are on a spiritual pilgrimage.

"Are we there yet?" Have you been on a trip and had someone in the car constantly asking that question? Maybe it was a younger sibling or one of your teammates as you were on a long drive to an away game. When we're on a physical trip, we can be impatient to get there, and sometimes our impatience can annoy our fellow travelers. With regard to our spiritual journey as a pilgrim people, the answer to "Are we there yet?" is both yes and no. In one sense, we *are* already there, because Christ established the Kingdom of God through his saving life, death, and Resurrection. In another sense, we are *not* there, because the Kingdom of God has not yet been fully realized. Until all people are fully united as one family of God, we are still "on the road."

And while we're "on the road," we need nourishment to keep us going. The Church sustains us on our pilgrim journey through the sacraments, especially the Eucharist, and through the witness of all those who have gone before us. The saints, all holy women and men, and our own loved ones who have died form a "a great cloud of witnesses" (Hebrews 12:1) whose example of faith can inspire and direct our own pilgrim journey toward the Kingdom of God. ✳

UNIT 3

HMMMMMM. . . Think of someone—living or dead—whose example of faith can support your own spiritual journey. Why is this person's life inspiring to you?

Article 31

Pope Francis: The Church in the Heart of the Action

As Andre boarded the chartered bus early Friday morning, he was psyched for a day off from classes. He was less excited about where the bus was headed. Today was the annual junior class field trip to Gettysburg Park. They were studying the Civil War in U.S. history, and so they were going to Gettysburg to see the battlefield and the museum. Not exactly his idea of a good time, but it was better than sitting in class.

Why do you think the author chose to relate the story of Andre's field trip to a Civil War battlefield in an article about the Church in action?

To Andre's surprise, the day actually turned out to be kind of interesting. The park ranger who guided them was enthusiastic and knowledgeable and, amazingly, not boring. He helped them imagine what the battlefield scene would have been like both during and after the battle. It would have been gruesome, with thousands of injured people screaming and crying. There would have been a terrible smell of rotting flesh mixed with gunpowder. Nurses tried to tend the wounded from both sides, but for many, it would be too late. They would die anyway.

A few weeks later, Andre was researching online and came across a quote from Pope Francis that described the Church as a "field hospital after battle." Instantly, Andre was back imagining the scene at Gettysburg. "What a cool way to think of the Church," he reflected. "Out there in the thick of things, helping people who are suffering, and not afraid to get bloody and dirty." That, he thought, was a Church that he could be proud to be a part of.

Do you identify with Pope Francis's image of the Church as a field hospital after battle?

UNIT 3

Tending the Wounded: The Field Hospital

Pope Francis first used the image that Andre found online in an interview conducted shortly after he became Pope. In that interview, he stated:

> The thing the Church needs most today is the ability to heal wounds and to warm the hearts of the faithful; it needs nearness, proximity. I see the church as a field hospital after battle. It is useless to ask a seriously injured person if he has high cholesterol and about the level of his blood sugars! You have to heal his wounds. Then we can talk about everything else. ("Interview with Pope Francis by Anthony Spadaro," August 19, 2013)

When Pope Francis talks about the Church's ministry of healing wounds, he doesn't necessarily mean physical wounds. He is using figurative language to refer to spiritual and emotional wounds. Maybe you know people your age who are wounded in this way. They may be feeling some of the following emotions:

- loneliness and longing for a friend
- anger about their parents' divorce
- serious depression after a betrayal or breakup
- self-isolation because of concerns about their physical appearance
- anxiety about their future

Pope Francis's vision of the Church as a field hospital calls us to reach out with compassion and care to people who are suffering in situations like these. We cannot solve everyone's problems, but we can listen and offer reassurance, a new perspective, and even a little humor. We can even share the hope that belief in Christ brings to our life. Pope Francis invites us to sacrifice some of our own comfort and security in order to place ourselves right at the heart of someone's need and to not turn away until that person is healed and whole again.

© Antonio Guillem / iStock.com

We are called to be Christ for one another in very tangible ways. Being a good listener, offering comfort, making a personal sacrifice in order to help another . . . These are all ways we can live out our faith in our everyday lives.

CATHOLICS **MAKING** A **DIFFERENCE**

Archbishop Juan José Gerardi of Guatemala was truly a shepherd who was unafraid to be close to his sheep, even at the cost of his own life. During Guatemala's thirty-six-year civil war, he defended the human rights of the country's native Mayan peoples, most of whom were poor farmers. He received numerous death threats and even had to temporarily leave Guatemala, but he would not be silenced. On April 24, 1998, he released a report that found the Guatemalan military to be responsible for the systematic oppression and attempted genocide of the Mayan people. Two days later, Archbishop Gerardi was found beaten to death in his garage. Three former military officers were convicted of his murder.

Archbishop Gerardi defended his people, his "sheep," against all those who would harm them. He exemplified the kind of Church Pope Francis envisions: a Church that is "bruised, hurting and dirty" because of self-sacrificial love ("The Joy of the Gospel," number 49).

Serving until We Smell

Just two weeks after he was elected, Pope Francis gave a homily at Saint Peter's Basilica in which he directed priests to "be shepherds, with the 'odor of the sheep.'" So priests should smell like barnyard animals? What point was Pope Francis trying to make?

What do you think the reaction was to Pope Francis's homily in which he directed priests to "be shepherds with the odor of the sheep" (Pope Francis, "Chrism Mass, Homily of Pope Francis, Holy Thursday," March 28, 2013).

UNIT 3

If you've spent any time on a farm, you know that sheep and other farm animals smell. Sheep smell like wet wool, grass, hay, and just that general animal scent that you find in a barn. In the time of Jesus, shepherds were with the sheep 24/7, and daily bathing or showering was definitely *not* the norm. So shepherds would literally smell like their sheep, which is part of why no one wanted to hang around shepherds for very long.

In his homily, then, Pope Francis used this shepherding metaphor to describe the Church's ministry. Although he directed his words to priests, this metaphor is relevant to the entire Church. Pope Francis is saying that if we want to serve other people, we cannot keep our distance from them. Instead, we have to be *with* people who are sick, suffering, poor, imprisoned, depressed, or just in need of companionship. In accompanying them and helping them, we lighten their burden by sharing in the "odor" of their suffering.

Several months later, in the apostolic exhortation "The Joy of the Gospel" (*"Evangelii Gaudium"*), Pope Francis continued to develop this theme using a different metaphor. He talked about the Church, in its work of evangelization:

> It never closes itself off, never retreats into its own security, never opts for rigidity and defensiveness. It realizes that it has to grow in its own understanding of the Gospel and in discerning the paths of the Spirit, and so it always does what good it can, even if in the process, its shoes get soiled by the mud of the street. (Number 45)

Later in the same document, he stated:

> I prefer a Church which is bruised, hurting and dirty because it has been out on the streets, rather than a Church which is unhealthy from being confined and from clinging to its own security. I do not want a Church concerned with being at the center and which then ends by being caught in a web of obsessions and procedures. (Number 49)

© Friedrich Stark / Alamy Stock Photo

A Church that is out on the streets serves people where they are. This volunteer is feeding a dying man in one of the houses run by the Missionaries of Charity.

Like a Church that has the "odor of the sheep," a Church that is "out on the streets" is also closely allied with those who are suffering. The Church that Pope Francis wants us to be is unafraid to go where the need is greatest, and is characterized by compassion, courage, and self-sacrifice.

We shouldn't be afraid to get close to people or to get our hands dirty—either literally or metaphorically! What are some ways that you could respond to Pope Francis's invitation to be like shepherds who have "the odor of the sheep?" For example, could you . . .

- choose a new, challenging placement for your community service hours, like an after-school program for children with special needs or a community garden that provides fresh vegetables for people who are poor?

- deliver food or clothing donations to a domestic violence shelter?

- visit your grandparents once or twice a month, to keep them company and listen to them when perhaps they don't have many visitors?

- reach out to a student who is crying in the bathroom or looking for a place to sit in the cafeteria, instead of looking away or pretending that you don't see?

Pope Francis's images of the Church challenge us to get out of our comfort zone. He invites us to take risks—not risks that are foolish or dangerous, but risks that allow us to proclaim, in both our words and actions, the Gospel message of God's redeeming love. When we do this, we may be uncomfortable. We may get "dirty." We may even smell! Some of our friends or even family members might not understand. But we can take comfort in knowing that we are faithfully following the example of Jesus and creatively responding to Pope Francis's call. ✳

HMMMMM. . . What "wound" in our nation, society, or world do you think is most in need of healing?

1. What three insights into the Church can we find in the *Magnificat?*

2. What is significant about the words that Jesus speaks from the cross in John's Gospel?

3. How did Pope Francis bring new attention to the Blessed Virgin Mary as the Mother of the Church?

4. What does it mean to praise God? Why should we do it?

5. What two images of the Church did Vatican II highlight, and why are they important?

6. What are three ways in which the Church is different from other groups that we belong to?

7. What medical image has Pope Francis used to emphasize the Church's ministry of healing people who are wounded? Why is it important?

8. What did Pope Francis mean when he said that priests should have "the odor of the sheep"?

9. What is Archbishop Juan José Gerardi most known for?

My soul proclaims the greatness of the Lord,
my spirit rejoices in God my Savior
for He has looked with favor on His lowly servant
From this day, all generations will call me blessed.
The Almighty has done great things for me
and holy is His Name

Be not afraid

UNIT 3

THE MAGNIFICAT

1. Based on this artist's depiction of Mary, what emotions do you think Mary is experiencing as she prays the *Magnificat*?

2. How do the colors, shapes, and images in this painting draw you into the image? How do they make you feel?

CHAPTER 9
The Church and Other Religions

WHAT DOES THE CATHOLIC CHURCH THINK OF OTHER RELIGIONS?

SNAPSHOT

Article 32   Page 191
What Are Ecumenism and Interreligious Dialogue?
• Pre-read: John 17:20–26

Article 33   Page 196
The Church's Relationship with Judaism

Article 34   Page 201
Matthew's Message: The Jewish Gospel
• Matthew 1:1–2:23

Article 35   Page 206
The Church's Relationship with Islam

Article 36   Page 212
Focus on Pope Francis: "The Joy of the Gospel"
• "The Joy of the Gospel," numbers 244–258

Article 32

What Are Ecumenism and Interreligious Dialogue?

All her life, Abby has gone to church twice for Christmas every year. It isn't that her family is "super religious." They go twice because her dad is Catholic and her mom is Lutheran. So every year they go to the Christmas Eve Mass at Saint Thomas More Catholic Church and then to the Christmas morning service at Our Savior Lutheran Church. Abby doesn't really mind. She likes singing all the Christmas carols, and the songs are mostly the same at both churches. The rest of the year they usually just go to Saint Thomas More, unless there is something special going on at Our Savior. Abby knows that there are real differences between Catholic and Lutheran beliefs and practices. But when she sits there with her parents and brother each year on Christmas morning, it is the things that they share in common—like Baptism, the Bible, and faith in Jesus—that seem so much more important.

UNIT 3

© ShoeShare / iStock.com

Have you ever had the opportunity to participate in services at churches of different denominations like Abby? What similarities did you notice? what differences?

The many images of the Church that you have explored help to clarify the Church's essential mission: to faithfully preach the Gospel of Jesus Christ through both words and actions, at all times, and in every age. Yet, as the pilgrim people of God, the Church is on a journey in a very diverse world. Even as the Church witnesses to her faith in Jesus as Messiah and Lord, she is called to accompany all people, including those of other religions, and to participate in meaningful dialogue with them. The Church's efforts to engage with other Christians—such as the Eastern Orthodox, Anglicans, Lutherans, and Baptists—are called **ecumenism**. Her work with non-Christian religions, including Judaism, Islam, and eastern religions like Hinduism and Buddhism, is called **interreligious dialogue**.

© Gwengoat / iStock.com

The Catholic Church is called into dialogue with not only other Christian denominations but also other religions.

The Fullness of Christ's Church

The fullness of Christ's one Church—the Church that he established according to God the Father's eternal plan—subsists in the Catholic Church. As Vatican II's *Dogmatic Constitution on the Church* (*Lumen Gentium*, 1964) states: "The one Church of Christ . . . constituted and organized as a society in the present world, subsists in the Catholic Church (number 8)." Yet, the document also affirms that "many elements of sanctification and of truth are found outside [the Church's] visible confines" (number 8).

---

ecumenism ➤ The movement to restore unity among all Christians, the unity to which the Church is called by the Holy Spirit.

interreligious dialogue ➤ The efforts to build cooperative and constructive interaction with other world religions.

Another Vatican II document, the *Decree on Ecumenism* (*Unitatis Reinte-gratio*, 1964), echoes this idea and identifies some of these elements of shared belief and practice: "the written Word of God; the life of grace; faith, hope, and charity" and "the other interior gifts of the Holy Spirit" (number 3). To put it more simply, these documents humbly acknowledge that the Catholic Church does not have a monopoly on holiness and truth. They recognize that God works both within the Church and beyond it. This recognition drives the Church's efforts to dialogue and find common ground with other religions.

Ecumenism: That They May All Be One

Shortly before being arrested, knowing that "his hour had come to pass from this world to the Father" (John 13:1), Jesus prays that his disciples may be united as one: "Holy Father, keep them in your name that you have given me, so that they may be one just as we are" (17:11). These words, spoken so shortly before his death, tell us that Christ desires and wills that all divisions among his followers cease in favor of unity, which is a sign of his unity of being with the Father. This unity is a gift from Christ, even though, "the Church must always pray and work to maintain, reinforce, and perfect the unity that Christ wills for her" (*CCC*, number 820).

UNIT 3

TAKE IT TO GOD

God,
I see you at work, bringing people of many
  different religions together today.
I see people sharing their beliefs, accepting differences,
  and working together despite them.
Help me to be a part of this great dialogue and outreach.
Give me the commitment to seek peace and understanding
  with all those I meet, despite our differences.
Give me the courage to share my faith
  and listen respectfully as others share theirs.
Give me the wisdom to see where we can come together
  and where we must agree to disagree.
Amen.

Dialogue between the Church and other Christian denominations is called ecumenism. Ecumenical relationships are based in the shared Sacrament of Baptism.

Recall from chapter 3 that disunity in the Christian community occurred during the schism that separated the Roman Catholic Church and the Eastern Orthodox Church in 1054 and, later, during the Protestant Reformation. The Church has made great efforts to work at unity with these separated Churches and ecclesial communities. These include, most recently, Pope Francis's meeting with Patriarch Kirill of the Russian Orthodox Church and his participation in commemorating the 500th anniversary of the Protestant Reformation. Ecumenical efforts like these are rooted in our shared Baptism, the Sacrament of Christian unity. As Vatican II's *Decree on Ecumenism* (*Unitatis Redintegratio*, 1964) states: "All who have been justified by faith in baptism are incorporated into Christ; they therefore have a right to be called Christians, and with good reason are accepted as brothers by the children of the Catholic Church" (number 93). In addition to our baptismal unity, Pope Francis has also emphasized the shared willingness of Christians—Catholics, Orthodox, and Protestants—to die for their faith. In a 2017 meeting in Cairo, Egypt, with the Coptic Orthodox leader Tawadros II, Pope Francis referred to the witness of these Christian martyrs as an "ecumenism of blood" ("Address of His Holiness Pope Francis, Cairo," April 28, 2017). The willingness of Christians to sacrifice everything for the sake of their faith is surely one way in which Jesus' vision of Christian unity is realized.

Practically Speaking

What does ecumenism actually look like in practice? For Church leaders and theologians, ecumenism can involve engaging in respectful dialogue focused on **doctrine**, prayer, worship, or social issues. It may also include training priests, deacons, and lay ministers how to relate well with people of varied religious backgrounds.

For everyday people, like you or like Abby, small actions can make a significant contribution toward Christian unity. You can start by simply getting to know people who belong to various Christian **denominations**. These people may be your neighbors, classmates, friends, or, in Abby's case, even members of your own family! You could pray with them, study Scripture together, or organize a service project. Such efforts are not meant to ignore or minimize the real differences that exist among Christ's followers; rather, they are meant to strengthen our shared baptismal identity as disciples called to courageously proclaim the Gospel message and generously serve those in need, all in the name of Christ. ✳

UNIT 3

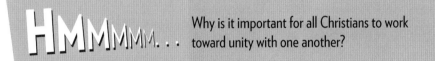

HMMMMM. . . Why is it important for all Christians to work toward unity with one another?

doctrine ➤ An official, authoritative teaching of the Church based on the Revelation of God.

denomination ➤ A group of churches or local congregations that are united by a common creed or shared faith under a single governmental structure (for example, the Episcopal Church or the Presbyterian Church).

Article 33
The Church's Relationship with Judaism

Since Vatican II (1962–1965), the Church has encouraged Catholics to engage in interreligious dialogue. Pope Francis has gone one step further in declaring such dialogue to be "a duty for Christians as well as other religious communities" ("The Joy of the Gospel" *["Evangelii Gaudium"]*, number 250). This strong push toward constructive interaction and conversation with people who are not Christian is rooted in the Church's recognition of the goodness, holiness, and truth that exist in many of the world's religions. For example,

the Vatican II document *Declaration on the Relation of the Church to Non-Christian Religions (Nostra Aetate,* 1965) praises Hindu philosophy and the Buddhist way of life (see number 2). Even more, Catholic teaching acknowledges that God can, in ways known to himself, bring to eternal salvation people who seek him with a sincere heart. Acknowledging the spiritual and moral truths found in other religions does not negate or lessen one's own religious faith. It is possible *both* to witness to one's own faith *and* affirm the goodness and dignity of people who practice other religions.

Traditional Tibetan prayer beads are called Malas. They are used for counting mantra recitations. The most common type of mala is a string of 108 beads or stones.

UNIT 3

Judaism and Catholicism: Uniquely Connected

Of all non-Christian religions, the Church is most uniquely connected with Judaism, both historically and theologically. The Jewish People—initially known as Hebrews and later as Israelites—were the first to hear the Word of God. Their faith is a response to God's revelation. As Saint Paul, who was himself Jewish, explains about the Jewish faith, "theirs the adoption, the glory, the covenants, the giving of the law, the worship, and the promises; theirs the patriarchs, and from them, according to the flesh, is the Messiah" (Romans 9:4–5). And not only Jesus the Messiah, but also Mary, Joseph, the Twelve Apostles, and most of the disciples were Jewish. Judaism and Christianity are so closely related in a shared spiritual heritage that Pope Saint John Paul II described Jews as the "dearly beloved . . . elder brothers" of Christians ("The Roots of Anti-Judaism in the Christian Environment," April 13, 1986).

Some Christians mistakenly believe that the New Covenant established through the life, death, and Resurrection of Jesus Christ replaces the Old Covenant. This is not the case! Think about this: You wouldn't give your best friend a special birthday gift and then ask for it back a few months later. That wouldn't be a gift at all. At best, it would be a loan, and, at worst, a really mean joke. Similarly, God would never take back the gift that he gave the Israelites when he formed a covenant with them. That covenant will endure forever. In the words of Saint Paul, "the gifts and the call of God are irrevocable" (Romans 11:29). They cannot be taken back.

The Church has a unique and intimate relationship with Judaism. There is a shared ancestry and spiritual heritage unlike any other.

UNIT 3

© StunningArt / Shutterstock.com

The Holocaust and Anti-Semitism

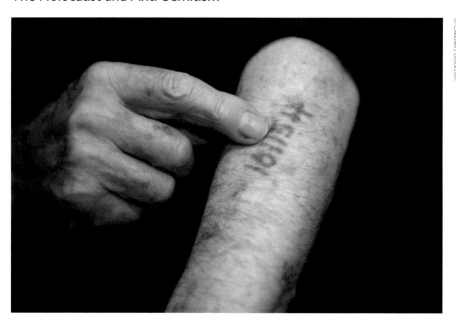

A sign of a Holocaust survivor is an identification number tattooed on their arm. The Holocaust was the attempt by Hitler's Nazi regime to eradicate the Jewish people.

At many times in their history, Jews have been the targets of **anti-Semitic** words and actions, including prejudice, discrimination, and violence. The most horrific example of this was the **Holocaust**, also known as the *Shoah*, which occurred during the Second World War. During the Holocaust, the Nazi regime—which quickly spread throughout western Europe from its original base in Germany—attempted **genocide** against the Jewish people. As a result, six million Jews, plus five million other victims, were murdered from 1933 to 1945.

The Holocaust raises difficult questions regarding Jewish-Christian relations. For example, the 1998 Vatican document *We Remember: A Reflection on the Shoah* asks this: "[During the Holocaust] Did Christians give every possible assistance to those being persecuted, and in particular to the persecuted Jews?"

---

anti-Semitism ➤ Prejudice against the Jewish people.

Holocaust ➤ In the Old Testament, this refers to a sacrifice consumed by fire. It is now the widely used term to designate the attempted extermination of the Jews by the Nazis during the Second World War (1939–1945).

Shoah ➤ A Hebrew word meaning "calamity" that is often used to refer to the Holocaust.

genocide ➤ The systematic and planned extermination of a national, racial, ethnic, or cultural group.

Irena Sendler, pictured here, smuggled thousands of Jewish children out of Nazi-occupied Poland, and delivered them to safety with Christian families.

Miep Gies hid Anne Frank and her family for more than two years until they were discovered and sent to concentration camps.

For sure, some Christians did assist Jewish friends, neighbors, and even strangers. For example, you may know the story of Miep Gies, the Catholic woman who hid Anne Frank and her family for more than two years in Nazi-occupied Amsterdam, Holland. She did so at great risk to herself. A lesser-known example is that of Irena Sendler, also Catholic, who smuggled more than two thousand Jewish children out of the ghetto in Warsaw, Poland. She placed the children with Christian families, where they could be safe until the war ended.

Yet, not all Christians extended this kind of help to Jews. Some actively participated in the persecutions; others simply failed to protest, speak up, or resist. *We Remember* expresses deep regret for "the errors and failures of those sons and daughters of the Church."

A Way Forward

In his 2014 visit to Jerusalem, Pope Francis challenged Jews and Christians to work together to ensure that a tragedy like the *Shoah* will never happen again: "Ever mindful of the past, let us promote an education in which exclusion and confrontation give way to inclusion and encounter, where there will be no place for anti-Semitism in any of its forms or for expressions of hostility, discrimination or intolerance towards any individual or people" ("Welcoming Ceremony Address of Pope Francis, Tel Aviv," May 25, 2014).

Pope Francis's words can inspire all of us to take concrete steps to nurture positive and productive Jewish-Christian relations. We can study and pray with the Old Testament, which both Jews and Christians revere as God's Word. We can learn more both about the Jewish roots of Christianity and about contemporary Judaism. We can use the lessons of history to remind us of the importance of challenging anti-Semitic words, actions, and attitudes. Perhaps most importantly, we can give thanks for the gift of God's faithful love, a love first revealed to Abraham, Sarah, and their descendants and made fully visible in Jesus Christ. ✳

CATHOLICS MAKING A DIFFERENCE

Sr. Rose Thering was a Dominican sister and university professor who devoted her life to reducing prejudice and promoting understanding between Jews and Christians. During her doctoral studies at St. Louis University in the late 1950s, she researched the history of anti-Semitism in Catholic publications and sermons. When the Second Vatican Council opened in 1962, the Council Fathers used her findings to draft portions of Vatican II's *Declaration on the Relation of the Church to non-Christian Religions* (*Nostra Aetate,* 1965).

Prior to Vatican II, some Catholics had charged all Jews with the crime of deicide. They blamed the Jews of Jesus' lifetime and those of the present day for killing God. *Relation of the Church to Non-Christian Religions* condemned this erroneous belief: "What happened in His passion cannot be charged against all the Jews, without distinction, then alive, nor against the Jews of today" (number 4).

Sister Thering died in 2006 at the age of eighty-five, her faith-filled and critical scholarship having left a lasting mark on Catholic theology and on Catholic-Jewish relations.

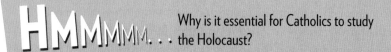

HMMMMM. . .
Why is it essential for Catholics to study the Holocaust?

Article 34
Matthew's Message: The Jewish Gospel

Here's a quick quiz for you:

- Which of the four Gospels contains 130 quotes from, and references to, the Old Testament?
- Which Gospel uses the phrase "Son of David" more times than all the other Gospels put together?
- In which Gospel does Jesus narrowly escape death as a baby?
- In which Gospel does Jesus go up a mountain to teach a crowd of people?

If you answered "Matthew" to all of these, you are correct. The Gospel of Matthew is sometimes called "The Jewish Gospel," and the questions above give you some hints as to why. Matthew roots the story of Jesus firmly in Jewish history and Jewish identity, making it clear that Jesus is the Messiah whose arrival had been anticipated for many generations. For this reason, Matthew is particularly important when considering the relationship between Christians and Jews. It can help us to understand the historical context in which Christianity arose from Judaism. It can also help us to find common ground with Jewish people today.

Biblical scholars believe that the Gospel of Matthew was written to a Jewish Christian community. The members of this community would have still identified themselves as Jewish, but they professed belief in Jesus Christ. The first two chapters of Matthew, called the **infancy narrative**, demonstrate how the author tries to appeal to this audience and to affirm their faith in Jesus.

Matthew's Genealogy

The Gospel of Matthew begins with a **genealogy** that traces Jesus' ancestry all the way back to Abraham. In the first verse of the first chapter, Matthew identifies Jesus as "the son of David, the son of Abraham" (1:1). This doesn't mean literal, biological son. Remember that Jesus was born about eighteen hundred years after Abraham and about a thousand years after King David. This means that Jesus is the descendant, both physically and spiritually, of these great leaders of the Jewish People.

---

infancy narratives ➤ The accounts of Jesus' birth and early childhood.

genealogy ➤ Known as family history, is the study of families and the tracing of their lineages.

Genealogies are not the most exciting thing to read. So-and-so was the father of so-and-so who was the father of so-and-so gets tiresome very quickly, especially when the names are difficult to pronounce! However, if you take the time to carefully read Matthew's genealogy of Jesus, you'll recognize the names of many famous Old Testament figures, like the

Though reading a genealogy may not be very exciting, tracing our ancestors provides a link from our past to our present.

UNIT 3

patriarchs Abraham, Isaac, and Jacob and the kings David and Solomon. Notice, also, that Matthew includes four Old Testament women in a genealogy that otherwise consists entirely of men. If you don't know or remember the stories of Tamar (see Genesis, chapter 38), Rahab (see Joshua 2:1–21, 6:22–25), Ruth (see Ruth, chapters 1–4), and Bathsheba (the wife of Uriah, see 2 Samuel 11:1–12:25), it's worth your time to read about them. Each of these women, in some way, falls outside of mainstream Israelite society. Yet, Matthew makes clear that they are an essential part of Jesus Christ's family history.

The Jewish-Christian community who was the Gospel's audience would have been immersed in God's Word. They would have recognized the names and stories of many of Jesus' ancestors. Matthew's message would have been clear to them: Jesus comes from a long line of faithful Jewish People—and even some God-fearing, Gentile ancestors.

Old Testament Connections

The Gospel of Matthew quotes from and refers to the Old Testament more than any other Gospel. The author's goal is to portray Jesus as the fulfillment of various Old Testament prophecies. In the infancy narrative alone, Matthew quotes from the Old Testament five times, including quotes that state that **Emmanuel** will be born of a virgin (see Matthew 1:22–23) and that a ruler of Israel will come from Bethlehem (see 2:4–6). This pattern continues throughout the Gospel, as the author builds the case for his audience that they don't need to keep looking or waiting for a Messiah. The one God promised to send is already here.

Emmanuel ➤ A Hebrew word meaning "God is with us."

© Chronicle / Alamy Stock Photo

The Gospel of Matthew was written for Jewish Christians. The connection the author makes between Joseph, Mary's husband, and Joseph, son of Jacob, would be clear to this audience.

Another interesting connection between the Gospel of Matthew and the Old Testament is Joseph, Mary's husband. Do you remember Joseph from the Book of Genesis? He was one of the sons of Jacob (Israel) and had the gift of interpreting dreams. This talent leads him to freedom, success, and a reunion with his long-lost brothers. Similarly, in Matthew, Joseph is a dreamer. In the course of the infancy narrative, Joseph has four different dreams in which God speaks to him and guides him. In the first of these, God tells him that it's okay to marry Mary, his fiancée, even though she is pregnant. In reading these stories, Matthew's audience would have made the connection with the Old Testament dreamer, Joseph, and the story of Jesus Christ would have been that much more appealing to them.

© Renata Sedmakova / Shutterstock.com

Joseph, son of Jacob, interprets dreams for the pharaoh. And Joseph, Mary's husband, has four dreams in which God speaks to him and guides him.

A New Moses

The Gospel of Matthew also uses another technique for connecting Jesus' life with Jewish history. Beginning in the infancy narrative, the author writes about Jesus in ways that connect his life and ministry with Moses. As a baby, Jesus' life is in danger, just as Moses's life was. Recall that Pharaoh (the king of Egypt), feeling threatened by the Hebrews, decreed that all Hebrew baby boys be killed. Moses survives because of the quick thinking of his mother and sister and the compassion of Pharaoh's daughter, who adopts and cares for baby Moses (see Exodus 1:8–2:10).

Another connection between the Gospel of Matthew and the Old Testament is the story of Moses. As babies, both Moses's and Jesus' lives were in danger.

Similarly, King Herod, frightened by the reports of the birth of a new king, orders the murder of all boys aged two and under. Jesus survives because Joseph obeys what an angel tells him in a dream: to take Mary and Jesus to Egypt, until Herod is dead. Later, the Holy Family comes out of Egypt and returns to Israel, just as Moses, centuries before, led the Israelites out of slavery in Egypt to freedom in Israel.

The Gospel of Matthew's portrayal of Jesus as a new Moses continues throughout the Gospel. For example, just as Moses went up a mountain to receive the tablets of the Law (see Exodus 19:3–25), so too does Jesus go up a mountain to teach the people a New Law in the Sermon on the Mount (see Matthew, chapters 5–7). Also, biblical scholars have identified five longer speeches that Jesus makes in the course of Matthew. Along with the Sermon on the Mount, there is a speech about being a missionary (see 10:5–42), a collection

UNIT 3

Both Moses and Jesus were whisked away to safety. The Gospel of Matthew continues to make these connections of Jesus as the new Moses throughout.

of parables (see 13:3–53), instructions on how to live together as a community of faith (see 18:1–35), and a speech about **eschatology** (see 23:1–25:46). Scholars think that the author intentionally organized these teachings into these five sections in order to remind his Jewish audience of the five books of the Torah.

When you consider all these things together, the Gospel of Matthew gives evidence to the deep and unbreakable connection between the Jewish People and the Christian Church. The Vatican II document *Relation of the Church to Non-Christian Religions* (*Nostra Aetate*, 1965) refers to the mutual history of Jews and Christians as it condemns anti-Semitism: "The Church, mindful of the patrimony she shares with the Jews . . . decries hatred, persecutions, displays of anti-Semitism directed against Jews at any time and by anyone" (number 4). Matthew makes clear that Judaism and Christianity spring from the common root of God's merciful, redeeming love. ✳

HMMMMM. . .

How would you explain why it helps to know something about the audience each Gospel was written for?

eschatology ➤ The area of Christian faith having to do with the last things: the Last Judgment, the particular judgment, the resurrection of the body, Heaven, Hell, and Purgatory.

Article 35

The Church's Relationship with Islam

Ben made his way across the crowded cafeteria and grabbed an empty seat by his classmate Fouad. "Dude, aren't you hungry? This fried rice is great!" Ben exclaimed, as he dug into his lunch. A moment later, he got a sinking feeling in his stomach, realizing what he had said. "Fouad, sorry! I totally forgot that you're fasting. When does Ramadan end, anyway?"

"Two more weeks," Fouad replied.

"I don't know how you can do that—not eat or drink at all during the day," Ben said.

"It's not that weird. Muslims fast for Ramadan, Jews fast for Yom Kippur—lots of religions fast. Don't you fast during Lent?"

"Yeah, but . . . not eating meat on Fridays isn't that big of a deal. It's not the same as not eating at all!"

"I guess. Hey, Ben, why don't you come to my house for dinner sometime before Ramadan finishes? We don't eat during the day, but, man, do we chow down once that sun sets! You should come."

"Sure, that'd be fun. Text me, okay?"

Friendships like Ben and Fouad's are not always the norm. Though Christians and Muslims have often had very positive relations in the last sixteen centuries, we have also experienced tension and even violence in our shared history. Narrow interpretation of the **Quran** can result in intolerance of Christians by Muslims. And Christians, nervous and hesitant to accept a new religion, became territorial and prejudiced. Too often tension, misunderstanding, and prejudice have polarized the two religious groups.

Islam and the Catholic Church

Along with Judaism and Christianity, Islam is the third **monotheistic** religion that claims Abraham as its spiritual ancestor. This means that Judaism, Christianity, and Islam are all Abrahamic faiths. People who follow Islam are known as Muslims. Historians trace the beginning of the Muslim faith to the life of the prophet Mohammed in the early seventh century AD. Mohammed lived in the cities of Mecca and Medina, which are located in modern-day Saudi Arabia.

Quran ➤ The book of sacred writings accepted by Muslims. Muslims believe the Quran is composed of revelations made to Mohammed by Allah through the angel Gabriel.

monotheism ➤ The belief in and worship of only one God.

The Vatican II document *Relation of the Church to Non-Christian Religions* (*Nostra Aetate*, 1965) states that "the Church regards with esteem also the Muslims" (number 3) and emphasizes the things Christians and Muslims have in common. Most important, both religions worship the same one God. Muslims call God "Allah," which is simply the Arabic word for "God." (Even Arabic-speaking Christians call God Allah.) In addition, Muslims respect Jesus as a prophet, honor the Blessed Virgin Mary, and believe in the resurrection of the dead. Like Christians, they practice prayer, **fasting**, and **almsgiving**.

Though the Church recognizes the many differences and even hostilities that have arisen between Christians and Muslims, the Church takes great care to focus on what we have common, namely that both religions worship the same one God.

Relation of the Church to Non-Christian Religions also acknowledges the many "quarrels and hostilities" that have arisen over the centuries between Christians and Muslims. The document urges that both religions to put the past behind them. In this way, they can move forward in a way that achieves "mutual understanding" and promotes "social justice and moral welfare, as well as peace and freedom" (number 3).

---

fasting ▶ The penitential practice of going without food and/or water for a given period of time.

almsgiving ▶ Freely giving money or material goods to a person who is needy, often by giving to a group or organization that serves poor people. It may be an act of penance or of Christian charity.

MAKE IT SO

Globally, Muslims make up the second largest religious group after Christianity, with 1.8 billion people, or 24 percent of the world's population. Make a resolution to educate yourself about this religion that shares so much in common with Christianity and yet is so often misunderstood. Get to know Muslims in your school or in the wider community. Ask them about their beliefs and practices, so that you can understand what is similar to and different from your own faith. With this knowledge to empower you, you can speak up when someone makes an anti-Islamic comment, including equating Muslims with terrorists. You can also be a friend and advocate for refugees, many of whom come from Muslim-majority countries that have been torn apart by war. Above all, pray for peace in our world, especially among all the children of Abraham.

Saint Francis of Assisi (c. 1181–1226) shocked his contemporaries by traveling to Egypt to meet with the Muslim leader, Sultan Malik al-Kamil, to negotiate an end to the Crusades. Demonstrating respect and understanding towards a leader of another religion was groundbreaking.

© Lanmas / Alamy Stock Photo

Saint Francis and Pope Francis

More than seven hundred years before *Relation of the Church to Non-Christian Religions*, Saint Francis of Assisi made a courageous decision that models how Christians and Muslims could develop greater understanding of one another and cooperate in efforts toward peace. The year was 1219. The **Crusades** were in full

---

Crusades ➤ The military expeditions that were launched under Church authority during the eleventh to thirteenth centuries in order to retake the Holy Land from Muslim control.

swing. In an effort to stop these religious wars, Saint Francis traveled to Egypt to meet with the Muslim leader, Sultan Malik al-Kamil. Against the crusaders' advice—who thought that he was foolishly risking his life—Saint Francis entered the Sultan's camp. He remained there for several days, dialoging with the Sultan and his religious advisors.

Saint Francis's visit with the Sultan did not end the war. In fact, the Crusades would continue for another seventy-two years! Yet, his mission was not a failure. As a Christian, he was ahead of his time in demonstrating extraordinary respect and understanding toward a Muslim leader. This prayerful, open attitude and commitment to a peaceful encounter are an essential foundation of interreligious dialogue, both then and now.

I DIDN'T KNOW THAT!

Judaism, Christianity, and Islam are the world's three major monotheistic religions. All three claim that their faith originates with Abraham and all worship the one merciful God. In addition, all three believe the city of Jerusalem to be sacred. For Jews, Jerusalem was the city of King David and the location of the Temple, where God dwelled and the people offered sacrifice. For Christians, Jerusalem is where Jesus preached and healed, and, most important, where he died and rose. Muslims hold that the prophet Mohammed was taken to Jerusalem on a winged horse-like creature, ascending a ladder to Heaven, meeting with biblical figures, and returning to Earth.

In modern-day Jerusalem, the sites sacred to Jews (the Western Wall, the only surviving part of the ancient Temple), to Christians (the Church of the Holy Sepulcher), and to Muslims (the Dome of the Rock) are all located in the Old City. Jerusalem's Old City is tiny: only a little more than half a square mile. Unfortunately, the three religions' competing claims to such a small area have often resulted in tension and violence. How would Jerusalem, and, with it, the whole world, be different if these three monotheistic religions focused less on what divides them and more on what they share in common?

Pope Francis's approach to Islam seems inspired by the example of his namesake. Even before he became Pope, when he was the archbishop of Buenos Aires, he was the first Catholic bishop to visit Argentina's Islamic Center. As Pope, he has traveled to several Muslim-majority countries, including Bangladesh, Egypt, Jordan, Turkey, and the Palestinian territories. In his 2017 visit to Egypt, he warmly embraced the Grand Imam (Muslim spiritual leader) of Al-Azhar mosque in Cairo and addressed him as "my brother."

Saint Francis and Pope Francis both demonstrate a willingness to reach across divisions, barriers, and boundaries in order to find common ground and engage in meaningful dialogue with Muslims. Such dialogue does not diminish or ignore the real differences between these two religions; rather, it seeks to enable both Christians and Muslims to recognize in each other the image and likeness of the one true God, Creator of all. ✳

Taking a page out of Saint Francis's book, Pope Francis visited the Grand Imam of Al-Azhar in Egypt. This interreligious dialogue is critical to finding common ground and treating one another with respect.

UNIT 3

Common Terms Associated with Islam	
Term	Definition
Islam	Along with Judaism and Christianity, Islam is the third monotheistic religion that claims Abraham as its spiritual ancestor.
Muslims	People who follow Islam are known as Muslims.
Mohammed	The founder of Islam, Mohammed lived in the early seventh century AD.
Allah	The Arabic word for God.
mosque	A building used for public worship by Muslims.
Ramadan	The ninth month of the Islamic year observed as sacred with fasting practiced daily from dawn to sunset.
Imam	The prayer leader of a mosque.

UNIT 3

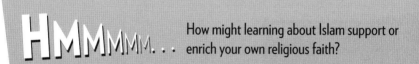

How might learning about Islam support or enrich your own religious faith?

Article 36
Focus on Pope Francis: "The Joy of the Gospel"

So far, we've looked at two of Pope Francis's major documents: "The Joy of Love" (*"Amoris Laetitia"*) and "Rejoice and Be Glad" (*"Gaudete et Exsultate"*). Next up is the apostolic exhortation "The Joy of the Gospel" (*"Evangelii Gaudium"*).

First of all, do you see a pattern in the titles of these documents? Joy . . . rejoice . . . more joy . . . It seems that Pope Francis is trying to tell us something! His point is clear: being a follower of Christ is a great gift that should fill us with deep, lasting joy. Of course, this does not mean that life will always be easy or happy. Experiences that make us sad, angry, or frustrated are a normal part of everyone's life. But, it means that even when we suffer or encounter any kind of difficulty, we can rely on our faith. We can be peaceful and confident, knowing that we are beloved children of God the Father, redeemed by Jesus Christ, and blessed with the power and presence of the Holy Spirit. If that's not good and joyful news, what is?

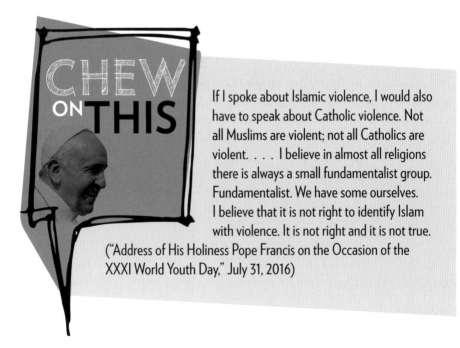

CHEW ON THIS

If I spoke about Islamic violence, I would also have to speak about Catholic violence. Not all Muslims are violent; not all Catholics are violent. . . . I believe in almost all religions there is always a small fundamentalist group. Fundamentalist. We have some ourselves. I believe that it is not right to identify Islam with violence. It is not right and it is not true.

("Address of His Holiness Pope Francis on the Occasion of the XXXI World Youth Day," July 31, 2016)

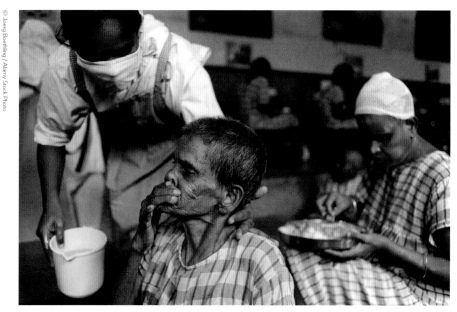

© Joerg Boethling / Alamy Stock Photo

Part of the joy of the Gospel message is sharing it with others. When we purposefully seek to assist those who cannot return the favor or pass it forward, or when we help with the purest of intentions, we are the face of Christ for others.

UNIT 3

"The Joy of the Gospel" begins by reaffirming both the joy of the Gospel message itself and the joy of sharing that message with others. Pope Francis says that the Church is called to go out to all the world like "a mother with an open heart" (number 46) who seeks out those who are lost, confused, or in any kind of need. He acknowledges that the world, which the Church is called to serve, is facing many challenges, including materialism, economic inequality, corruption, social unrest, and violence. Yet, these problems should not scare us away from our responsibility to proclaim the Gospel. All of us—the whole People of God—are called to be "missionary disciples" (number 120), with the help of the Blessed Virgin Mary, "mother of evangelization" (number 284).

Companions on a Shared Journey

In the heart of "The Joy of the Gospel," in a chapter titled "The Social Dimension of Evangelization," Pope Francis turns his attention to ecumenism and interreligious dialogue. Speaking of ecumenical relations with other Christians, he asks that we "never forget that we are pilgrims journeying alongside one another" (number 244). Our conversations and interactions must be based on trust, not suspicion. Pope Francis urges us to focus on what we have in common with other Christians, while also recognizing that we can learn a lot from our differences.

Do you approach those who have different religious beliefs, cultures, and attitudes with openness and acceptance, or with fear and mistrust?

When dialoguing with people of other (non-Christian) religions, Pope Francis recommends that, first, we simply "learn to accept others and their different ways of living, thinking, and speaking" (number 250). Think about steps you could take to practice this kind of acceptance. People of other religions may dress differently than you do, celebrate different holidays, speak a different language, or eat different foods. Can you approach these differences with "an attitude of openness in truth and in love" (number 250), rather than with fear or mistrust? Once we have this foundation of trust and acceptance, then we can work together to bring about peace, harmony, and justice.

Relations with Judaism and Islam

In "The Joy of the Gospel," Pope Francis echoes earlier Church documents on Catholic-Jewish relations in several key ways. For example, he affirms the Jewish faith as "one of the sacred roots of [the Church's] own identity" (number 247). He states that "God continues to work" (number 249) among the Jewish people, in faithfulness to the covenant he made with them many centuries ago. He also expresses regret for the persecutions Jews have endured, "especially those that have involved Christians" (number 248).

Pope Francis visited the concentration camp at Auschwitz in July of 2016. Emphasizing a strong relationship between Judaism and Christianity, Pope Francis said, "[The Jewish faith] is one of the sacred roots of [the Church's] own identity" (cf. Romans 11:16–18).

To be sure, basic differences between Judaism and Christianity remain. Most significantly, the Church proclaims Jesus Christ as Lord and Messiah, a belief that Jews do not accept. And yet, Pope Francis urges Christians and Jews to be friends with one another, to collaborate on solving social problems, and to study the Old Testament together. Such shared, interreligious activities enrich both the Jewish community and the Church.

UNIT 3

Pope Francis notes the growth of Islam, including in many countries that have historically been mostly Christian. Because we are now more likely to have Muslims as our neighbors and friends, we need to learn more about Islam. This will help us to dialogue with one another intelligently and respectfully. He also asks that we show particular concern for Muslim immigrants, newly arrived in our country, often after having suffered terrible hardships. Finally, recognizing that Muslims are often the targets of harmful stereotypes, Pope Francis states that "authentic Islam and the proper reading of the Quran are opposed to every form of violence" (number 253).

Pope Francis calls us to show particular concern for Muslim immigrants, such as these refugee children.

Truly Ourselves, Truly Engaged with Others

For the first time, Brianna was excited about her spring break plans. Ever since she'd heard about the French Club's annual trip to Canada, she'd been saving her babysitting money so that she could go. She had never been out of the United States before, and she couldn't wait to see what a new, different place was like.

But, she was a little nervous too. Part of the trip was a four-night home stay with a Canadian family, and she didn't know what that would be like. What if they thought she was weird? What if *they* were weird? What if she asked stupid questions? Her French teacher had told her to be ready to talk about her school and her life in the United States, but what if they weren't interested?

"Brianna," her dad said, when they were talking about this a few days before the trip, "just be yourself. That's all you can do, right? Share with them who you really are, and try to be open to who they are."

"But what if I say the wrong thing, or offend them, or . . ."

"Then you say the wrong thing! It's okay. They wouldn't have signed up to host an American student if they didn't want to learn about you, and have a fun time showing you around a new place. And hey, if it turns out that you like them, maybe they can come here and stay with us sometime."

Brianna grinned. "Really? That'd be awesome."

"Yes, really," her dad said. "Now go finish packing."

Brianna's dad was inviting her to be true to herself, even as she met new people and experienced a new country and culture. In discussing interreligious dialogue in "The Joy of the Gospel," Pope Francis states that "true openness involves remaining steadfast in one's deepest convictions, clear and joyful in one's own identity" (number 251). In other words, in order to relate with other religions honestly, we must not be afraid to be who we are and to proclaim what we believe. From this firm, clear foundation, we can then interact and dialogue with others. This will not change our core beliefs. But, it will transform our perspective on the world, and strengthen and enrich our own faith. ✳

HMMMMMM. . . Why is being true to ourselves essential for having a healthy, open relationship with another person?

UNIT 3

1. What is the difference between ecumenism and interreligious dialogue?

2. What did Jesus pray for shortly before his death?

3. What sacrament is the source of unity for all Christians? Why?

4. Why did Pope Saint John Paul II call Jews the "elder brothers" of Christians?

5. Why was the Holocaust the most horrifying example of anti-Semitism?

6. Name two Catholics who tried to save Jews during the Holocaust.

7. Why is the Gospel of Matthew sometimes called the "Jewish Gospel"?

8. What are the three monotheistic religions that trace their origins back to Abraham?

9. What lesson can we learn today from Saint Francis's meeting with the Sultan?

10. According to Pope Francis, why is it important for us to learn more about Islam?

UNIT 3

MADONNA OF THE HOLOCAUST

1. What points do you think the artist is trying to make with this painting?

2. What are some of the Jewish and Christian symbols in this artwork?

3. In what ways could this image be the basis for dialogue between Jews and Christians?

CHAPTER 7   The Church in Scripture

Images of the Church

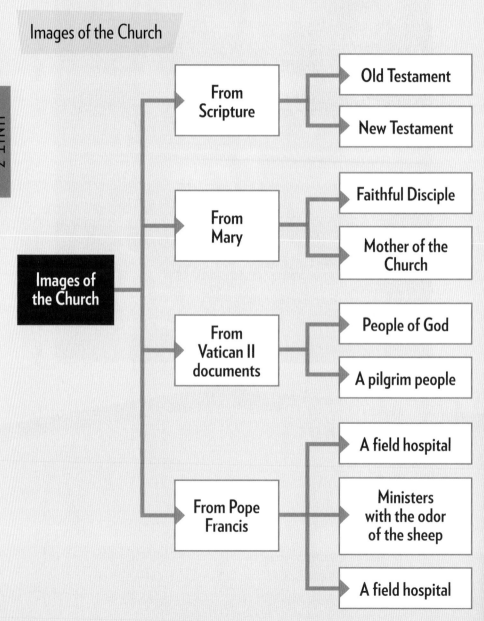

Old Testament Images that Foreshadow the Church

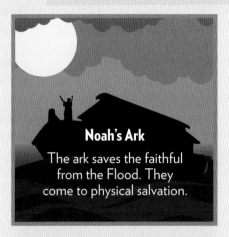

Noah's Ark

The ark saves the faithful from the Flood. They come to physical salvation.

The Church

The Church saves the members through Christ's saving work. Members come to spiritual salvation.

Abraham

God forms his Chosen People starting with one faithful family: Abraham, Sarah, and Isaac.

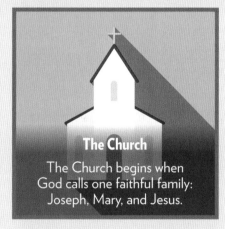

The Church

The Church begins when God calls one faithful family: Joseph, Mary, and Jesus.

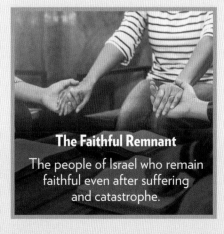

The Faithful Remnant

The people of Israel who remain faithful even after suffering and catastrophe.

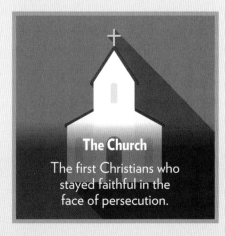

The Church

The first Christians who stayed faithful in the face of persecution.

New Testament Images that Foreshadow the Church

Images from the Gospels

Good Shepherd

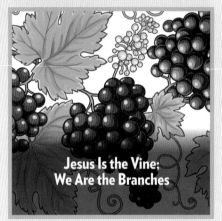

Jesus Is the Vine; We Are the Branches

Images from the Epistles

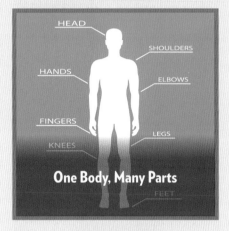

HEAD
SHOULDERS
HANDS
ELBOWS
FINGERS
LEGS
KNEES
FEET

One Body, Many Parts

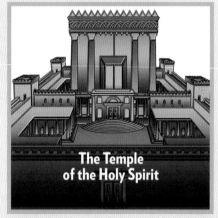

The Temple of the Holy Spirit

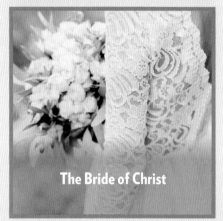

The Bride of Christ

CHAPTER 8   Traditional and Contemporary Images of the Church

Mary, the *Magnificat,* and the Church

The *Magnificat* is a prayer of praise to God.

- Praising God is recognizing with gratitude something God is or that God does.

The Church is called to always give praise to God.

- We offer God praise at every Mass and other liturgies.

The *Magnificat* gives us an image of service.

- Mary praises God's concern for people who are in great need.

The Church must be a servant to the world.

- We are called to renounce privilege and to serve others in a spirit of true holiness, humility, and compassion.

Mary as Mother

- Mary physically gave birth to Jesus.
- As the mother of Christ, Mary was a faithful follower of her son, leading her to holiness.
- As Jesus is crucified, he calls his mother and the Beloved Disciple into a new relationship: he entrusts Mary to his disciples as their mother and his disciples to her as her children.

Implications for the Church

- This call to new relationship is an invitation for Jesus' followers to form a new family—the Church.
- Mary is not only the mother of Jesus, not only of the Beloved Disciple, but of the entire Church.
- Through the sacraments and the Word, the Church gives birth spiritually to new sons and daughters of God.

CHAPTER 9   The Church and Other Religions

Three Monotheistic Religions

Judaism

1. Began with Abraham around 1800 BC.

2. They were the first people to hear the Word of God.

3. God's covenant with them will last forever.

4. They are the "elder brothers" of Christians.

Islam

1. Began with Mohammed, early seventh century.

2. Followers are known as Muslims.

3. They respect Jesus as a prophet and honor the Blessed Virgin Mary.

4. They share some spiritual practices in common with Jews and Christians.

All three believe in and worship the same one, true God.

Christianity

1. Began with Jesus Christ, the Son of God, who lived on Earth from approximately 4 BC–AD 30.

2. This religion is closely related to Judaism.

3. Jesus is the fulfillment of many Old Testament prophecies.

4. Has received the fullness of Revelation and is the source of salvation for all people.

5. Christians are called to proclaim the Gospel and dialogue with all people.

The Gospel of Matthew: The Jewish Gospel

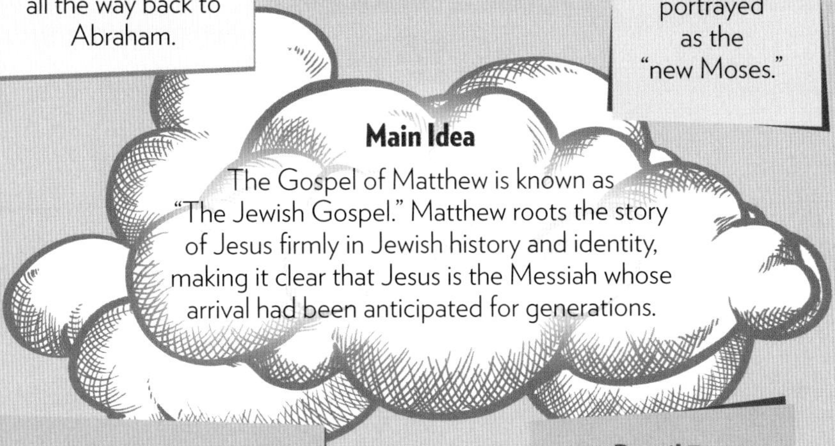

Detail 1
Matthew has a genealogy tracing Jesus' family tree all the way back to Abraham.

Detail 4
Jesus is portrayed as the "new Moses."

Main Idea
The Gospel of Matthew is known as "The Jewish Gospel." Matthew roots the story of Jesus firmly in Jewish history and identity, making it clear that Jesus is the Messiah whose arrival had been anticipated for generations.

Detail 2
Matthew has 130 quotes and references to the Old Testament.

Detail 3
Joseph, Mary's husband, is a "dreamer" like Joseph from Genesis.

UNIT 3

Images: Vecteezy.com

UNIT 3
BRING IT HOME

WHAT DOES GOD WANT THE CHURCH TO BE LIKE?

FOCUS QUESTIONS

CHAPTER 7   What images from Scripture can help us understand the Church?

CHAPTER 8   How do different images of the Church help us understand what the Church really is?

CHAPTER 9   What does the Catholic Church think of other religions?

ROSA
Totino-Grace High School

After reading the unit, I realize that there are some other ways God reveals what he wants the Church to be like. Pope Francis teaches us that we are meant to listen to not only people who are similar to us but also to those who are different in their beliefs. Maybe that isn't the traditional way people have thought of the Church, but it makes sense to me. Pope Francis also talks about the importance of interreligious dialogue, because we have to acknowledge that we can learn from other faiths. He reminds us that when we are fully experiencing the Church, we should feel happy and content as a follower of Christ.

REFLECT

Take some time to read and reflect on the unit and chapter focus questions listed on the facing page.

- What question or section did you identify most closely with?

- What did you find within the unit that was comforting or challenging?

UNIT 4
Ministry in the Church

HOW DO
WE ALL
SHARE IN
CHRIST'S
MISSION?

LOOKING AHEAD

CHAPTER 10 Page 230

The Ministry of Leadership

CHAPTER 11 Page 262

Mission and Holiness

All people are working toward sharing Christ's mission, whether or not we are fully conscious of it. Christ's mission is the root of humanity, the root of all that is good, and the root of love. His mission is to save us from sin and evil by his grace and bring us into union with him. While not all people believe in Heaven, or even in God himself, we should all strive to live in harmony and in peace with one another. By working toward this, it becomes how Christ's mission connects to us all; it is the mission that we as humans, religious or not, naturally aspire to achieve.

HANNAH
Cotter High School

CHAPTER 10
The Ministry of Leadership

WHAT DOES IT MEAN TO BE A LEADER IN THE CHURCH?

SNAPSHOT

Article 37 Page 231
The Structure of the Church

Article 38 Page 236
Matthew's Message: The Ministry of the Pope
- Pre-read: Matthew 16:13–20

Article 39 Page 240
The Ministry of Bishops

Article 40 Page 244
The Ministry of the Magisterium

Article 41 Page 248
The Ministry of Priests and Deacons

Article 42 Page 254
Lay Ministry

Article 37

The Structure of the Church

Do you know where the principal's office is? Do you know who to talk to if you need a late pass? How about where to go to pick up your cross-country uniform? What room does your history class meet in? Where do you go on campus if you need help with a research project? What if you need tutoring in Spanish? Who collects the permission forms for retreats and field trips?

What structures does your school have in place that make it easy for new students to navigate their way to their classes, understand the schedule, and participate in sport and activities?

Just like understanding the structure of your school with all of the various roles and responsibilities of its leaders can seem confusing, the structure of the Catholic Church might seem confusing at first as well. With different roles, such as the Pope, bishops, priests and deacons, the laity, lay ecclesial ministers, and those in consecrated life, the structure of the Catholic Church is vast. However, with over one billion Catholics worldwide, strong leadership and an organized structure is vitally important to the mission of the Church.

UNIT 4

© Monkey Business Images / Shutterstock.com

If you know the answers to these questions, then you are familiar with how your school is run. You know where to go and who to talk to in order to get something accomplished. Now, imagine if your school didn't have these systems in place. For example, what if the classrooms didn't have numbers? What if no one knew which adult was in charge of different programs? What if teachers and administrators switched offices and classrooms with no warning? What if your history class sometimes met in the physics lab and your English class sometimes didn't meet at all? Though changing your school's routine could seem exciting for a while, it would probably not take very long for you to get completely frustrated!

Any organization—whether a business, farm, factory, or workplace, or school—needs structures and systems in order to run smoothly and accomplish its goals. Otherwise, everything can easily fall into complete chaos, and nothing will get done.

UNIT 4

TAKE IT TO GOD

God,
Being a leader of your flock can be challenging.
Today I pray for those who are leaders in the Church.
May they be worthy of their calling to serve you.
May they proclaim the Gospel boldly.
May they keep their eyes focused on you,
    and not be distracted or rely on their own strength.
May they be wise in leading us,
    with hearts that are open to your plan.
May they take the time alone to listen to your voice,
    and pray in order to minister to your people.
And help me grow in my leadership skills and to fearlessly
    spread the Good News in my actions and words.
Amen.

Layers of Leaders

The Church also needs leaders, policies, and systems to fulfill her mission of faithfully proclaiming the Gospel. Globally, the Church's leadership is organized with a visible, hierarchical communion. The word *hierarchy* comes from a Greek root meaning "sacred rule." It refers to the Church's leaders—everyone from the priest at your local parish to the Pope at the Vatican. All members of the hierarchy work together to help the Church run smoothly.

The Catholic Church is organized in a hierarchical structure. The Pope is the center of Church leadership. Pope Francis was elected by the College of Cardinals in 2013.

UNIT 4

At the center of the Church's leadership is the Pope. His role as shepherd of the entire Church takes several forms. First, he is the Bishop of Rome. He is also the head of the **Holy See**, which is the central administration of the whole Church, located in Vatican City. Last, and perhaps most important, he is the head of the worldwide **College of Bishops**. In and through all of these roles, the Pope has supreme authority over the whole Church. To put all this a little more simply, the Pope is the main man, the head honcho, the big kahuna, the guy in charge.

Holy See ➤ This term is a translation of the Latin *sancta sedes*, which literally means "holy seat." The word *see* refers to a diocese or seat of a bishop. The Holy See is the seat of the central administration of the whole Church, under the leadership of the Pope, the Bishop of Rome.

College of Bishops ➤ The assembly of bishops, headed by the Pope, that holds the teaching authority and responsibility in the Church.

You'll recall from earlier in this book that Christ chose the Twelve Apostles, with Saint Peter as their leader, to carry on his mission and ministry. This original community that Jesus established continues today in the community of the Pope and bishops. The Pope is the successor of Saint Peter. Bishops are the successors of the Apostles, according to the authority that has been passed down to them through the Holy Spirit.

Worldwide, the Church is organized into regions or territories known as **dioceses**. Each diocese (larger dioceses are known as archdioceses) has a bishop (or archbishop) as its head. In a larger diocese or archdiocese, one or more auxiliary bishops may assist him with the many tasks involved in running a diocese.

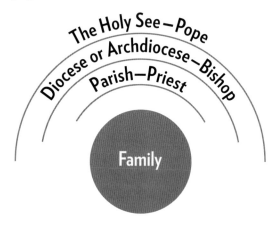

The ministry of bishops has a twofold focus. On the one hand, they must give their full attention to the People of God who have been entrusted to them—the people of their own diocese. Bishops are responsible for anything Catholic within their diocese: parishes, schools, hospitals, social service agencies, and other Church-sponsored ministries and projects. On the other hand, as members of the worldwide College of Bishops, bishops also must demonstrate care and concern for the Universal Church. In particular, they must defend and advocate for those who are poor, for missionaries, and for those who are persecuted because of their faith.

Within each diocese, the Church is organized into **parishes**. Each parish covers a particular geographic area in the diocese and is run by a pastor: a priest appointed to this role by the bishop. Sometimes a priest may be pastor of more than one parish. The pastor may be assisted by other priests, deacons, lay ministers, and members of religious orders.

---

diocese ➤ Also known as a "particular" or "local" Church, the regional community of believers, who commonly gather in parishes, under the leadership of a bishop. At times, a diocese is determined not on the basis of geography but on the basis of language or rite.

parish ➤ The local Christian community under the care of a pastor, appointed by the bishop of the diocese. A parish is a local center for celebration of the Eucharist and other sacraments, the preaching of the Gospel, and works of charity and social concern.

Think Globally, Pray Locally

What qualities do you think make a strong student leader? What types of organizational support can help student leaders be more successful?

UNIT 4

Arturo had been involved in the youth group at Saint Cecilia's since the sixth grade. Now he was part of the senior high group and also a leader for the middle school and junior high students. He loved every minute of it. He really enjoyed meeting students from other high schools who, like him, were trying to live their faith. Plus, it was fun to have the younger students look up to him. He was already sad at having to leave the group when he went away to college! But, that was more than a year away, and Arturo intended to make the very most of that year.

Arturo didn't know it, but, the great experience he was having with his youth group was possible because of the Church's organizational structure. His pastor had started the youth group years ago and continued to encourage the lay leaders who currently directed it. The bishop supported and guided the pastor, and the Pope, in turn, supported the bishop. And because of that cooperation among the Church's hierarchy, Arturo was able to grow in his own faith and help lead others to Christ. ✳

HMMMMM. . . What are the three most important qualities of a good religious leader? Explain why you chose these three.

Article 38

Matthew's Message: The Ministry of the Pope

If the Pope is important enough to be at the very center of the Church's leadership, then where did this idea of having a pope come from? Although the actual word *pope* appears nowhere in the Gospels, the role of the Pope has a clear scriptural basis in a passage that appears only in Matthew's Gospel (see 16:13–20).

We find scriptural evidence for the role of the Pope in Matthew's Gospel. Jesus declares that Peter is blessed and states, "You are Peter, and upon this rock I will build my church" (16:18). In the very next verse, he tells Peter that he will give him "the keys of the kingdom of heaven" (verse 19).

The Bible uses a key as a symbol of authority. In Isaiah 22:22, the priest, Eliakim, receives a key: "I will place the key of the house of David on his shoulder." This is significant as a servant to the king would wear the key to the king's house on a hook on his shoulder. Holding the keys was typically the responsibility of the chief steward of a house. This symbolism is also used in Revelation, which references Jesus having the key of David. Holding they key implies power: ". . . who opens and no one shall close, who closes and no one shall open" (Revelation 3:7).

UNIT 4

The "Keys" to the Kingdom

In this story, Jesus asks his disciples, "Who do people say that the Son of Man is?" He is referring to himself: **Son of Man** is one of several titles for Jesus used in the Gospels. The disciples tell Jesus that people think that he is a prophet who has returned to life. Some believe he is one of the Old Testament prophets, such as Elijah or Jeremiah; others think he is John the Baptist. Then Jesus asks a much more personal question: "Who do you say that I am?" Before anyone else can get a word in, Simon Peter jumps in. Peter is like the student who always wants to answer first—whose hand shoots into the air before the teacher has even finished asking the question. And, in fact, his response is perfect A+ material: "You are the Messiah, the Son of the living God" (Matthew 16:16). Peter knows *exactly* who Jesus is.

Jesus responds to Peter with excitement and enthusiasm, like a teacher pleased by a really good answer. He declares that Peter is blessed and that his faith is a gift from God. Then, he states: "You are Peter, and upon this rock I will build my church" (16:18). The Greek word for Peter is *Petros*, and the Greek word for rock is *petra*. Jesus is using a play on words as he designates Peter to be the first leader of the Church. Peter will be the rock-solid, stable foundation that will allow the Church to form, grow, and thrive.

Finally, Jesus tells Peter that he will give him "the keys to the kingdom of heaven" (16:19). Of course, Jesus does not literally give Peter a key. The Kingdom of Heaven does not have a literal, physical door that needs to be unlocked. But, the "keys" symbolize Peter's ultimate authority as well as the authority of his successors, the popes. This authority means that the Pope has supreme, ordinary, and immediate jurisdiction--that is the power to make decisions and judgments--for the Universal Church. Every pope since Peter can trace his ministry back to this same Gospel passage.

UNIT 4

Son of Man ➤ A messianic title from the Book of Daniel, used to describe a figure who receives authority over other nations from God; the only messianic title in the Gospels used by Jesus to describe himself.

The Pope: A Dad Who Builds Bridges

Recall from chapter 3 that a key aspect of the Pope's ministry is to develop and strengthen unity in the Church. As the pastor of the entire Church, the Pope is called to unite the bishops, as the Church's leaders, as well as uniting all people of faith. The meaning of the word *pope* can help us to understand this ministry of unity.

The word *pope* comes from the Greek word *pappas,* an affectionate term for a father. So the Pope is "Papa" to all the Catholic faithful throughout the world. Like the father of any family, he is called to unite us in one community of mutual love, care, support, and service. Every family—including the Church—suffers setbacks, experiences disagreements, and struggles with hurts and misunderstandings. But the Pope's dedicated, humble leadership can remind us that, no matter what, the Church is still one family of faith, united in Christ.

© Sergeiev / Shutterstock.com

Why do you think the Pope is called the "Supreme Pontiff" or bridge-builder?

© WENN US / Alamy Stock Photo

I DIDN'T KNOW THAT!

Pope Benedict XVI was the first Pope to use Twitter. On December 12, 2012, he tweeted: "Dear friends, I am pleased to get in touch with you through Twitter. Thank you for your generous response. I bless all of you from my heart." The papal Twitter handle is @Pontifex, and Pope Francis tweets daily. In this digital age, the Pope's bridge-building ministry must happen not only in person but also online. If you're not already following @Pontifex, do it today!

Another title for the Pope is **Supreme Pontiff**. The word *pontiff* comes from the Latin word *pontifex*, which means "bridge-builder." As a unifier, the Pope is called to bring together people who are on the opposite sides of a conflict or issue. He can support them as they make connections, create peace, and move forward in a spirit of mutual cooperation. We see Saint Peter doing this in the Acts of the Apostles, as he comes to understand that God is calling both Jews and Gentiles to be part of the Church (see 10:34–35).

The Pope is also called to build bridges to those who have been forgotten by the Church or by society, so that they can once again experience a sense of belonging. These may include people who suffer from drug or alcohol addiction, people who are homeless or poor, people who are elderly or have a disability, or people who identify as gay or lesbian. In a world that so often defines people as one of us or one of them, the Pope's mission is to proclaim that there is no "them." Rather, there is only "us": God's beloved children, the whole human family. *

UNIT 4

HMMMMM. . .

Who is a "rock" for your own life of faith? Whom can you count on for reliable help and prayerful support whenever you need it?

Supreme Pontiff ➤ Another title for Pope, the Bishop of Rome, successor to Saint Peter. Comes from the Latin term *pontifex*, meaning "bridge-builder."

Article 39
The Ministry of Bishops

Bishops are the ordinary ministers of Confirmation. This is one of the many roles and responsibilities of the office of a bishop.

The leadership role of the bishop is an ancient one, going back to the Apostles, who were the original bishops of the Church. The Apostles taught and trained other men who also took on this role in the early Church. The Pastoral Letters to Timothy and Titus describe the qualifications of a bishop. Here's the description from First Timothy:

> Whoever aspires to the office of bishop desires a noble task. Therefore, a bishop must be irreproachable, married only once, temperate, self-controlled, decent, hospitable, able to teach, not a drunkard, not aggressive, but gentle, not contentious, not a lover of money. He must manage his household well, keeping his children under control with perfect dignity; for if a man does not know how to manage his own household, how can he take care of the church of God? (1 Timothy 3:1–5; see also Titus 1:7–9)

If you are like most Catholics, you probably see your bishop only rarely, if you have even met him at all. Many people only see their bishop at a Confirmation liturgy or maybe at a special visit he makes to their parish or school. This may leave you wondering what bishops do all day! As pastors, bishops are called to guide the Church in the path of holiness and truth. In order to do that, they have three jobs, which the Church calls "offices." All bishops—including the Pope who is the Bishop of Rome—must teach, sanctify, and govern.

Teaching

As teachers, bishops' primary task is to preach the Word of God, authentically interpreting that Word in Scripture and Tradition. Bishops may do this through homilies, speeches, writings, and in their daily interactions with both the clergy and the laity of the diocese. Ideally, the bishops' ministry of teaching helps us to value God's Word, to be faithful to the Apostles' teachings on faith and morals, to follow the Church's moral laws, and to understand the **hierarchy of truths** that comprise our faith. The bishops must not only strengthen the faith of those who are already Christ's disciples but must also obey the mandate for evangelization, trying to bring new people into the Church.

The bishops' role as authoritative teachers also means they are responsible for the law of the Church. These are pastoral laws or norms that guide the faithful in participating in the life of the Church. The precepts of the Church would be an example of these laws. When circumstances call for it, the bishops may adjust certain Church practices that fall under these laws. For example, in 2015, Ash Wednesday and the Lunar New Year both fell on February 17. Ash Wednesday, the beginning of Lent, is a day of fasting and abstinence for Catholics. The Lunar New Year is one of the most important and festive holidays of the year for Asian people—with feasting, not fasting! So most bishops declared that Asian Catholics could celebrate the Lunar New Year as usual, even though it was Ash Wednesday. The bishops asked that these Catholics choose another day during Lent to fast and abstain, to take the place of Ash Wednesday.

The bishops sometimes change Church practices, such as when they excused Asian Catholics from fasting on Ash Wednesday in 2015, in order to allow them to participate in the Lunar New Year festivities.

UNIT 4

© Hung Chung Chih / Shutterstock.com

---

hierarchy of truths ▶ The ordering of Catholic doctrines according to their relation to the Trinity, the central foundation of Christian belief.

Sanctifying

Here's part of a job description that would make anyone nervous: Duties and responsibilities: (1) Make sure everyone gets to Heaven.

It's true! The bishops' role of sanctifying means that they must, to the best of their ability, try to get everyone in their care to eternal life with God in Heaven. Of course, there's no way to ensure this 100 percent. Nonetheless, bishops must do their best to help the faithful who have been entrusted to them to become holy. Bishops can accomplish this through their prayer, work, preaching, and by setting a positive example of humble **servant leadership**. Most important, bishops train and encourage the priests of their diocese. The ministry of these parish priests, supported by the bishop, makes it possible for us to be become holy through participation in the sacraments, and most especially, through sharing in the Eucharist.

CATHOLICS **MAKING** A DIFFERENCE

As leaders of the Church and pastors of all God's people, bishops must always be open to God's grace, even if that grace appears in unexpected ways or through unlikely people. On December 9, 1531, a poor Native Indian named Juan Diego arrived to see Juan de Zumarraga, the Bishop of Mexico. Diego had an urgent message. The Blessed Virgin Mary had appeared to him, asking for a chapel to be built in her honor on a hill near Mexico City. Bishop Zumarraga thought Diego's story sounded like crazy talk, and he did not believe him. He demanded that Diego come back with a sign that his story was true.

Three days later, Diego returned, clutching his cloak, which he had filled with roses. As he opened his cloak, the roses tumbled to the floor, and both the bishop and Diego gasped. On the cloak was an image of the Virgin Mary, looking exactly as she had when she appeared to Diego. The bishop fell to his knees. The chapel, of course, was built. Today, that chapel is the Basilica of Our Lady of Guadalupe, which attracts more than twelve million pilgrims each year.

servant leadership ➤ A type of leadership based on humble service to all God's people.

Governing

Like a parent running a household, a principal running a school, or a CEO running a company, a bishop must oversee, or govern, his diocese. He must use his sacred power responsibly, following the example of Jesus the Good Shepherd. In other words, he must exercise real leadership and authority, but with humility, compassion, an openness to others, and a willingness to listen. He must always have his people's best interests at heart.

If something is good, like your daily breakfast sandwich, why change it? Bishops can change how things work if they think it will help their community. We trust them to know what works best.

In his own diocese, a bishop is not like a branch manager of a company who has to rigidly follow certain corporate policies. For example, let's say that you usually have a fast-food sausage biscuit with egg for breakfast. You know that it's always the same and always good, even if you go to the same fast-food restaurant in a different town or a different state. That's because the manager of each restaurant has to follow the company's rules for how to prepare the food. A manager can't decide one day, "You know, I'll think I'll try a new biscuit recipe."

Unlike managers in a restaurant chain, bishops have a lot of freedom in how they govern their dioceses. They can set policies, determine priorities, and begin new programs, and they don't need to check with the Pope or anybody else about any of it. Bishops are trusted to know best what works for their own people, in their own area.

For example, when the Most Rev. Michael C. Barber, SJ, the bishop of the Diocese of Oakland, California, became aware of the large number of teenage girls in his diocese who were being sexually exploited through **human trafficking**, he asked Catholic Charities to investigate this problem. He wanted to explore ways the Church could help. As a result, several years later, the diocese opened Claire's House, a home for girls ages twelve to seventeen, who have been victims of sex trafficking. Bishop Barber did not have to get the Pope's, or anyone else's, approval before moving ahead with this project. He simply saw a need and responded to it in the name of Christ. ✳

UNIT 4

HMMMMMM. . .
What do you see as the greatest needs in your city or town? How do you think your diocese could help?

---

human trafficking ➤ Modern-day slavery; the use of force, fraud, or coercion to obtain some type of labor or commercial sex act.

Article 40
The Ministry of the Magisterium

The official teaching office of the Church is called the **Magisterium**. This word comes from the Latin word *magister*, which means teacher. The Magisterium is not a physical office like where your parents may work or where you go for a dental appointment. The Magisterium is a group of people: all the bishops throughout the world, in union with the Pope.

© Sueddeutsche Zeitung Photo / Alamy Stock Photo

The Magisterium is the official teaching authority of the Church and includes the Pope and all of the bishops of the Church.

Practically speaking, what does this mean? God wants to guarantee that we have access to the truth that we need for our salvation. He does not want to leave us fumbling around, trying to figure things out on our own. The Magisterium is that guarantee. Two gifts from the Holy Spirit help the Magisterium to accomplish this: indefectibility and infallibility.

Magisterium ➤ The Church's living teaching office, which consists of all bishops, in communion with the Pope, the Bishop of Rome. Their task is to interpret and preserve the truths revealed in both Sacred Scripture and Sacred Tradition.

Indefectibility

The **indefectibility of the Church** ensures that the Church will always teach the Gospel correctly, in spite of the "defects" of her members. *Defect* might seem like a strange word to use in reference to a person. It sounds more like something that you bought on online that you have to send back because it's defective and not working properly. However, when we talk about the defects of the Church's members, we are talking about the sins, imperfections, and mistakes of both ordained people and laypeople.

The gift of indefectibility assures us that even though no person in the Church is perfect, we can trust that the Magisterium will still accurately proclaim the truth of the Gospel message.

Infallibility

The Church's indefectibility and her **infallibility** are related. If the Church is without defect, she must also be without error, or infallible, in her teachings. You have learned that infallibility is the Holy Spirit's gift to the whole Church by which the leaders of the Church—the Pope and the bishops in union with him—are protected from error when teaching on a matter of faith and morals. This infallibility includes all elements of doctrine. The gift of infallibility ensures that the truths of the faith are preserved for all generations, are correctly taught, and are properly observed by the faithful. The gift of infallibility can take more than one form.

For many people, the most familiar form of the Church's infallibility is the gift of papal infallibility. Specifically, as the supreme pastor and teacher of all the faithful, the Pope may proclaim infallible teaching on his own authority. When a pope makes such a definitive teaching, we say it is issued *ex cathedra*, which is a Latin term meaning "from the chair." The term refers to the Pope's authority as the successor to Peter, an authority symbolized by

---

indefectibility of the Church ➤ The Church's remaining uncorrupted and faithful to Christ's teachings, until the end of human history.

infallibility ➤ The gift given by the Holy Spirit to the Church whereby the Magisterium of the Church, the Pope and the bishops in union with him, can definitively proclaim a doctrine of faith and morals without error.

ex cathedra **➤** A Latin term literally meaning "from the chair," referring to pronouncements concerning faith or morals made by the Pope, acting with full Apostolic authority, as pastor and teacher of all Christians.

the image of the Pope sitting in Peter's chair. The Pope's gift of infallibility applies only in very specific circumstances when the Pope officially acts as the Church's supreme pastor and with the authority of the Apostles to define a specific matter of faith or morality for the belief of the whole Church. When the Pope makes such a pronouncement, he is speaking as the supreme teacher of the Universal Church, not as a private individual.

Not everyone knows about a second form of the Church's gift of infallibility. The worldwide College of Bishops has this gift of infallibility when, in union with the Pope, it agrees that a certain doctrine regarding faith and morals must be definitively held by the faithful. This infallible authority is exercised when they either teach together dispersed throughout the world, or when they meet in an Ecumenical Council, a gathering of all Catholic bishops that is convened by the Pope and acts under his authority and guidance. The last Ecumenical Council was Vatican Council II, which was convened by Pope Saint John XXIII in 1962 and concluded under Pope Venerable Paul VI in 1965.

© sedmak / iStock.com

An example of the first form of infallible authority occurred in 1950 when, as Pope, Venerable Pius XII (1876–1958) proclaimed *ex cathedra* that the Assumption of Mary is a dogma of faith, a teaching that every Catholic must acknowledge as true. An example of the second form of

The Assumption of Mary is a unique way that God's grace is extended to Mary. Once Mary's time on Earth was completed, Mary's body and soul were assumed, or taken up, into Heaven.

infallibility, exercised by the bishops in union with the Pope, is a teaching from the Council of Chalcedon (AD 451). At that time, Christians had been debating the exact relationship between Christ's human and divine natures. Guided by the teaching of Pope Saint Leo I, the Council of Chalcedon stated infallibly that Christ's two natures exist "without confusion, change, division, or separation" ("Christ, the Eternal King" *["Sempiternus Rex Christus"]*, number 23), that Jesus Christ is one Divine Person with two natures.

All infallible declarations—whether issued by the Pope alone or by the entire College of Bishops—put forth doctrines that are the divinely revealed teachings of Christ. They must be accepted and obeyed by all Catholics. However, our faith cannot be limited *only* to those teachings that have been declared to be infallible. The bishops, in union with the Pope, always have the assistance of the Holy Spirit as they help us to understand Revelation in matters of faith and morals. Therefore, we must accept their teachings, even when they are not pronounced definitively or infallibly. This does not mean that our obedience needs to be blind or uninformed; rather, it means that we can trust that the bishops have our best interest at heart, and that the Holy Spirit is guiding their ministry. ✳

HMMMMMM. . . How would you explain the importance of the Magisterium to a Christian who is not Catholic?

UNIT 4

Article 41
The Ministry of Priests and Deacons

Our primary experience with leadership in the Church is often witnessing the ministry of priests and deacons. Priests such as Fr. Greg Boyle, who founded Homeboy Industries, work and pray with those in their community not just on Sundays, but every day.

For many Catholics, their primary experience with the Church's leaders and ministers is through **priests** and **deacons**. Most of us will never personally meet the Pope, and we may rarely see our local bishop. Priests and deacons are much more available and accessible to us on a regular basis. We see them at Sunday liturgy, and they are with us at many of life's most significant moments. Maybe you have known a priest or deacon who prayed with you before you had surgery or who comforted you and your family when a grandparent passed away. Maybe you still remember the priest or deacon who baptized your new baby cousin. Or maybe a priest or deacon has just given you good advice, the way that an older sibling or trusted friend might. If you have experienced these or similar situations, then you know the power and the importance of these ordained ministries.

---

priest ➤ One who has received the ministerial priesthood through the Sacrament of Holy Orders. The priest serves the community of faith by representing and assisting the bishop in teaching, governing, and presiding over the community's worship.

deacon ➤ Along with bishops and priests, one of the three Holy Orders conferred by the Sacrament of Holy Orders. Deacons are entrusted with various ministries, including baptizing, preaching, and witnessing marriages.

Priestly Ministry

Historically, the ministry of bishop arose from the Apostles and their successors. As more and more people joined the Church, bishops were unable to care for all those people by themselves. So, the ministry of deacons and priests developed, ordained ministers who assist the bishops with their responsibilities. The emerging ministry of priests and deacons can be seen in the Acts of the Apostles and some of the New Testament letters. Deacons served bishops by writing letters, assisting in proclaiming the Gospel, and serving those who are poor and needy on behalf of the bishop. Although the word *priest* is not used, the New Testament letters refer to the role of presbyters, who have roles that will become the role of priests as we know them today. Priests eventually began to preside at the Sunday Eucharist when the bishop could not be present.

Today, priests and deacons are recognized as coworkers of bishops, called to support them, trust them, and cooperate with them in serving God's people. Together, bishops, priests, and deacons continue the ministry of Christ, the Head of the Church. Like all ministries, priestly ministry is rooted in the Sacrament of Baptism. However, priestly authority and power come from the Sacrament of Ordination. Through ordination, priests share in the mission that Christ entrusted to the Apostles. They preach the Gospel, guide us toward holiness, and lead us in celebrating the sacraments. A priest's most special and unique role is presiding at Mass—at "the Eucharistic assembly of the faithful" (*Catechism of the Catholic Church*, number 1565). The importance of this responsibility cannot be overestimated, because the Eucharist is the center of life in the Church. It is the best way we have to be fully united both with God and with the Catholic community of faith.

UNIT 4

I DIDN'T KNOW THAT!

Did you ever think what priests' lives were like before they became priests? Many priests had careers before entering the seminary. Ignatius of Loyola joined the army at seventeen and dreamed of fame before becoming a priest and eventually founding the Jesuit order. Even Jorge Bergoglio from Argentina worked normal jobs before becoming a priest and eventually Pope! Pope Francis has a chemical technician's degree and worked in the food section of a laboratory. He also worked as a bar bouncer and a janitor before becoming a priest.

Steps to Becoming a Priest

Though each diocese and religious order will have its own particular approach, the following general steps are typical for most men who enter the priesthood.

Entering the Clergy at a Young Age	Becoming a Priest Later in Life
Meet the basic requirements: • Male • Unmarried • At least twenty-five years old	Meet the basic requirements: • Male • Unmarried • Usually not older than fifty-five years of age
Step 1: Discernment: • Get to know the priests at your parish. • Ask if you can assist them during services or when they go to visit the sick from the community. • Pray for God's assistance in discerning your situation. • Ask for advice from a vocational director or spiritual advisor.	Step 1: Consider your life experiences: • If you demonstrate intellectual, spiritual, and pastoral qualities, you are more likely to be accepted to the seminary. • Educational and career experience may help, but teaching or providing emotional and spiritual guidance can also help prepare you.
Step 2: Attend college (recommended): • Having a bachelor's degree makes it easier to be accepted into the seminary. • While in college, get involved in campus ministry.	Step 2: Enter the seminary: • Consists of graduate-level coursework. • Without a bachelor's degree, length of time in the seminary could be eight years. • Some seminaries cater to older students and focus on areas that fit their life skills.

UNIT 4

Entering the Clergy at a Young Age	Becoming a Priest Later in Life
Step 3: Seminary Formation: • Apply through your diocese or through a religious order. • Seminaries also look at your physical health, emotional well-being, knowledge of Church doctrine, and conformity of behavior with Catholic tradition. • You will study philosophy, Gregorian chant, dogmatic and moral theology, exegesis, canon law, Church history, and perhaps Latin. • If you have your bachelor's degree, the seminary typically lasts four years.	**Step 3: Become ordained:** • Serve as a deacon for at least six months. • You may be ordained as a diocesan priest serving in a parish. • You may take vows and live in a religious community.
Step 4: Become ordained: • First you will be ordained as a transitional deacon. You will serve as a deacon for at least six months. • During your time as a transitional deacon, you will typically serve at a parish, under the mentorship of a seasoned priest and the bishop. • Then you will be ordained as a priest. You could be ordained as a diocesan priest. Bishops assign diocesan priests to parishes, as chaplains, religious teachers, and other positions. • You could also be ordained as a religious order priest. These priests are part of a vowed community and participate in the particular charism, or work, of that community.	

UNIT 4

There are two types of priests: diocesan priests and religious order priests. Diocesan priests promise obedience to the bishop of their diocese. This means they have to serve wherever the bishop assigns them. The bishop may assign a particular priest to a parish, school, university, or other ministry within the diocese. The assignment may not be the priest's first choice. But the priest must trust that the bishop knows where the needs in the diocese are greatest. The priest is called to rely on the Holy Spirit as he responds to those needs to the very best of his ability, in a spirit of generous service.

Similarly, religious order priests make a vow of obedience to the superior of their community, who may send them to any place where their priestly ministry is needed. Many religious orders operate internationally. So, unlike a diocesan priest—who serves only within the geographic boundaries of his diocese—a religious order priest could end up serving at a parish in Haiti, teaching at a university in Kenya, or working at an administrative role in Rome.

MAKE IT SO

If anyone ever tells you that young people are the future of the Church, respectfully tell them that they wrong! Young people like you are the Church *now*. And you can be leaders in the Church now too. Consider taking on a visible role in liturgical leadership at your parish or school: you could serve as an altar server, cantor, lector, or, if you are confirmed, as an Extraordinary Minister of Holy Communion. Or, think about being a leader in community service: get your school involved with the Saint Vincent de Paul Society's food pantry, or help to organize a pro-life project with the Knights of Columbus. You could also volunteer to take on a leadership role on your school's Campus Ministry Team, in your parish's youth group, or even on the Parish Council. Whatever you choose to do, exercise your faith-centered leadership with integrity and humility—and have fun!

Diaconal Ministry

The word *deacon* comes from the Greek word *diakonia*, which means "service." Those who are ordained as deacons share in the grace, mission, and ministry of Christ, the Servant of all. Deacons have two primary areas of responsibility: liturgical ministry and charitable works. Regarding liturgy, deacons assist the

Deacons are primarily responsible for liturgical ministry and charitable works. Do you have any deacons active at your parish? If so, what do you perceive their role is?

bishop and priests at Mass, including by proclaiming and preaching the Gospel. Even when a priest is not present, deacons are able to witness marriages and to baptize. However, deacons cannot preside at Mass or at the Sacrament of Penance and Reconciliation. Regarding charity, deacons may organize efforts to alleviate hunger and poverty, to support single parents, or to minister to those in jails, prisons, or juvenile detention facilities.

There are two types of deacons: transitional deacons and permanent deacons. Transitional deacons will, one day, be ordained as priests, usually after about a year of diaconal ministry. Permanent deacons, who can be married men, will remain deacons and not ever become priests. ✳

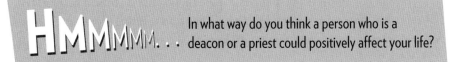

HMMMMMM. . . . In what way do you think a person who is a deacon or a priest could positively affect your life?

Article 42
Lay Ministry

As usual, Chloe had left something with a firm deadline until the absolute last minute. The "something" was her application for the Confirmation program at Our Lady of Grace parish. She was looking forward to her Confirmation, and she knew that it meant a lot to her parents too. So, she didn't want to flake out and miss the deadline—which was exactly two hours away.

Most of the questions were pretty simple, but she got stuck on one of the essay prompts: *Describe one person who's been particularly important to your journey of faith.* One? Chloe didn't think she could name just one. She thought first of David and Ellen, the married couple who were her parish's youth

If you had to write a Confirmation essay like Chloe did, about someone who has been particularly important to your journey of faith, whom would you describe?

ministers. They had gotten her involved with the youth group, which had really given her faith a boost. Then there was Ms. Mueller, the campus minister at her school, who had pushed her to go on her first overnight retreat. That had been a totally awesome experience. She thought of her Uncle Steve, who was actually Brother Steve—a Marianist Brother who was a college professor in Hawaii but who usually spent Christmas with Chloe's family. They always talked about deep stuff when he was visiting. She supposed she could write about Father Tom, her pastor. She didn't really know him that well, but she liked his homilies. If she went *way* back, she could write about Sister Louisa, who had prepared her for First Holy Communion and whom she still saw at Mass sometimes.

Thinking of all these possibilities, Chloe tapped her fingers impatiently on the keyboard. Time was ticking by. The deadline was getting closer and closer. She had to make a decision. Smiling to herself, she started typing.

UNIT 4

One Man, Many Ministers

Chloe's story illustrates some powerful truths about the Church. On the one hand, the Church is a "one-person show," because it's all about Jesus Christ. Without Jesus' life, death, and Resurrection, we would not have a Church. On the other hand, when it comes to furthering the Church's mission, it's most definitely *not* a one-person show. Spreading the Gospel, inviting new people into the Church, and supporting people of faith throughout their lives takes many people working together. So many of the Church's leaders and ministers have nourished Chloe's faith up to this point. In the future, she will meet even more people who will help her faith continue to grow and mature.

This chapter on the ministry of leadership has, so far, focused on the ministry of people who are ordained. These bishops, priests, and deacons play important, unique roles in the Church. They are indispensable because, without them, we would not have access to the sacraments, which are the heart of our Catholic Christian identity.

Yet, bishops, priests, and deacons cannot possibly do it all alone. So other people also function as leaders in the Church—people like those whom Chloe considered as she worked on her Confirmation application. Some of these people are religious sisters and brothers. You will learn more about their **consecrated life** later in this course. We are all called to minister to the world, but some of the lay faithful have a calling to serve in leadership roles within the Church. There are two kinds of lay ministry: some Catholics are called as

UNIT 4

CATHOLICS **MAKING** A DIFFERENCE

Steve Angrisano is an international musical performer and storyteller. Though he majored in music and business at the University of Texas, he applied for youth ministry jobs because he felt that "being in the business of encouraging and cultivating faith was the most worthwhile thing I felt I could do." He spends more than forty weeks a year on the road performing at conferences, concerts, and events such as World Youth Day, the Los Angeles Religious Education Congress, the National Catholic Youth Conference, and many more. Without being ordained or taking any religious vows, Steve Angrisano has dedicated his life to sharing his faith and the Good News!

consecrated life ➤ A state of life recognized by the Church in which a person publicly professes vows of poverty, chastity, and obedience.

volunteer lay leaders, and others are called to work full- or part-time for the Church. Those who work for the Church in these paid, professional ways are known as **lay ecclesial ministers**. They work alongside of the ordained to serve God's people and to advance the Church's mission.

Lay Ecclesial Ministers

"Lay ecclesial minister" is not, in itself, a job title; rather, it is a general term that simply refers to a layperson who works for the Church full- or part-time. The actual jobs or roles that laypeople fill can vary. In a parish, lay ecclesial ministers may serve as the Director of Religious Education or as the Director of Youth Ministry. In Catholic schools, they may be religious studies teachers,

Have you met any lay ecclesial ministers at your school, parish, or even on a retreat who have helped you feel a connection to your faith community?

campus ministers, or principals. At Catholic colleges and universities, they may work as retreat directors or mission trip coordinators. In hospitals and prisons, they may serve in the chaplain's office, supporting individuals and families in times of great difficulty. They may also work in social service agencies, like Catholic Charities. In short, lay ecclesial ministers seek to offer a reassuring, Christlike presence anywhere that the Gospel needs to be proclaimed, or where God's people are in need of care, companionship, education, and support.

---

lay ecclesial ministers ➤ Those who are not ordained but serve in a leadership capacity by ministering to others in either a full- or part-time capacity within the Church.

Looking more closely at the term *lay ecclesial minister* can help us to better understand this role, including how it is different from ordained ministry. Lay ecclesial ministers are, by definition, laypeople. The sacramental basis of their ministry is the Sacrament of Baptism, not the Sacrament of Holy Orders. Obviously, as laypeople, they do not exercise ministries that are limited to ordained ministers. They do not preside at any of the sacraments, and they do not serve as pastors of parishes. However, their ministries are vital to the Church.

The work of lay ecclesial ministers is *ecclesial* because it occurs within the community of the Church (recall that the Greek word *ekklesia* means "church"). Their ministry serves the Church's mission, promotes unity among all the faithful, and is both authorized and supervised by the Church's hierarchical leadership. In fact, many types of lay ecclesial ministry require training and even advanced degrees and certification. Many lay ecclesial ministers even see their work as something God is calling them to as a lifelong commitment.

Lay ecclesial ministry is *ministry* because it is a real sharing in the mission and ministry of Christ. It supports the continuation of Christ's mission to proclaim the Reign of God in the world.

New Horizons in Lay Ecclesial Ministry

In the summer of 2018, Pope Francis made two decisions that help us to see new possibilities for lay ecclesial ministry, even at the highest levels of the Church. In June, he appointed a layman, Vincenzo Buonomo, as the rector of the Pontifical Lateran University in Rome. At this university, which is under the Pope's direct oversight, four thousand students—including priests, men and women religious, and laypeople—study theology, philosophy, and **canon law**. Buonomo is the first layperson ever to hold this important position in the school's 250-year history.

Just one month later, Pope Francis appointed another layman, Paolo Ruffino, as the head of the Vatican's Communications Office, which has a staff of more than six hundred people. Ruffino is the first layperson ever to lead a major department at the Vatican. Usually, these roles are filled by bishops. Pope Francis's decision to appoint laypeople to prominent roles in Church leadership can help to us to consider new areas of the Church where the expertise and background of lay ecclesial ministers may be particularly helpful and important.

UNIT 4

---

canon law ➤ The name given to the official body of laws that provide good order in the visible body of the Church.

Lay ecclesial ministers do far more than play the guitar and plan retreats. They function as chaplains, teachers, lawyers, social workers, ministers to the homebound, and more.

Sign of Christ's Enduring Love

Chloe clicked "send" on her application, pleased by whom she had chosen to write about. Linda—Chloe couldn't even remember her last name—worked in the chaplain's office at the hospital where her grandfather had passed away from leukemia last year. Her grandfather had gone downhill quickly, so he was only in the hospital a few days before he died. But over those days, Linda had prayed with Chloe's family, listened to them, comforted them, and helped them to accept that God was calling her grandfather home. Chloe had never met anyone who was so clearly in touch with God's presence, and who reflected Christ's love with such compassion. She hoped that someday she could do that for other people.

Volunteer Lay Ministers

It is very possible that you are already a lay minister at your parish or school. Have you ever helped to plan a school Mass? Have you been a lector or Eucharistic minister at your church? Do you sing in the choir? These are just a few of the many ways laypeople can participate in leadership roles within the Church.

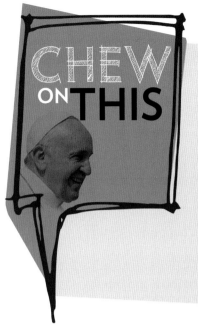

CHEW ON THIS

How beautiful it is to see young people who embrace the call to dedicate themselves fully to Christ and to the service of his Church! Challenge yourselves, and with a pure heart do not be afraid of what God is asking of you! From your "yes" to the Lord's call, you will become new seeds of hope in the Church and in society. ("Address of His Holiness Pope Francis on the Occasion of the XXX World Youth Day," January 31, 2015)

Volunteer lay ministry is a way for many people to fulfill their call to ministry by serving others within their parish community. It isn't something you have to wait until you graduate from high school or have a family to do. The Church could not function without lay ministry volunteers. Lay ministry is a way for you to take on a leadership role within your faith community and deepen your relationship with God. And by volunteering, you are helping the Church to fulfill its mission to bring the Good News to others by fleshing out ministries that are in desperate need of help.

For example, faith formation programs need volunteer catechists in order to provide religious education for elementary and middle school children. The Director of Religious Education might be a paid, lay ecclesial minister, but the people who teach religious education classes are volunteers. If parishes didn't have volunteers to staff the classes, then the programs would not be available. Would you consider stepping up to a leadership role within your church community by volunteering to teach religious education classes to younger kids? Would you help with Vacation Bible School? Serving as a lay minister is something you can start right now. Are you ready? ✳

HMMMMMM. . . Why are lay ministers vital to the Church?

1. Name three ways in which the Pope is the center of leadership for the entire Church.

2. What is the scriptural basis for the ministry of the Pope?

3. What is the significance of the title Supreme Pontiff?

4. Name the bishops' three "offices" or jobs, and briefly describe each.

5. Name and define the two gifts from the Holy Spirit that help the Magisterium teach the Gospel message accurately.

6. What two criteria must be met for the Church to exercise infallibility?

7. What are the unique roles and responsibilities of priests?

8. What are deacons' two primary areas of responsibility?

9. What is a lay ecclesial minister?

10. How has Pope Francis helped us to consider new possibilities for lay ecclesial ministry?

The Church's Leadership

BISHOPS

There are almost 5,000 bishops worldwide. Around 456 of them are in the United States.

THE LAITY

There are over 1 billion Catholics worldwide. Almost 68.5 million are in the United States.

PRIESTS

There are over 414,000 priests worldwide. Just over 37,000 of them are in the United States.

The Pope

UNIT 4

LAY ECCLESIAL MINISTERS

There are over 39,000 lay ecclesial ministers in parish ministry in the United States, and many more the world over.

DEACONS

There are approximately 45,000 permanent deacons worldwide. More than 18,000 of them are located in the United States.

CONSECRATED LIFE

There are over 650,00 religious sisters and over 52,000 religious brothers in the world today. In the United States, we have about 45,000 religious sisters and approximately 4,000 religious brothers.

CHAPTER 11
Mission and Holiness

WHAT DOES A HOLY PERSON LOOK LIKE?

SNAPSHOT

Article 43   Page 263
The Universal Call to Holiness

Article 44   Page 268
Focus on Pope Francis: "The Light of Faith"
• Pre-read: "The Light of Faith," numbers 37–46, 50–51, 57

Article 45   Page 272
Priest, Prophet, and King

Article 46   Page 278
Consecrated Life

Article 43

The Universal Call to Holiness

When he got to school on Monday morning, Brandon groaned inwardly. "Called to Holiness: Vocation Awareness Week!" the brightly colored posters proclaimed. Every year around this time, Brandon heard a priest, sister, or brother talk about how the Church needs vocations and how he and his class-mates should pray about whether God was calling them to be a priest, brother, or sister. The speakers were nice people, and it was a break from the regular class routine. But no matter how much he prayed, Brandon was pretty sure he wasn't called to be a priest.

When he got to his religious studies class, Brandon was surprised to see that their guest speaker wasn't a priest at all. It was Mr. McMahon, who ran the faith formation program at his parish. "You'll be hearing from Father Mel and Sister Felicia at tomorrow's assembly," he explained. "For today, I'm here to talk about this year's theme: Called to Holiness. Now, when I say the word *holy*, what do you think of?"

Students called out their answers. "The Pope," someone said. "Priests and nuns," said someone else. "Mass." "Jesus." "Mary." "The saints." "People who pray all the time." Then Mr. McMahon turned off the lights and started a PowerPoint presentation. As the slide show scrolled by, it took a minute for Brandon to realize what he was looking at. Each slide was a picture of one of his classmates, and each slide had the same caption: the student's name, followed

Simple demonstrations like Mr. McMahon's slide-show can oftentimes be very impactful. Seeing your name with the phrase "called to holiness" can make you stop and think about what that might look like in your life.

by "Called to Holiness." The class got really quiet. Brandon wasn't sure where Mr. McMahon was going with this, but he was curious to find out.

UNIT 4

TAKE IT TO GOD

God,

Holy is the last word that I would use to describe myself.

And yet, I know that you want me to be close to you.

You want me to serve your people.

You want me to make the world a better place.

You want me to take up my cross and follow your Son, Jesus.

Give me strength, God, to grow in holiness.

Help me to remember that I cannot do it alone,

But with the support your Church offers, I can do what I am called to.

Amen.

The Vocation to Holiness

Like Brandon, you may have heard the word *vocation* most commonly used to refer to a call from God to serve him as an ordained minister, the consecrated life, or a married person. However, there is another, more general way to use the word *vocation*. It refers to the common vocation that *all* Christians share: the vocation to be holy. We receive this vocation at our Baptism. How we live it out will vary, depending on our age; our gifts, talents, and other resources; and many other personal circumstances.

The Vatican II document *Dogmatic Constitution on the Church* (*Lumen Gentium*, 1964) put it well when it stated that "all the faithful of Christ of whatever rank or status are called to the fullness of Christian life and to the perfection of charity (love)" (number 42). Perhaps the most important word in that sentence is *all*. All Christians—not just priests, nuns, or other leaders in the Church—are called to live their faith by engaging in loving service of others, in the name of Jesus. In other words, all Christians are called to be holy. When we dedicate ourselves to responding to this call, we not only grow in personal sanctity but also help the Church fulfill the mission she received from Jesus Christ. Whether this awesome responsibility makes you feel humble or proud, eager or nervous, let's look in more detail at what it involves.

Being Holy: The Basics

Living out your vocation to holiness means making God a priority in your life. Practically speaking, this involves being a person of prayer, trying to live a morally good life, and engaging in works of charity and justice.

© FatCamera / iStock.com

Making time for prayer can seem like a tough challenge. But starting small with prayer before meals or a prayer before practice or a performance can help you get in the habit of making prayer a priority.

Making time for prayer can be hard. If you are like many high school students, both your days and weekends are chock full of school, sports, clubs, family responsibilities, and social life. If your weekly Mass attendance is a little spotty, start by making a solid commitment to participating in Sunday Eucharist every week. This is particularly important as Sunday Mass attendance is obligatory as a precept of the Church. From there, consider other ways you could carve out time to pray. If you want to pray with others, maybe you could take a moment to pray with your family before you eat together. Or maybe you could join a prayer group at your school or parish. If you want to pray alone, think creatively about how you could find the time to do that. Could you finish your lunch a few minutes early and pray in your school's chapel? If you take a bus to school, could you use that time to listen to a prayer podcast? Take advantage of the opportunities that your church provides. Holy hours, Stations of the Cross during Lent, Bible study groups, and Adoration are a variety of ways that the Church has in place to help us in our efforts to be more holy. There isn't one right way to pray. The right way is the way that works for you—the way that allows you to connect with God, to experience God's great love for you, and to listen attentively to God's voice.

Living a morally good and holy life requires making decisions according to the Ten Commandments and the teachings of the Church. It may seem easy to say "yes" to this in theory, but when actually faced with a decision, it can be quite challenging. Can you be honest with your parents even when it means you might get in trouble? Can you be courageous and defend someone who is being bullied even if you also may be ridiculed? Can you practice chastity when faced with sexual pressure? Your life of prayer will strengthen you to make these decisions wisely. And when you fail—and sometimes you will—you can seek out the Sacrament of Penance and Reconciliation. The Church offers us opportunities to get back on the right track. We can't do it alone. This Sacrament will comfort you with God's mercy and support you in your weakness. In addition, seeking the counsel of a priest, deacon, nun, youth minister, or lay minister encourages us to recognize that we can't fulfill our call to holiness alone. We must rely on God and the help that the Church provides.

© arindambanerjee / Shutterstock.com

Being an active part of your faith community includes works of charity and justice, such as collecting food for the food pantry, serving the homeless and hungry, contacting your elected officials about issues of affordable housing, protecting, the environment, and more.

Works of charity and justice should help you not only to grow in holiness but also to proclaim God's love to the world. You know that in your local community and around the world people suffer from hunger, poverty, addiction, violence, and discrimination. What are you doing to respond to these needs?

Though you can't completely solve these problems, you can make a real difference. You can organize or participate in food drives, clothing drives, or toiletry drives. You can volunteer at a shelter, soup kitchen, or food pantry. Even if you are not yet old enough to vote, you can still contact elected officials and express your views about affordable housing, protecting the environment, the rights of people with disabilities, and other important issues. The Church also provides pathways to holiness through charity and service. The Society of Saint Vincent de Paul feeds the hungry and assists those who have fallen on hard times. You don't have to look online for ways to help others. Often your own parish has organizations and plans in place to help others. Participating in these organizations and plans can also foster your call to grow in holiness as you serve others. Whatever you choose to do, the most important thing is to do *something*. Make a conscious decision to act in the name of Christ, the One who calls you to holiness, both now and in the future.

The Way of the Cross

In all three synoptic Gospels, Jesus teaches his disciples about following the call to holiness. He states: "Whoever wishes to come after me must deny himself, take up his cross, and follow me. For whoever wishes to save his life will lose it, but whoever loses his life for my sake will find it" (Matthew 16:24–25). This is a stark message. Jesus is trying to tell us that living out the vocation to holiness isn't easy.

We may have to sacrifice some of our free time in order to make time for prayer and service. We need to make conscious choices to have Christian friends and mentors who support our beliefs and moral choices. We may have to endure rejection from people who don't understand or support our priorities. We may have to suffer. But in all of this, we can find reassurance in our faith in the Resurrection. On the other side of any kind of suffering, we will always find the promise of new life and hope. As Saint Paul put it, "For if we have grown into union with [Jesus Christ] through a death like his, we shall also be united with him in the resurrection" (Romans 6:5). ✳

UNIT 4

What is one concrete step you could take to take advantage of an opportunity your church offers for prayer, community, or service?

Article 44
Focus on Pope Francis: "The Light of Faith"

Think for a moment about light and darkness. When we are in darkness, light becomes irresistible. Light attracts us, beckoning us to pay attention to it and to draw closer. Maybe it's a single candle burning in a darkened church or the stars in the black night sky. It could be a cell phone screen in the middle of the night, a campfire in the woods, or the one room in the house with a light on in the middle of the night. Light of any kind is powerfully appealing. It pulls us in, offering the possibility of comfort and warmth.

© Andrey Prokhorov / Shutterstock.com

Just as stars can illuminate the night sky, the light of faith can illuminate every aspect of human existence. When we see with the light of faith, we can see where hope and help are needed.

In his first **encyclical**, issued just three months into his pontificate, Pope Francis suggests that faith is a lot like light. "The Light of Faith" *("Lumen Fidei")* describes faith as a light that is "capable of illuminating every aspect of human existence" (number 5). Like physical light, faith exerts a pull on us. It offers hope and guidance, and it reminds us that we are not alone. In addition, faith is the firm foundation that enables us to live out our vocation to holiness and to make our own unique contribution to the Church's mission. In the light of faith, everything else that helps to grow in holiness becomes possible, including prayer, wise decision making, and a commitment to compassionate service, charity, and justice.

---

encyclical ➤ A teaching letter from the Pope to the members of the Church, or even the whole world, expressing Church teaching on an important topic.

The Path of Faith

Pope Francis begins the encyclical by talking about faith as something that illuminates our path through life: "Faith opens the way before us and accompanies our steps through time. Hence, if we want to understand what faith is, we need to follow the route it has taken, the path trodden by believers, as witnessed first in the Old Testament" ("The Light of Faith," number 8). He then goes on to summarize how faith guided the way of the many biblical people we have already studied: Abraham, Moses, the Israelites. He makes the point that these Old Testament saints were saved by faith in Christ, the "Christ who was yet to come."

Pope Francis then goes on to remind us that faith finds its fulfillment in Jesus Christ and the Paschal Mystery: "All the threads of the Old Testament converge on Christ; he becomes the definitive 'Yes' to all the promises, the ultimate basis of our 'Amen' to God (cf. 2 Corinthians 1:20)" (number 15). What does all this mean for us? Pope Francis summarizes the meaning with these words:

> Our faith in the Son of God made man in Jesus of Nazareth enables us to grasp reality's deepest meaning and to see how much God loves this world and is constantly guiding it towards himself. This leads us, as Christians, to live our lives in this world with ever greater commitment and intensity. (Number 18)

UNIT 4

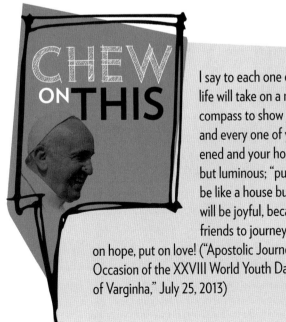

I say to each one of you "put on faith," and life will take on a new flavor, life will have a compass to show you the way; "put on hope" and every one of your days will be enlightened and your horizon will no longer be dark, but luminous; "put on love," and your life will be like a house built on rock, your journey will be joyful, because you will find many friends to journey with you. Put on faith, put on hope, put on love! ("Apostolic Journey to Rio De Janeiro on the Occasion of the XXVIII World Youth Day, Visit to the Community of Varginha," July 25, 2013)

Most people will say that they want their life to mean something, that they want to make a difference in the world. But it isn't always easy to do. How do we get past the discouragements, the mistakes, our own sin and weakness? In "The Light of Faith," Pope Francis makes the case that the surest way to get past these challenges is to keep our eyes on Christ.

A Bright and Lively Faith

As he expands on this metaphor of faith as light, Pope Francis explores three ways that faith impacts our lives. First, faith opens our eyes to see the reality of God in the world. He laments the fact that "our culture has lost its sense of God's tangible presence and activity in the world. We think that God is to be found in the beyond, on another level of reality, far removed from our everyday relationships" ("The Light of Faith," number 20).

Maybe you know people who believe some version of what Pope Francis is describing: that God is busy in Heaven and doesn't really want or need to have anything to do with us on Earth. This mistaken belief could not be further from the truth. God is involved and active in our world, and the light of faith helps us to notice his presence. Even very small and simple things—like a friend's smile, a beautiful sunset, a parent's support, or a delicious lunch—can be signs of God's love and care.

© FatCamera / iStock.com

Finding God's presence in the normal and ordinary is a gift of faith. When you have fun with your friends or enjoy a delicious meal, you are given the opportunity to thank God for his loving presence in your life.

UNIT 4

© Alexandros Michailidis / Shutterstock.com

Have you ever felt as though you didn't want to go to Church? Many young people choose not to attend for a variety of reasons. However, sharing our faith can strengthen our faith. Our gift of faith is not mean to be hidden under a basket; we are called to share it with others.

UNIT 4

Second, the light of faith guides and directs us in making morally good decisions. Faith "sheds light on every human relationship" ("The Light of Faith," number 69), so it should have a real impact on our lives, especially on how we treat other people. It should motivate us to serve others, especially those who are suffering, and to act in ways that promote love, mercy, justice, and peace.

Last, the light of faith is meant to be shared. Pope Francis is clear that faith is not something we should keep to ourselves, like a secret, special gift that is only for us: "Those who have opened their hearts to God's love, heard his voice and received his light, cannot keep this gift to themselves" ("The Light of Faith," number 37). And when that gift is shared, the light of faith grows ever brighter and stronger. Maybe you have attended an Easter Vigil and seen how the Paschal candle (or Easter candle) lights many smaller candles carried by members of the assembly. The light grows and grows, until the whole Church is bathed in it. Faith is like this. Sharing faith does not weaken or diminish it. Sharing faith strengthens faith: it grows and grows, until the whole world has experienced God's merciful, redeeming love. ✳

HMMMMM. . . Pope Francis uses the metaphor of light to describe faith. What image would you use to explain or describe faith?

Article 45
Priest, Prophet, and King

"He now anoints you with the Chrism of salvation, so that you may remain members of Christ, Priest, Prophet and King, unto eternal life" (*The Rites of the Catholic Church,* page 429). At every celebration of Baptism, the bishop, priest, or deacon prays these words as he anoints the person with **Sacred Chrism**. If you were baptized when you were very young, you probably don't remember hearing this prayer. And yet, these powerful words are worth remembering! They teach us something very important about our vocation to holiness. Through Baptism, we share in Christ's ministry as priest, prophet, and king.

Sharing in Jesus' Priestly Ministry

As baptized people, we participate in the **common priesthood of the faithful**, sometimes called the baptismal priesthood or the priesthood of all believers. Jesus Christ is the High Priest of the New Covenant. Because we, through Baptism, become members of his body, then we too share in his priesthood.

This common priesthood is distinct from the ministerial priesthood, which is received through the Sacrament of Holy Orders. Those who are baptized but not ordained do not have the authority and sacred power that ordination confers. Most notably, they cannot offer the sacrifice of the Mass.

What we *can* offer is spiritual sacrifice. Saint Paul advised the Colossians that their faith should be something that they think about more than once a day or once a week, when they are praying or celebrating the Eucharist. Rather, their Christian faith should pervade their whole lives. He said, "Whatever you do, in word or in deed, do everything in the name of the Lord Jesus" (Colossians 3:17).

Sacred Chrism ➤ Perfumed olive oil consecrated by the bishop that is used for anointing in the Sacraments of Baptism, Confirmation, and Holy Orders.

common priesthood of the faithful ➤ The name for the priesthood shared by all who are baptized. The baptized share in the one priesthood of Jesus Christ by participating in his mission as priest, prophet, and king.

You might not think of doing homework, folding laundry, washing dishes, or bringing coffee to a friend as prayer. However, if you offer up your daily words and actions to God, you are, in essence, praying.

Paul's advice to the Colossians applies to us too. In faith and in love, we can offer God our work, our service, our relationships, our joys, and our struggles. Practically speaking, this means turning to God in prayer throughout our day, to express gratitude or to ask for help. It means recognizing, honoring, and responding to God's presence in each person we encounter. And, it means accepting that every single experience we have—whether good or bad, easy or hard—is a chance for us to grow in faith. In this way, through our efforts and in cooperation with God's grace, we can help to consecrate the whole world to God. We can make our very lives—every word we speak and every action we undertake—a form of prayer and worship that glorifies God and that leads others to holiness. This is the way we live out the priesthood of the faithful.

Sharing in Jesus' Prophetic Ministry

In the Old Testament, prophets like Amos, Isaiah, and Jeremiah called the Israelites back to fidelity to the covenant. They reminded the people of God's love and mercy and tried to get them back on track when they strayed into sinful behaviors. In a similar way, Jesus proclaimed the Kingdom of God. His preaching urged people to be a part of that Kingdom: to share in the New Covenant that he would establish through his death and Resurrection.

UNIT 4

As sharers in Christ's prophetic ministry, we are called to evangelize: to proclaim our faith "by a living testimony as well as by the spoken word" (*Dogmatic Constitution on the Church*, number 35). In many cases, the old saying "actions speak louder than words" is true. The testimony of your holy life is more powerful than any amount of words. And yet, the prophetic work of evangelization does sometimes involve speaking about your faith, either with believers whose commitment may need a boost or with those who do not yet believe.

This doesn't mean you have to stand on a street corner talking about Jesus or hold up a "John 3:16" sign at the football game on Friday night. Instead, find a way that comes naturally to you. Let people know that your faith is important to you and invite them, with gentleness and love, to consider accepting the gift of faith in their own lives. Maybe you invite a couple of friends to join you at a parish youth group meeting, or to sign up for your school's overnight retreat. If they say no, don't sweat it. Trust that God is present and active in their lives, as he is in the lives of all people, and pray that they may be more and more open to God's grace.

© snagrafie / Shutterstock.com

We are called to evangelize, but that doesn't mean we have to force our beliefs on others. Inviting a friend to go to a youth-group activity or sticking by our beliefs when challenged are non-threatening ways to share our faith.

UNIT 4

Have you ever made a suggestion and felt like no one paid any attention to you? Maybe you have a new idea for a service project, or you've thought of ways to make your school's liturgies more appealing for students. It may surprise you to know that as a sharer in Jesus' prophetic ministry, you have both the right and the responsibility to express your opinions "on matters which pertain to the good of the Church" (*The Code of Canon Law*, canon 212). The rules of canon law are critical to understanding what we believe. The Roman Catholic Church is governed by canon law. The word *canon* is derived from the Greek work *kanon*, which means "measuring line or rule." Essentially, these are the standards against which we measure pretty much anything that has to do with being Catholic, from Baptisms to burials, penance to parishes. Let's break down what this means.

1. The Church's leaders and ministers care what you think, especially regarding issues that have a unique impact on young people in the Church. On that topic, you are the expert.

2. You have the right to your opinion on Church matters, even if your opinion is not totally correct or not perfectly informed.

3. You have the right to respectfully share your opinion both with the Church's leaders and with other faithful people.

Have you ever considered that Church leaders and ministers care about your opinion regarding issues that impact young people in the Church?

UNIT 4

4. In expressing your opinion, keep in mind that the Church is here to proclaim the Gospel and to serve all people, not just you. Concern for the common good means that everyone may not get what they want.

You can rely on the Holy Spirit to give you the courage to speak up and share your views. If you feel scared or doubtful, remember the words of the First Letter to Timothy: "Let no one have contempt for your youth, but set an example for those who believe, in speech, conduct, love, faith, and purity" (4:12).

CATHOLICS MAKING A DIFFERENCE

Saint Pedro Calungsod (1654–1672) committed himself to living out his baptismal call to holiness while he was still a teenager. In 1654, at the age of fourteen, he volunteered to travel with Spanish Jesuit missionaries from his home in the Philippines to island communities in the western Pacific. Many people were open to the Gospel message, but others were suspicious of the missionaries' intentions. Some local leaders even began spreading rumors that Saint Pedro and his companions were trying to poison the people with holy water. On April 2, 1672, these tensions reached a breaking point. Saint Pedro and Fr. Diego Luis de San Vitores were attacked by a village chief and died of their wounds.

Saint Pedro is an inspiring example of a young lay leader who took his baptismal priesthood seriously, served Christ with prophetic courage, and willingly took on a leadership role in the Church, even at great risk to himself.

UNIT 4

Sharing in Jesus' Kingly Ministry

Naomi read the ballot and considered her options. Brett was such a nice guy. She thought she should probably vote for him. On the other hand, Arun was kind of the underdog candidate, so maybe he needed her support. Then there was Jaime. . . .

"Hurry up!" Naomi's best friend, Isabella, interrupted her thoughts. "It doesn't matter. Prom king doesn't mean anything. All he's going to do is stand up there, smile and wave, and wear a plastic crown."

"I guess you're right," Naomi said. Sighing, she marked her ballot and headed back to the dance floor.

Isabella was right. Prom king is a symbolic role. It adds to the excitement of the evening and makes for a fun photo op, but no one expects the prom king to have any real power.

When we talk about Jesus as King, we are not talking about a symbolic figurehead. Instead, Jesus is a ruler or leader with true power and authority. He revealed this authority through his preaching: "For he taught as one having authority, and not as their scribes" (Matthew 7:20). He revealed it through his miracles: Jesus' command over nature was a sign of his divine authority and power. Most important, he demonstrated his authority through his self-sacrifice: only a person who truly loves us really has the power to change us.

Jesus' power and authority as King were not just symbolic. He demonstrated his divine authority through his miracles and self-sacrifice.

As sharers in Jesus' kingly ministry, we are called to use our own authority and power to shape the world into a more just and peaceful place. We are called to live a virtuous and moral life and to share our gifts and talents with the Church and with the wider world. The Vatican II document *Dogmatic Constitution on the Church* affirms that each layperson is "a witness and the living instrument of the mission of the Church itself" (number 33). This means that we are not simply observers of the Church's mission, or passive recipients of God's grace; rather, we are a primary means by which the mission of the Church will be fulfilled.

Think about it: There are more than one billion Catholics in the world, and only a tiny fraction of them are priests or consecrated religious. They can't carry out the Church's mission alone! All those one billion Catholics—including you—are called to live out the vocation to holiness, in service to the Church and world. We are called to be the hands of Christ serving those who are poor and hungry. We are called to take on the heart of Christ in extending compassion to the suffering. We are called to take on the mind of Christ by thinking creatively about how to make the world more just. We are called to be his feet walking with the oppressed, so that they are not alone. And we are called to pray always, so that all of our work and ministry may bear fruit, through the power of the Holy Spirit.

These are awesome responsibilities! Are you ready? ✳

UNIT 4

HMMMMM. . . Which way of sharing in Christ's ministry—prophet, priest, or king—do you most feel called to take on?

Article 46

Consecrated Life

At Baptism, each of us received a call to holiness and a share in Christ's ministry as priest, prophet, and king. And yet, the specific path of living out this call is different for every person. Those who are called to the consecrated life as religious sisters or brothers live out their baptismal vocation in a uniquely powerful way. Their example of total dedication to Christ, and their desire to serve God and God's people, can inspire and encourage our own life of faith.

Consecrated religious life is a gift from Christ to the Church. From the earliest centuries of the Church all the way to the present day, members of men's and women's religious communities have played crucial roles in helping the Church to grow and flourish. Those who are members of active, apostolic orders witness to God's love by serving in schools, hospitals, and in service-oriented agencies and missions. The Christian Brothers, the Dominicans, the Sisters of Mercy, the Franciscans, the Sisters of the Presentation, and the Society of Jesus (Jesuits) are examples of active orders. Those who are members of contemplative orders focus their ministry on prayer, interceding with God for the needs of the world. The Carmelites, the Cistercians, and the Trappists are examples of contemplative orders.

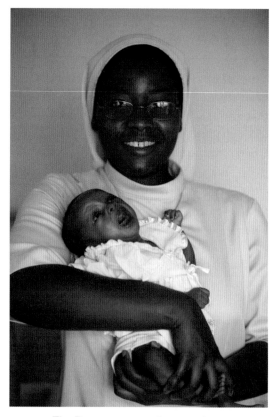

This Franciscan sister is living out her vocation and dedication to Christ by caring for babies at an orphanage in West Africa.

© robertharding / Alamy Stock Photo

UNIT 4

© Bill Witt

Cistercian monks belong to a contemplative order. Their ministry focuses primarily on prayer.

All members of religious orders and religious societies are consecrated to Christ through the publicly professed **religious vows** of poverty, chastity, and obedience. These vows are sometimes called the **evangelical counsels**.

UNIT 4

Members of religious communities publicly profess the vows of poverty, chastity, and obedience. Yet all of us are called to embrace the evangelical counsels as guides for our Christian living. Think about what this could mean for you. How can you limit your attachment to material possessions and share what you have, especially with people who are in need? How can you renew your commitment to chastity by avoiding situations that might lead to sexual temptation? How can you surrender to God's holy will, listening attentively and obediently to His voice? Incorporating the evangelical counsels into your own spiritual life can support you as you journey on the path to holiness.

religious vows ➤ The promises made by members of religious communities to follow the evangelical counsels of poverty, chastity, and obedience.

evangelical counsels ➤ The call to go beyond the minimum rules of life required by God (such as the Ten Commandments and the Precepts of the Church) and strive for spiritual perfection through a life marked by a commitment to chastity, poverty, and obedience.

Poverty, Chastity, and Obedience

The vow of poverty doesn't mean that religious sisters and brothers live without adequate food, clothing, or shelter; rather, it means that these and other basic needs are met, but religious brothers and sisters often don't have additional funds for things that are nonessential. Also, the members of the community share all things in common. For example, they live communally in a house or convent, but the house is owned by the religious order. Likewise, a religious sister may have the use of a car in order to get to the school or hospital where she ministers, but she does not own the car—the order does.

© Photononstop / Alamy Stock Photo

Nuns who serve at this school and orphanage in Togo, West Africa, live communally. They have taken a vow of poverty. So, they have their basic needs met, yet they share all things in common.

For all people, practicing **chastity** involves recognizing our sexuality as a tremendous gift from God and respecting the limits that God has established for sexual expression. For single people, this requires abstaining from sexual activity until marriage. Married people must be exclusively faithful to each other and, at times, abstain from sexual intercourse. For people in the consecrated life, their vow of chastity involves a lifelong commitment to **celibacy**.

chastity ➤ The virtue by which people are able to successfully and healthfully integrate their sexuality into their total person; recognized as one of the fruits of the Holy Spirit. Also one of the vows of religious life.

celibacy ➤ The state or condition of those who have chosen or taken vows to remain unmarried in order to devote themselves entirely to the service of the Church and the Kingdom of God.

They will not marry or engage in sexual or romantic relationships for the rest of their lives. This allows them the freedom and flexibility to serve God's people with complete, undivided dedication.

The word *obedience* comes from a Latin verb meaning "to hear." Members of religious communities take a vow of obedience to their religious superior, the head of the community. This expresses their willingness to put aside their own personal needs, preferences, and desires in order to serve wherever the superior determines that they are most needed. More fundamentally, the vow of obedience reflects religious sisters' and brothers' complete and total openness to God's will. They are committed to listening attentively to God's voice and to following wherever God may lead them.

When you think of religious sisters or brothers, you probably picture them teaching in schools, working in hospitals, or serving people who are poor or homeless. But some members of religious orders engage in ministries that are a little less traditional. For example, the Eastern Orthodox Monks of New Skete, in Cambridge, New York, breed, sell, and train German Shepherds. The dogs remind them of the beauty of the natural world and of God's creative love. The Dominican Sisters of Patzcuaro, Mexico, raise *achoques*, an endangered species of salamander that is native to their region. More than three hundred *achoques* live with them in their convent—in aquariums, of course! Sr. Noella Marcellino, a Benedictine nun at Regina Laudis Abbey in Bethlehem, Connecticut, uses her doctoral degree in microbiology to make artisanal cheese that is sold in the abbey's gift shop. Those who are called to religious life must be completely ready and willing to serve God—even in ways they never expected!

UNIT 4

Other Forms of Consecrated Life

Some women who wish to consecrate themselves to Christ without joining a religious order serve the Church as consecrated virgins or widows. These single women take a vow of celibacy in the presence of their diocesan bishop. They remain in the world, working in **secular** careers, but support the Church through their prayer and volunteer work.

Secular institutes are communities of people who live consecrated lives but whose daily work takes place within the world. They witness to Gospel values in society, and they share in the work of evangelization. Members of secular institutes may share annual retreats, meetings, and daily common prayer. Caritas Christi, for example, is an organization of single Catholic women who desire to follow Christ more closely while still working in their secular jobs. Voluntas Dei is a secular institute comprised of both men and women, single and married, whose aim is to enliven the whole world with the Gospel message of love and salvation. Members live with their own families and have their own jobs, but they meet regularly in small, local teams for prayer, study, and reflection.

Societies of apostolic life, also called apostolic societies, are not, strictly speaking, a form of the consecrated life. But they are similar to religious orders. They consist of laity or clergy who usually live in community for a particular purpose but do not make public religious vows. For example, the Catholic Foreign Mission Society of America, also called Maryknoll, is an apostolic society dedicated to foreign missions. The Oratory of Saint Philip Neri fosters a greater devotion to prayer, preaching, and the sacraments.

---

secular ➤ Relating to worldly concerns rather than religion.

secular institutes ➤ Ecclesiastically approved communities whose members commit themselves to the evangelical counsels but work in the world as witnesses to Christ.

societies of apostolic life ➤ Communities whose members strive to live according to the Gospel yet do not take religious vows. They may exercise a particular ministry or sponsor a particular apostolate.

Those who live an apostolic life, like this Maryknoll sister serving in Vietnam, do not make public religious vows. However, they live in a very similar way to those who have taken consecrated vows.

UNIT 4

The laity can be connected to those in the consecrated life through membership in a **third order**. Third orders consist of laypeople—married or single—who wish to formalize their relationship with a particular religious community without taking religious vows. These people commit to incorporating the community's spirituality into their daily lives and to participating in the community's ministries to whatever extent is possible. They may meet regularly with vowed members of the community for retreats, communal prayer, study groups, and social opportunities. Examples include the Lay Dominicans, the Mercy Associates, and the Secular Franciscans.

third order ➤ People who are affiliated with a religious order; generally, lay or secular members who promise to live according to the spirit of the order and to participate in its ministries to the extent possible.

Options for Consecrated Life	Examples of Consecrated Organizations
Active Orders Witness to God's love by serving in schools, hospitals, and in service-oriented agencies and missions.	Christian Brothers Dominicans Sisters of Mercy Franciscans Jesuits Sisters of the Presentation
Contemplative Orders Focus their ministry on prayer, interceding with God for the needs of the world.	Carmelites Cistercians Trappists
Secular Institutes Live consecrated lives, but their daily work takes place within the world.	Voluntas Dei Caritas Christi
Societies of Apostolic Life Similar to religious orders, they consist of laity or clergy who usually live in community for a particular purpose but do not make public religious vows.	Maryknolls Oratory of Saint Philip Neri
Third Orders Consist of laypeople—married or single—who wish to formalize their relationship with a particular religious community without taking religious vows.	Lay Dominicans Mercy Associates Secular Franciscans

UNIT 4

Sent Forth to Love and Serve

God calls every baptized person to serve him in a unique way. This includes you! God has a plan for how you can live out your baptismal vocation to holiness and help fulfill the Church's mission. You may not know yet whether you are called to marriage, to ordination, or to the consecrated life. But whatever your particular vocational path turns out to be, this much is certain: You are a member of Christ's own body, called to witness to the Gospel and to serve others with joy and generosity. God, who created you in love and redeemed you in mercy, will continue to sanctify and strengthen you for this holy work each day, until you are, at last, fully united with him forever.

HMMMMM. . . What is something that you could learn from the lives and ministries of religious sisters and brothers?

UNIT 4

1. What is the common vocation that all baptized people share?

2. What opportunities does the Church offer to help us grow in holiness?

3. What metaphor does Pope Francis use to describe faith?

4. How does faith help us to see the world differently?

5. What three aspects of the ministry of Jesus Christ do all baptized people share in? Briefly describe each.

6. How is the common priesthood of the faithful different from the ministerial priesthood?

7. Under what conditions was Saint Pedro Calungsod martyred?

8. What are the different types of consecrated life a person might enter?

9. What are the three evangelical counsels?

10. What does the Latin root of the word *obedience* mean? How does this give us deeper insight into the meaning of the vow of obedience?

11. How can the laity be formally connected with those in the consecrated life?

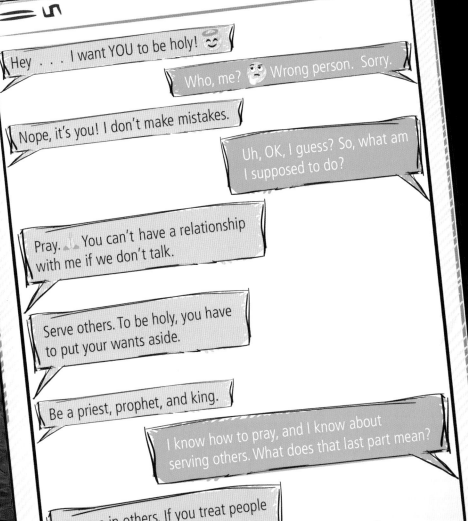

GOD TEXTED ME

How can the Church help and support young people who are reluctant to accept their call to holiness?

UNIT 4 HIGHLIGHTS

CHAPTER 10 The Ministry of Leadership

Ministry of the Pope:
Develop and Strengthen Unity in the Church

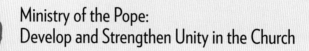

The word *pope* comes from
the Greek word *pappas,* an
affectionate term for father.

• Like the father of any family,
  the Pope is called to unite us
  in one community.

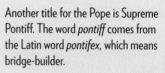

Another title for the Pope is Supreme
Pontiff. The word *pontiff* comes from
the Latin word *pontifex,* which means
bridge-builder.

• The Pope is called to bring together
  people who are separated by nationality,
  social status, income—even political and
  religious differences.

Images: Shutterstock.com • Ve-teezy.com

Ministry of Bishops

Twofold Ministry
- Service to people of their diocese
- Concern for the worldwide Church

Teaching
- Members of the Magisterium
- Called to preach God's Word

Bishops

Sanctifying
- Lead all people to holiness and Heaven
- Pray, preach, and set a good example

Governing
- Run the diocese as a servant leader
- Respond to local needs

UNIT 4

Ministry of the Magisterium

Infallibility
This is the Holy Spirit's gift to the whole Church, by which the leaders of the Church are protected from making errors when teaching on matters of faith and morals. Both the Pope and the College of Bishops can speak and teach infallibly.

Indefectibility
This is one of the gifts given to the Magisterium to ensure that the Church will always teach the Gospel correctly. Though no person in the Church is perfect, we can trust that the Magisterium will accurately proclaim the truth of the Gospel message.

Magisterium
All the bishops throughout the world, in union with the Pope, who function as the teaching office of the Church.

CHAPTER 11 Mission and Holiness

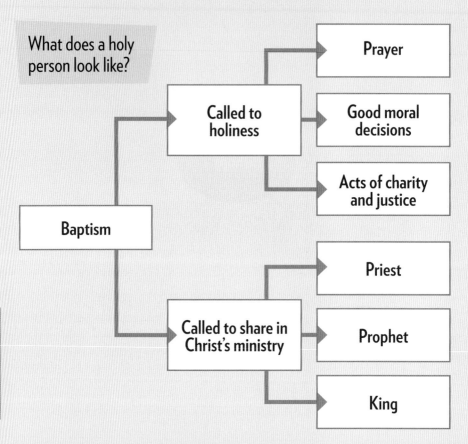

What does a holy person look like?

- Baptism
  - Called to holiness
    - Prayer
    - Good moral decisions
    - Acts of charity and justice
  - Called to share in Christ's ministry
    - Priest
    - Prophet
    - King

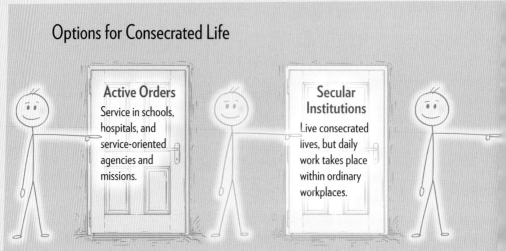

Options for Consecrated Life

Active Orders
Service in schools, hospitals, and service-oriented agencies and missions.

Secular Institutions
Live consecrated lives, but daily work takes place within ordinary workplaces.

The Vows of Religious Societies and Orders

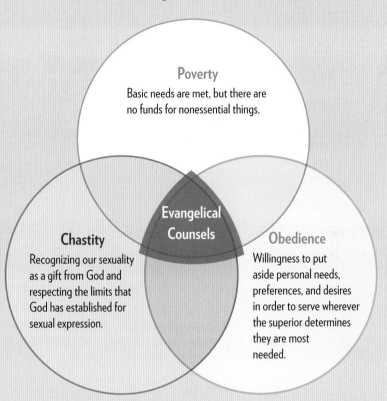

Poverty
Basic needs are met, but there are no funds for nonessential things.

Evangelical Counsels

Chastity
Recognizing our sexuality as a gift from God and respecting the limits that God has established for sexual expression.

Obedience
Willingness to put aside personal needs, preferences, and desires in order to serve wherever the superior determines they are most needed.

Third Orders
Laypeople, married or single, who formalize their relationship with a religious community without taking religious vows.

Contemplative Orders
Focus their ministry primarily on prayer, interceding with God for the needs of the world.

Societies of Apostolic Life
Similar to religious orders, but they live in a community for a particular purpose. They don't make public, religious vows.

Images: Shutterstock.com

UNIT 4

UNIT 4
BRING IT HOME

HOW DO WE ALL SHARE IN CHRIST'S MISSION?

FOCUS QUESTIONS

CHAPTER 10   What does it mean to be a leader in the Church?

CHAPTER 11   What does a holy person look like?

HANNAH
Cotter High School

UNIT 4

Our actions, our words, and our invitations are the basis of the Church and her mission. I believe that while most of us firmly believe God should come first, we fall short on our execution. School, the arts, sports, homework, and so on, all demand a certain amount of dedication, time, and effort. With every other aspect of our lives being so overwhelming, it is hard to find time to just breathe, yet alone turn to God. It is in these exhausting moments that it is important we turn to God. Though it is challenging, during these times when we are spread thin is probably when we evangelize most effectively.

REFLECT

Take some time to read and reflect on the unit and chapter focus questions listed on the facing page.

- What question or section did you identify most closely with?

- What did you find within the unit that was comforting or challenging?

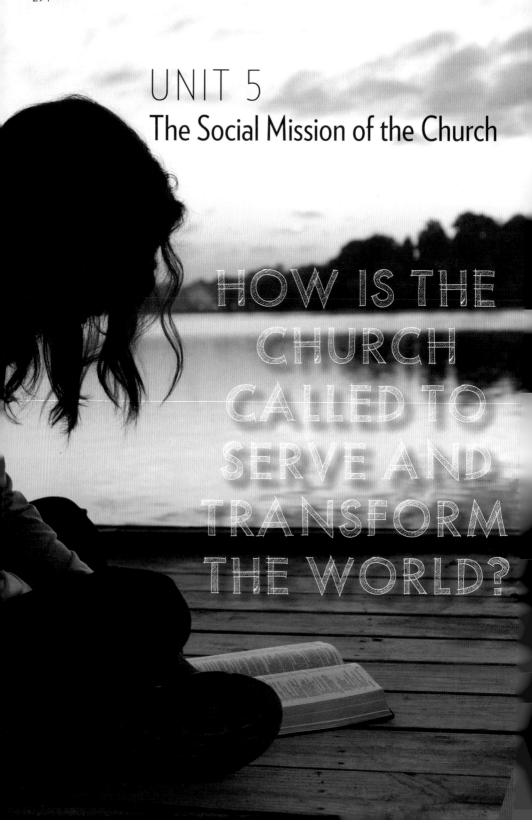

UNIT 5
The Social Mission of the Church

HOW IS THE
CHURCH
CALLED TO
SERVE AND
TRANSFORM
THE WORLD?

LOOKING AHEAD

CHAPTER 12 Page 296
The Gospel Message
of Service and Justice

CHAPTER 13 Page 320
Strength in Numbers:
Catholic Service Organizations

CHAPTER 14 Page 346
The Gift of Oneself:
Gospel-Centered Volunteer Service

UNIT 5

The Church, meaning each living
individual, is called to live
following Jesus' example. In
other words, each person should live
humbly, charitably, truthfully, and
peacefully. Each person should work
to serve others and to help build
harmony between all people. If only
humanity united like this, then
humanity could be truly united
with God. This is the work of
the Church.

COLIN
Father Judge High School

CHAPTER 12
The Gospel Message of Service and Justice

HOW AM I CALLED TO BE HOLY?

SNAPSHOT

Article 47   Page 297
Reading the Signs of the Times
- Pre-read: Luke 12:54–56

Article 48   Page 301
A Call to Conversion: The Parables
- Pre-read: Luke 12:16–21, Luke 16:19–31

Article 49   Page 307
Matthew's Message: The Corporal Works of Mercy
- Pre-read: Matthew 20:1–16
- Pre-read: Matthew 25:31–46

Article 50   Page 313
The Washing of the Feet
- Pre-read: John 13:1–17

Article 47
Reading the Signs of the Times

As Todd heard the last few notes of the song of sending forth drifting out of the open church door, he got his clipboards ready. For his service project this semester, he was volunteering with his parish Social Justice Committee to collect signatures for a petition to prevent funding decreases for food stamps. As people left the church, some stopped to sign, or to ask questions, but a lot just walked by him and headed to the parking lot. Then a man came right up to Todd and said: "I'm not signing that! Politics is none of the Church's business. The Church should stay out of it." Startled, Todd had

How would you respond if you were in Todd's position?

trouble getting his thoughts together. "It's so people have enough to eat," he said weakly. The man just scowled and walked toward his car. Todd took a deep breath, tried to compose himself, and continued to pass out the clipboards.

On the one hand, the man's outburst reflected a valid point. The Church's primary business is the salvation of all people, through Jesus Christ. In this regard, the Church's mission transcends history because she is concerned with the eternal salvation of souls. On the other hand, this doesn't mean that the Church should *not* be concerned with politics. After all, the Church exists in the world and is a part of history. God has been at work in human history since the very beginning of creation—most importantly in the act of sending Jesus Christ to live as one of us and to redeem us. As members of the Church, we can't say that what is going on in the world has nothing to do with us, or that our only focus is getting to Heaven. We can't turn away from our families, our friends, our school, our neighborhood, and people in need. Because Christ came to redeem the world, we must always be concerned for the world's welfare—for the well-being of all people and all creation.

UNIT 5

TAKE IT TO GOD

"You have been told, O mortal, what is good,
and what the LORD requires of you:
Only to do justice and to love goodness,
and to walk humbly with your God?" (Micah 6:8)

When I serve others, I know I am following in your footsteps.
When I am helping others directly, or when I am working toward
social change,
I know I am demonstrating charity and justice.
As I walk humbly with you, Lord, let my actions be a signpost for others.
Through my service to you,
I ask the Holy Spirit to bring others to know you.
Amen.

The Signs of the Times

A short passage in Luke's Gospel (Luke 12:54–56) can help us to understand the Church's mission to be actively engaged with the world. In this story, Jesus addresses a crowd of people, and he's frustrated with them. He calls them hypocrites. A hypocrite is a person who's inconsistent—whose words and behaviors don't match. For example, if your older sister says that you shouldn't vape, but you know that she vapes all the time, she is being hypocritical. Her advice to you doesn't match her own actions.

So why is Jesus criticizing the crowd? Why does he call them hypocrites? He says that the people are able to understand "the appearance of the earth and the sky," but they cannot "interpret the present time" (Luke 12:56). In other words, they recognize when it's going to rain and when it's going to be sunny, but beyond this very superficial level, they are clueless about what is really going on around them. For example, they don't grasp the meaning of Jesus' message. They cannot notice hints of the Reign of God, which Jesus has already begun through his preaching and his miracles. They can't figure out how they should respond to the needs of those around them. Their viewpoint is so limited. It's like Jesus is telling them: "Snap out of it! Wake up! Open your eyes! Look at the world around you and *do something!*"

Luke doesn't tell us how the crowd responded to Jesus. Maybe they were so shocked and embarrassed at being called hypocrites that they did wake up and start to engage deeply with the world around them. Or maybe they just dispersed and went back to their regular lives, unchanged. In either case, the Church does take seriously Jesus' command to "interpret the present time" (Luke 12:56). The Vatican II document *Pastoral Constitution on the Church in the Modern World* (*Gaudium et Spes*, 1965) described this as the Church's responsibility of "scrutinizing the signs of the time and interpreting them in light of the Gospel" (number 4).

"Reading the signs of the time" means that the Church must be attentive to and learn from every aspect of the world around her, including art, culture, politics, science, and technology. The Church must stay informed about current events, with particular concern for the needs of people who are poor and vulnerable. On both local and national levels, the Church must advocate for laws, policies, and programs that protect people who are elderly, ill, unborn, undocumented, or in need of housing, education, and social services. The Church must seek to ensure that these groups of people, who are so often overlooked or neglected, are cared for. In this way, the Church fulfills her mission of being a sign and instrument of communion with God and the unity of the whole human race.

The Church has an obligation to care for those who are poor and vulnerable.

You probably know that being the Pope comes with many privileges, but did you know that one of them is having your very own observatory with some of the most powerful telescopes in the world? The Vatican Observatory is a Church-owned institution that conducts world-class scientific research. Its resident scientists study all areas of astronomy and astrophysics, including the stars, planets, meteorites, comets, and other heavenly phenomena.

Some people mistakenly think that the Church is opposed to science. But, in fact, for many centuries the Church has recognized that "reading the signs of the times" requires engaging in scientific research. Because science teaches us so much about the world around us, we need it to inform our efforts to serve others, create justice, and help the Reign of God to be fully realized.

© MachineHeadz / iStock.com

Todd's Redo

Lying in bed that night, Todd was kind of annoyed with himself. He felt like he should have had a better response to that guy who had confronted him after Mass, but he'd never been good at thinking on his feet. Now, though, hours later, he knew exactly what he should have said: "Sir, social justice *is* the Church's business. This isn't about politics. If we aren't involved in trying to help hungry people, who will? If we don't notice people who are poor and in need right here in our own neighborhood, who will? If we don't respond with love and generosity, who will? If you believe the amount the government is spending on food stamps is more than needed, I understand and respect that. Christians can disagree on the best response based on our judicious under-standing and judgment. But could I show you some statistics about how many families would be affected by a reduction in food stamp assistance?" Satisfied that he would know what to say if he ever got into a situation like that again, he drifted off to sleep. ✹

HMMMMM. . .

How would you respond to someone who said that the Church should stay out of politics?

Article 48
A Call to Conversion: The Parables

Jesus often taught using parables, or short stories that use everyday images to communicate a religious message.

Although many Gospel passages can support and guide our efforts to read the signs of the times, the parables are particularly helpful for this task. On one level, the parables used imagery from daily life that the people of Jesus' time could easily understand and relate to. Yet, on another level, the parables are often strange and even disturbing, with a plot twist or a surprise ending. These stories are meant to make people a little bit uncomfortable: to lead them to examine their lives and priorities and to make concrete changes as a result. Through the parables, Jesus invites people both to recognize and to be a part of the Reign of God.

In this article, we'll look at two key parables from the Gospel of Luke. The next article will focus on two parables from the Gospel of Matthew.

UNIT 5

The Parable of the Rich Fool

In the Parable of the Rich Fool (Luke 12:16–21), we meet an unnamed man. All we know about him is that he's rich, and that he has a problem—a good problem. His land has produced a bountiful harvest, and he doesn't know what to do with all his extra crops. He has so much food that he doesn't even have enough space in his barns to store it.

The man comes up with a plan. He decides that he will build bigger barns that will store all his grain and other goods. Then he can rest and enjoy himself. He won't have to worry about anything for many years to come—he can just relax.

The Parable of the Rich Fool is about a man who has so much extra wheat from his harvest that he doesn't know what to do with it. This parable is still relevant today. If we have excess, should we find a way to hoard it, or should we use it to help others?

UNIT 5

Imagine yourself in this scene as Jesus tells this story. His audience is probably nodding in agreement and smiling in admiration. Droughts and famines happened often enough that they didn't take having enough food for themselves and their families for granted. They think that this guy is the hero of the story, who is teaching them all a valuable lesson about how to protect their resources and prepare for an uncertain future.

But this is a parable, so things are not what they seem. The rich man's plan sounds good until God intervenes. Calling the man a fool, God reveals that the man will die that very night. Now, the audience gasps in horror. He won't get to enjoy all his good fortune! All his crops and other possessions will do him no good. As the old saying goes, "you can't take it with you."

God calls the rich man a fool because he has made two big mistakes. When first faced with his problem, he asks himself, "What shall I do, for I do not have space to store my harvest?" (Luke 12:17). This problem has a solution that the man overlooks, and it doesn't involve hiring a contractor to build him a new barn: give away his extra food. We know that in first-century Palestine, there certainly were very poor people who struggled to scrape together even a meager living. If the man had shared whatever didn't fit in his current barns with those in need, he still would have had more than enough for himself.

The fact that sharing his excess food doesn't even cross the rich man's mind indicates a deeper problem. He has forgotten that in a sense, his possessions aren't really his alone. Yes, he legally owns them, and he probably worked hard to build up his farm so that it could be so productive. But, in another sense, God had entrusted him with these possessions, in the hopes that he would use them to make the world a better place. In that regard, the man failed miserably, no matter how big his harvest was.

The man has also lost a sense of the big picture. He has forgotten that his greatest gift from God—his most precious possession—is his life. And he has forgotten that his *ultimate* destiny is not to accumulate material things or to build bigger barns but to be united with God forever in Heaven. This loss of a sense of perspective—this failure to recognize what really matters in life—has led him to make some very poor decisions. Unfortunately, it is too late to correct his mistakes.

This parable teaches us that all that we have—our gifts and talents, our material possessions and resources, our family and friends, our education, and every other blessing—comes from God. It invites us not only to share what we have in a spirit of generous service but also to take an honest look at our relationship to material things. For example, do you find yourself wanting the new iPhone or the new Xbox as soon as it comes out? How much money do you spend each month on new clothes, coffee, or other treats and luxuries? How much do you give away to people who are in need? When it's time for you to attend a formal dance or prom, what will be your budget for your outfit, transportation, food, flowers, and other expenses? There isn't one right answer to these questions. But this parable does call us to ask these questions of ourselves, to answer them honestly, and, perhaps, to make some changes in our actions or attitude as a result.

© sirtravelalot / Shutterstock.com

UNIT 5

The Parable of the Rich Fool doesn't reprimand us for spending money or having nice things. However, it is a nudge for us to examine how we are spending our money and if we are putting any of our extra to help those in need.

The Parable of Lazarus and the Rich Man

A few chapters later in Luke's Gospel (Luke 16:19–31), Jesus tells another parable with some similar themes. The first three verses of the Parable of Lazarus and the Rich Man take place on Earth. We meet two people: an unnamed rich man and a poor man named Lazarus. The two live very close to one another—the poor man lies at the rich man's door—and yet their worlds could not be farther apart. The rich man eats fancy food, while Lazarus is hungry. The rich man dresses in fine clothes, while Lazarus is covered only in sores. The story tells us that Lazarus longs to eat "his fill of the scraps that fell from the rich man's table" (Luke 16:21), but, as far as we can tell, the two men never speak to each other or have any kind of interaction.

Then both men die. In the afterlife, they switch places. The rich man, who had such a privileged life on Earth, is now tormented in the netherworld, while Lazarus rests in "the bosom of Abraham" (Luke 16:22). To put it more simply: the rich man is in Hell, and Lazarus is in Heaven.

The rich man makes two requests of Abraham, whom he can see, far off, at Lazarus's side. The first is for Abraham to send Lazarus to bring him water. Abraham refuses. The second is for Abraham to send Lazarus back to Earth to the rich man's five brothers. He wants to warn them, so that they can change their ways and not also end up in Hell when they die. Abraham refuses this request too, saying that the brothers should listen to Moses and the prophets.

What does this advice mean? Moses and the Old Testament prophets were long dead at the time Jesus told this story. But their teachings were found in the **Torah** and in the prophetic books, and those teachings were clear. We must protect the needy (see Exodus 23:6). We must do justice and love goodness (see Micah 6:8). We must share our bread with the hungry and welcome the homeless into our houses (see Isaiah 58:6–11). Abraham is saying that the rich man's brothers have all the information they need in order to make better decisions. They simply have to pay attention: to hear the Word of God and put it into practice.

Torah ▶ A Hebrew word meaning "law," referring to the first five books of the Old Testament. It can also refer to the Law of Moses.

In this parable, either the rich man was oblivious to Lazarus's plight, or he was aware of it but just didn't care enough to do anything about it. The parable invites us to address both of these potential problems in our own lives.

The Parable of Lazarus and the Rich Man challenges us to open our eyes. How do you react when you see someone by the side of the road asking for money or help?

The first step is to open our eyes—to read the signs of the times and notice people in need. So often, people who are poor are invisible to us. For example, you may walk by people who are homeless with barely a glance. You may be unaware that when a friend's or neighbor's family goes through an illness, a death, or a divorce, they may have trouble making ends meet. You may not notice that some of the students in your own school are struggling financially.

The second step is to care: to open our hearts so that we feel compassion for people in need. The third step is to do something. Although you may feel limited in what you can do now, as a young person, you certainly don't have to act alone. You can work through an existing program in your school or parish, or you can gather a group and initiate something new. In either case, remember to consider both immediate needs—that is, the fact that people need food, clothes, and other necessities right now—as well as long-term, systemic changes that will help to address the underlying reasons why people are poor in the first place. For example, when wages are higher, and housing is more affordable, people are less likely to slip into hunger and poverty.

UNIT 5

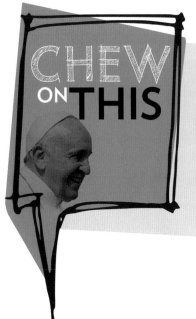

You young people have strength as you go through a phase of your lives where energy is not lacking. Make use of this strength and this energy to improve the world, beginning with the realities closest to you. ("Address of His Holiness Pope Francis on the Occasion of the XXXIII World Youth Day," February 11, 2018)

A Call to Conversion

Both of these parables, and, in fact, all of Jesus' parables, are calls to conversion. At its root, *conversion* means "turning." It refers to an interior shift, deep within us—a true change of heart that turns us away from sin and toward God. The rich men in both of these parables were completely focused on themselves. They didn't notice the suffering of others around them, even those who were literally at their doors. These parables invite us to broaden our gaze, to widen our perspective, and to expand the circle of our concern, so that those who are in need may find in us true friends and allies. ✳

 How might one or both of these parables help you to evaluate your own relationship to money and other material possessions?

Article 49

Matthew's Message: The Corporal Works of Mercy

Matthew's Gospel offers us some direction for how we are to serve others and help transform the world into a more just and peaceful place. In this article, we will look at two parables from the Gospel of Matthew and see how they can help us understand our call to serve and treat others with love and compassion in specific, concrete ways.

The Workers in the Vineyard

In Matthew 20:1–16, Jesus tells the Parable of the Workers in the Vineyard. You recall that a landowner goes out at dawn to hire laborers for his vineyard. He offers them an acceptable daily wage, and he sends them to work. He goes out four more times that day. Each time he hires more workers and promises to pay them a just wage. In the evening, he tells his foreman to gather the workers and pay them. All the laborers receive the same pay, whether they worked all day or just a few hours! Naturally, those who worked all day grumble about the laborers who only worked for an hour, yet received the same pay. The landowner chastises them for complaining, saying: "My friend, I am not cheating you. Did you not agree with me for the usual daily wage?" (Matthew 20:13).

Do the workers first hired have a good reason to be upset? The land owner had offered them a daily wage, and they had agreed. Does it matter how he chooses to pay the rest of the workers, whether they worked most of the day or just an hour? The landowner explains: "Are you envious because I am generous? Thus, the last will be first, and the first will be last" (Matthew 20:15–16). Do you know anyone who would have reacted the same way as the first-hired laborers?

This parable serves as a lesson for us today. Perhaps you identify with the first-hired workers. If you put in the hard work and effort, you want to be paid or rewarded more than someone who did less work. But Jesus reminds us that it isn't up to us to judge what a person earns or what they deserve. God is loving and just. We are called to serve others. Rather than trying to determine who deserves food, shelter, and other basic needs based on how hard they work, perhaps we need to share the bounty of our hard work with others. If "the last will be first," how can we serve them? How can we treat them with the love and compassion modeled for us by Christ? Let's look at another parable in the Matthew's Gospel to answer those questions.

The Sheep and the Goats

The last parable that Jesus shares, right before his Passion begins, is a powerful and thought-provoking story about the **Last Judgment**. In Matthew 25:31–46, the Son of Man (in other words, Jesus, who is also referred to as "the king" in this story) has come to judge all of humanity, so all the nations are assembled before him. He divides them into two groups, the way that a shepherd or farmer might divide a group of animals into two flocks. The "sheep" go on his right side, and the "goats" on his left. The king praises the people on his right side because they cared for him when he was hungry, thirsty, a stranger, naked, ill, and in prison. He condemns the people on his left side for failing to carry out these same actions.

Both groups of people are completely puzzled. They have no memory of ever seeing Jesus in any kind of need. Here's the parable's surprise punch line: "Whatever you did for one of these least brothers of mine, you did for me" (Matthew 25:40). In serving those in need, the "sheep" were, in fact, serving Jesus, even though they had no idea they were doing so. Likewise, in failing to serve those in need, the "goats" have failed to serve Jesus. The parable affirms a fundamental truth: although Jesus is present in all people, we have a special responsibility to recognize him in people who are poor or suffering.

UNIT 5

Last Judgment ▶ The judgment of the human race by Jesus Christ at his second coming. It is also called the Final Judgment.

The Corporal Works of Mercy

The Parable of the Workers in the Vineyard is the basis for a traditional Christian teaching: the **Corporal Works of Mercy.** The word *corporal* comes from the Latin word *corpus*, which means "body." All of the Corporal Works of Mercy involve responding to people's physical, bodily needs. Those that are mentioned explicitly in the passage are:

Which of the Corporal Works of Mercy do you find to be the most challenging?

- feeding the hungry
- giving drink to the thirsty
- welcoming the stranger (sometimes phrased as "sheltering the homeless")
- clothing the naked
- visiting the sick
- visiting the imprisoned

The setting of this parable—the Last Judgment—helps to highlight that the Corporal Works of Mercy are serious business. According to the parable, they are the criteria by which we will be judged. Therefore, these actions are a necessary component of the Christian life. They are not optional. They are not something that we fit into our schedule if we have extra time or if we're really bored and have absolutely nothing else to do. Rather, they should be at the top of our list of priorities.

The Parable of the Workers in the Vineyard has a hard truth at the end. The Corporal Works of Mercy are the criteria against which we will be judged. Are they at the top of your priority list?

Corporal Works of Mercy ➤ Charitable actions by which we help our neighbors in their bodily needs.

Additional Works of Mercy

Traditionally, one extra Corporal Work of Mercy has been added to the list of those that appear in the parable: "bury the dead." This addition reflects our call to care for people not only throughout their lives but also when they pass away. "Bury the dead" does not necessarily mean getting a shovel and literally digging a grave; rather, it directs us to reverence and honor of the memory of all those who have gone before us. We can do this by attending funerals and memorial services, visiting the graves of our deceased relatives and friends, and expressing our sympathy and support to those who are mourning the loss of a loved one.

How can you give honor and dignity to those who have passed away?

On September 1, 2016, the World Day of Prayer for the Care of Creation, Pope Francis proposed expanding the usual list of the Corporal Works of Mercy to include "care for our common home"—that is, care for the Earth, for nature, and for all of creation. This teaching demonstrates Pope Francis's deep concern for the environment. It also makes a great deal of sense when considered alongside the other works. Think about it: Are we supposed to feed the hungry with food grown in contaminated soil? Are we to give the thirsty polluted water to drink? Are we to visit people who are sick from exposure to toxic chemicals without trying to prevent others from becoming similarly ill? Science tells us that humanity is both connected with and sustained by all other living things. Our faith tells us that we must nurture and protect that connection, because justice for people cannot fully happen without justice for the Earth.

Why do you think Pope Francis proposed expanding the list of Corporal Works of Mercy to include care for our common home?

CATHOLICS MAKING A DIFFERENCE

What would you do if someone gave you a million dollars? When Venerable Catherine McAuley inherited a huge sum of money in 1824, she used it to build a "House of Mercy" in her native Dublin, Ireland. The House opened on September 24, 1827—the Feast of Our Lady of Mercy—and served as a school for the poor and a shelter for servant girls fleeing abusive situations. Four years later, McAuley and two of her companions professed vows as the first members of a new religious order: the Sisters of Mercy. Today, more than nine thousand Sisters of Mercy continue McAuley's legacy. Along with the usual vows of poverty, chastity, and obedience, these sisters take a fourth vow of service: a commitment to support those in need by carrying out the Corporal Works of Mercy.

UNIT 5

© Evgeny Atamanenko / Shutterstock.com

Eight-Day Challenge

Try to carry out all eight of the Corporal Works of Mercy in eight days! Here are some suggested actions to help you meet this challenge.

Corporal Works of Mercy	Living Out the Corporal Works of Mercy
Feed the hungry.	Donate money to your parish's Saint Vincent de Paul Society or a local hunger organization.
Give drink to the thirsty.	Educate yourself about the lack of clean, drinkable water in many parts of the world—even in the United States.
Welcome the stranger.	Introduce yourself to a new student at your school and invite him or her to join you and your friends for a meal or a movie.
Clothe the naked.	Go through your closet and donate all your clothes that you have outgrown or don't wear anymore. Make sure they are clean and in good condition—no rips, missing buttons, or broken zippers.
Visit the sick.	Spend time with a relative or family friend who is in a hospital or nursing home. Bring a handmade gift with you.
Visit the imprisoned.	Write a letter to someone who is serving in the military far from home. Service members are often "imprisoned" by loneliness and by the pain of being separated from their families. Collect Bibles and other spiritual reading materials to donate to a prison.
Bury the dead.	Pray for all those who are mourning the loss of a loved one due to war, violence, or natural disasters.

Care for our common home. Promote awareness of your school's recycling and composting program—or start such a program if your school doesn't have one! ✳

 Which of the Corporal Works of Mercy is most appealing for you to put into practice? Which seems most challenging? Why?

Article 50
The Washing of the Feet

Do you like your feet? What a weird question! Many people don't like feet, even their own, because feet are often smelly and sweaty—and sometimes just downright ugly!

Ugly or not, feet play a starring role in the Gospel of John's account of the Last Supper. Unlike the synoptic Gospels, John doesn't mention bread or wine in his version of this event. Instead, he tells a story none of the other Gospel writers do: that Jesus washed his disciples' feet (John 13:1–17). This action—which the Church remembers and celebrates each year on **Holy Thursday**—can help us to understand the Church's call to be of humble service to all the world.

Foot Washing: The Back Story

In biblical times, one of the responsibilities of a host was to have a servant or slave wash the feet of guests when they arrived. This might seem like a strange custom, until you consider the circumstances in which people traveled back then. Sandals were the footwear of choice, and people walked for miles along dusty roads littered not only with all kinds of garbage but also with both animal and human waste. Remember, this is way, way before indoor plumbing! Picture how dirty and disgusting people's feet might be when they finally reached their destination. So, to have one's feet washed upon arrival was a refreshing gesture of welcome and hospitality.

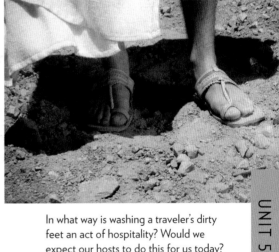

In what way is washing a traveler's dirty feet an act of hospitality? Would we expect our hosts to do this for us today?

© PeteWill / iStock.com

UNIT 5

Holy Thursday ❯ The beginning of the Easter Triduum, starting with the evening celebration of the Mass of the Lord's Supper.

Peter's Problem

How do you interpret the reactions of the other Apostles in this painting of Jesus washing the feet of Peter?

Imagine the awkward silence in the room as the disciples watch Jesus do the unthinkable: tie a towel around his waist, pour water into a basin, and wash and dry their feet. His actions would have been completely shocking, because the one they call "Master" and "Teacher" has taken on the lowly role of a servant.

Peter is the only disciple who breaks this silence. At first, he simply questions Jesus' behavior, but then he issues a direct challenge: "You will never wash my feet" (John 13:8). Jesus responds with his own ultimatum: "Unless I wash you, you will have no inheritance with me" (verse 8) In other words, Peter cannot remain a part of Jesus' mission unless he allows Jesus to wash his feet. What's the big deal? Why is Jesus washing Peter's feet so crucial that Jesus threatens to cut Peter out if he doesn't allow it to happen?

This action of Jesus—this washing of feet—is so important because it summarizes the whole pattern of his life and ministry. Jesus never failed to welcome all people with warm and generous hospitality, including those whom others would often reject, like women, the poor, and the sick. Jesus' ministry focused on serving others: healing the blind and the lame, raising the dead, extending mercy to sinners, and, ultimately, dying to save us. The Reign of God that Jesus preached is, in many ways, a world turned upside down. It's a world in which, as in the Parable of Lazarus and the Rich Man, those who were rich and powerful lose their privilege, and those who were poor are lifted up, blessed, and comforted. In his actions at the Last Supper, Jesus embodies this pattern by switching places with his disciples: the Master has become the Servant of All.

An Example to Follow

After washing their feet, Jesus tries to help the disciples grasp the significance of this deed. He tells them, "I have given you a model to follow, so that as I have done for you, you should also do" (John 13:15). Jesus' actions in this story can be an example for us in three key ways.

First, we are called to welcome others with gracious hospitality. Although this is unlikely to involve washing their feet—as this is no longer the custom in our society and culture—welcoming others can take many forms, depending upon the situation. Think, for example, about your school. When guests or visitors arrive at your school, how are they welcomed? How does your school treat new students, especially those with different ethnic or religious backgrounds? What about students who transfer in later in the academic year? How about seventh- and eighth-grade visitors who may become students there someday? Are they all welcomed with enthusiasm and respect? If so, then your school is a true model of Christlike hospitality. If not, then your school may have some work to do and some changes to make!

Foot washing isn't a common form of hospitality in our culture. What can you do to extend hospitality to newcomers to your school, youth group, team, or club?

Think about your city or neighborhood. How welcoming is your community for people of diverse ethnic and racial backgrounds or for families with different economic backgrounds? In short, is your school and your community a place where everyone feels respected and valued as God's beloved child?

Second, we are called to serve others in a spirit of generosity, selflessness, and humility. We all know that service is important, but serving others sometimes isn't glamorous. We may have to do the job that no one else wants to do or the work that seems messy or unpleasant. For example, it might be gratifying to pass a tray of food to a hungry person and see him or her smile in thanks. But someone has to scrub all the pots and pans and sweep the floor after everyone has eaten. It might be fun to coach middle school basketball, but someone has to work with the student who may never score a basket. It might be cute to play with babies and toddlers at a day care center, but someone has to change their diapers, wipe their runny noses, and clean up the mess when they spill their juice. As disciples, we must be ready to take on tasks like these. These tasks are far from glamorous, but they can help us to follow Jesus' example more completely and faithfully.

Last, as we try through our words and actions to help the Reign of God to be fully realized, we must be willing to embrace a world turned upside down. We must be willing, at times, to set aside our own privilege and power. We must be willing to reach out to those on the margins so that they may be included and lifted up. Like Jesus, we must be willing to become servants of all.

UNIT 5

The Story in Action

Each year on Holy Thursday, members of a nonprofit organization called the Care Through Touch Institute fan out through San Francisco's Tenderloin neighborhood. Their mission is to offer free foot massages to the many homeless people who. Because homeless people spend hours each day walking—sometimes pushing heavy carts that hold their belongings—their feet are often sore, calloused, and blistered. By offering some relief through a gentle massage—and a new pair of socks—Care Through Touch practitioners carry out Jesus' literal command to "wash one another's feet" (John 13:14), as well as the deeper meaning of his actions. They welcome with warm hospitality those whom society so often overlooks. They engage in service that others might find unappealing. And they place themselves in the role of a servant, kneeling beside a person in need to offer care and comfort. ✳

© K-Smile love / Shutterstock.com

Can you think of another example of the Corporal Works of Mercy in action other than the Care Through Touch program?

UNIT 5

HMMMMMM. . .
What shocking act of service might Jesus do today to get our attention?

1. What does it mean to "read the signs of the times"?

2. In the Parable of the Rich Fool, what problem does the main character encounter? How does he decide to solve this problem?

3. What two big mistakes does the rich fool make?

4. Why does Abraham refuse to send Lazarus to warn the rich man's brothers?

5. How does the setting of the parable that appears in Matthew 25:31–46 emphasize the importance of the Corporal Works of Mercy?

6. What two extra Corporal Works of Mercy have been added to those that appear explicitly in the Gospel of Matthew?

7. Who founded the Religious Sisters of Mercy? What additional vow do these sisters take?

8. In the Gospel of John, what was particularly shocking about Jesus' actions at the Last Supper? What example was Jesus setting for us by these actions?

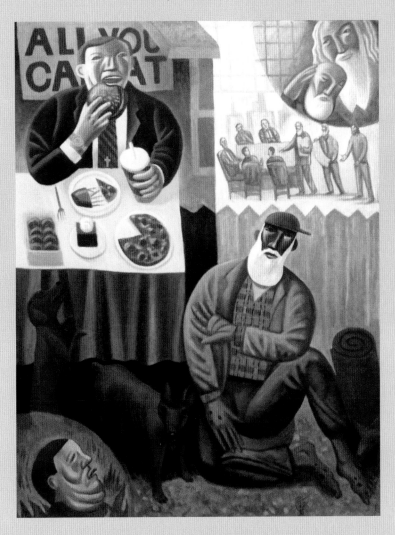

This painting is modern artist James B. Janknegt's depiction of the Parable of Lazarus and the Rich Man.

1. What elements of the original Gospel story do you see in this painting?

2. What elements of the painting speak to you or attract your attention? Why?

3. A cross appears on the rich man's necktie. What point do you think the artist is trying to make with this detail?

CHAPTER 13
Strength in Numbers: Catholic Service Organizations

HOW CAN I BEST SERVE OTHERS?

SNAPSHOT

Article 51   Page 321
Serving the Least among Us

Article 52   Page 330
Apostolic Religious Orders

Article 53   Page 336
Focus on Pope Francis:
"On Care for Our Common Home"

Article 51

Serving the Least among Us

What have been your most amazing and powerful experiences involving the Church? If you are like many teenagers, some of the most memorable experiences along your journey of faith have probably involved serving those in need. Maybe you visited a nursing home as part of your preparation for the Sacrament of Confirmation. Maybe you have worked with your school's campus ministry program to collect donations of food or clothing and deliver them to a food bank, shelter, or soup kitchen. Maybe your youth group has made bagged lunches and distributed them to hungry people. Maybe you have even participated in a more intensive service project, like an immersion program or mission trip.

These young adults traveled to Colombia for two weeks on a mission trip with an organization called Volunteers Without Borders. Mission trips and service-year programs are offered through churches, college organizations, and independent immersion programs.

Experiences like these highlight how seriously the Church takes the Gospel call to service and justice. They also demonstrate how important it is that the Church not simply rely on individual good will or good intentions but, rather, sponsor *collective* efforts to create a more just and peaceful world. We receive Christ's redemption as members of his Body, the Church. So, it makes sense for us to work together, as one Body and in the power of the Holy Spirit, to transform the world and help the Reign of God to be fully realized. When we do this, we experience the power of a shared life of faith characterized by prayer, unity, charity, service, and justice.

Think back on your experiences of serving those in need. How did you feel? Maybe you felt a deep connection with those with whom you were working, or proud that you were making a difference. Perhaps you felt grateful for the many blessings in your own life and for the ability to help others. Maybe you even felt close to Jesus. Emotions like these are not simply an opportunity to feel good about ourselves. Rather, they are spiritual gifts. Through gifts like these, Jesus Christ enriches us and supports us in our shared connection with others who want to follow him in the Church and live their faith authentically.

Numerous Catholic organizations are devoted to the work of service and justice. To study all of them would be a course in itself! This article will feature only two: Catholic Charities, which serves people in the United States, and Catholic Relief Services, which works overseas.

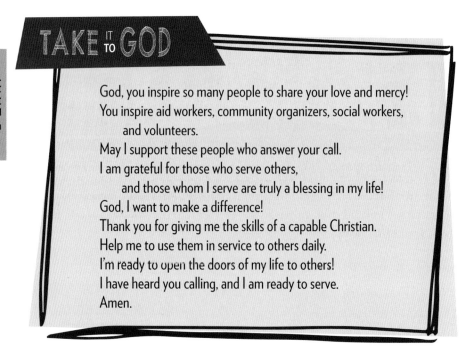

TAKE IT TO GOD

God, you inspire so many people to share your love and mercy!
You inspire aid workers, community organizers, social workers,
 and volunteers.
May I support these people who answer your call.
I am grateful for those who serve others,
 and those whom I serve are truly a blessing in my life!
God, I want to make a difference!
Thank you for giving me the skills of a capable Christian.
Help me to use them in service to others daily.
I'm ready to open the doors of my life to others!
I have heard you calling, and I am ready to serve.
Amen.

Catholic Charities

Founded in 1910, Catholic Charities provides service to people in need, advocates for justice in social structures, and calls the entire Church and other people of good will to do the same. Each U.S. diocese (or regional group of dioceses) operates a Catholic Charities agency. Although their projects and services vary greatly depending on local needs, they focus their ministry in three broad areas: disaster response, direct service, and advocacy.

Catholic Charities is the official domestic disaster response organization of the Catholic Church in the United States and its territories. Whether an earthquake, a wildfire, a flood, or other disaster, Catholic Charities staff are always among the first responders to help those who are suffering. For example, when Hurricane Florence tore through North Carolina in September of 2018, the Catholic Charities Mobile Response Center sprang into action. They

Catholic Charities focuses primarily on disaster response, direct service, and advocacy. There are a variety of ways for young people to be involved.

provided food, clothing, access to showers and laundry facilities, and other basic services to support people who had been displaced from their homes.

Even without the immediate threat of a natural disaster, many people throughout the United States are hungry, ill, or on the brink of homelessness. Catholic Charities responds to these needs through direct, charitable aid, which can take many forms. For example, they may offer a family cash assistance to pay rent and buy groceries for a few months while a parent looks for a new job. They may offer mental health counseling for those struggling with addictions, English language classes for newly arrived immigrants, and refugee resettlement services.

UNIT 5

Through political advocacy, Catholic Charities tries to address the root causes of social problems. Catholic Charities offices help inform and organize Catholics around such causes as livable wages; just immigration laws; access to affordable housing and health care; protection for the unborn, children, and the elderly; and poverty and homelessness. By working together to address these issues, we can offer powerful protection for vulnerable people, and, in many cases, lift people out of poverty.

© Catholic Charities USA

The need for direct service is constant. Beyond providing basic necessities, volunteers are needed to translate, assist in filling out forms, and help match those in need with programs that will best serve them.

Beyond these three general focus areas, Catholic Charities reads the signs of the times and responds accordingly. For example, in the summer of 2014, a record number of people crossed the U.S. southern border into Texas. Coming from Mexico and Central America, many of these families were traveling with very young children. Some were children and teens traveling alone. In response to this need, Catholic Charities of the Rio Grande Valley established the Humanitarian Respite Center in McAllen, Texas. Here, after a long and arduous journey, these newest immigrants could tend to their most basic needs—a warm meal, a shower, clean clothes, and rest—before boarding a bus to their final destination elsewhere in the United States The center continues to be staffed twenty-four hours a day, seven days a week, 365 days a year, as new immigrants arrive daily.

You can support and be involved in the work of Catholic Charities both now and in the future. Consider contacting your local Catholic Charities office to find out how young people can help. Perhaps your youth group can raise money to donate to Catholic Charities and their projects. Food and clothing drives are another way to assist Catholic Charities in meeting the needs of the community. Ask them what their greatest need is, and with your friends, family, youth group, or religion class, come up with a creative solution to address that need!

You might also think about how your future might involve Catholic Charities. If you start with projects now, you can carry that service forward as an adult. Clubs and organizations on college campuses are usually willing to fundraise for worthy organizations. Donating your time, talent, or treasure (funds) to Catholic Charities is probably the most accessible way for you to serve. But you could also work for them full-time as a social worker, counselor, case manager, or grant writer. Or, you could volunteer within your chosen career field. For example, if you become a lawyer, you could volunteer in a Catholic Charities immigration law clinic. If you become an accountant, you could help Catholic Charities' clients file their income taxes.

Whatever you do, now or in the future, remember that as the official charity of the Catholic Church in the United States, Catholic Charities is *our* charity. Their work is done on our behalf. They are a prime example of the Body of Christ supporting all its members, especially those who are most vulnerable and in need.

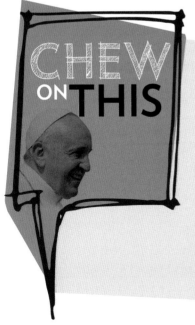

CHEW ON THIS

Dear young people, do not allow the spark of youth to be extinguished in the darkness of a closed room in which the only window to the outside world is a computer and smartphone. Open wide the doors of your life! May your time and space be filled with meaningful relationships, real people, with whom to share your authentic and concrete experiences of daily life. ("Address of His Holiness Pope Francis on the Occasion of the XXXIII World Youth Day," February 11, 2018)

Catholic Relief Services

Catholic Relief Services (CRS) is the international aid organization of the Catholic Church in the United States. CRS is governed by the U.S. bishops and is part of Caritas International, the international Catholic aid organization. The mission of CRS is to assist impoverished and disadvantaged people overseas. Within the United States, CRS tries to educate Catholics to live their faith in **solidarity** with the world's poor and vulnerable.

Hygiene kits stacked for distribution to displaced people along the Nile River, in Yolakot, South Sudan. Catholic Relief Services (CRS) has been responding with latrines, hand-washing stations, emergency shelter kits, and non food items to refugees fleeing conflict.

© Sara Fajardo / Catholic Relief Services

CRS was founded in 1943 with its initial focus being to assist the many refugees in Europe who struggled to rebuild their lives after World War II. Over the following ten years, CRS expanded its operations to include Africa, Asia, Latin America, and the Middle East. Today, it serves people in more than one hundred countries across the globe. U.S. Catholics can be very proud of the work of CRS; it is the largest non-governmental relief organization in the world!

---

solidarity ➤ Union of one's heart and mind with those who are poor or powerless or who face an injustice. It is an act of Christian charity.

Catholic Relief Services is focused on both works of charity and works of justice. The works of charity focus on responding to people's immediate physical needs. Whenever there is a crisis anywhere in the world—an earthquake or hurricane or act of war—CRS is one of the first organizations to respond. They provide food, shelter, medical care, whatever is most needed. And they stay as long as help is needed, often for many years.

CRS distributed emergency shelter materials to earthquake-affected communities in Mexico after a quake in 2017.

UNIT 5

Catholic Relief Service's justice work focuses on providing community-based, sustainable, development initiatives. This is a technical way of saying that they work together with local people on projects that will make long-term, positive differences in their quality of life.

For example, in a village in Ethiopia, Africa, children and adults were chronically sick and even dying. Representatives of CRS spent time in the village and helped the people diagnose the problem—contaminated drinking water. They determined that the village needed a well for clean, fresh drinking water. CRS didn't just come to town, dig the well, and leave. Instead, they organized a group of local people and supported them—with supplies, building plans, and general supervision—as *they* built the well. Within months, the people were healthier, there were fewer deaths, and children attended school more regularly (because they weren't weak and sick)—a huge difference in their quality of life. And, if, in a few years, the village needs another well, local people will know how to do it. This is just one example of development projects CRS supports around the world—helping people help themselves.

Catholic Relief Service's Youth Engagement Department includes two core programs, which you might consider exploring for your parish or school. The Food Fast program offers youth the opportunity to fast—for anywhere from three hours to twenty-four hours—in solidarity with the world's poor and to raise money to help alleviate poverty. The Global High School program recognizes and certifies schools for their outstanding commitment to CRS and to promoting global citizenship.

CRS has a dedicated Youth Engagement Department. You can participate in their Food Fast program or their Global High School program, or fundraise for CRS during Lent with Project Rice Bowl.

There is one more important way you can support the work of CRS. Every Lent, CRS sponsors Project Rice Bowl. This is a major fundraiser for the work of CRS, and almost every parish in the United States participates. Encourage your family to add money to the Rice Bowl as part of your Lenten almsgiving. and then turn it in to the parish before Easter. You can do this knowing that your donation will make a big difference in someone's life in another country.

UNIT 5

Find Your Niche

In addition to Catholic Charities and Catholic Relief Services, many other Catholic service organizations provide opportunities for us to serve the Body of Christ. Here are just a few examples:

United States Conference of Catholic Bishops (USCCB)	• Supplies information and resources that highlight the role of the Church in the formation of individuals' consciences. • "Issues and Action" section of their website provides action alerts so you can contact your elected representatives to express your concerns and opinions on upcoming legislation. • Provides special alerts related to migration and refugee issues.
Catholic Extension	• Builds up the Church in poor areas of the United States • This may involve literal building—renovating Church structures that have fallen into disrepair—or spiritual building, such as education, leadership training, and youth and young adult ministry.
The Catholic Worker	• Operates a grassroots network of houses of hospitality that offer food, shelter, and a place to belong. • Some Catholic Worker houses target their services to specific populations, such as refugees, people recovering from addictions, or people transitioning after incarceration.

Whatever your interests, gifts, talents, and desires, there is a Catholic service organization in which you can become involved. Take the plunge! Make a difference! Join forces with other faithful Catholics and make the Gospel message a living reality in our world. ✳

UNIT 5

How might your future career involve some element of serving those in need or working for justice?

Article 52

Apostolic Religious Orders

Members of religious orders are among those who are on the front lines of serving the suffering Body of Christ and working to create a more just and equitable world. As you learned in chapter 11, the hundreds of Catholic religious orders fall into two main categories: contemplative and apostolic. Members of contemplative orders live in **cloistered** monasteries. They seek to enter into deeper union with God through a life marked by intense prayer and solitude. They serve the world by daily praying for the world's needs. Often, they support themselves by making and selling homemade food or craft items.

Members of apostolic orders also engage in daily personal and communal prayer. However, they primarily share the Good News of God's love by ministering to those in need. Their specific ministry is determined by the order's charism. For example, the order may emphasize youth ministry, like the Salesians, education for justice, like the Jesuits, or health care, like the Religious Sisters of Mercy of Alma, Michigan.

Some form of cloister is present in all types of religious life. The Church recognizes three different types of cloister: a papal cloister, a constitutional cloister, and a monastic cloister. A papal cloister is the most strict form of enclosure, where nuns do not leave the monastery except for very serious reasons. Strangers are only admitted in rare cases of necessity. Constitutional cloisters are less strict than a papal cloister. The calling to cloistered life is also usually accompanied by some kind of apostolic or charitable work. Some constitutional cloisters run retreat houses. Monastic cloisters are one of the most ancient forms of contemplative life. They have always had a charism of hospitality, and welcome guests to stay at the monastery.

---

cloistered ➤ Adjective indicating a religious order whose members rarely leave the monastery or convent that is their home.

Youth Ministry: The Salesian Family

The Salesians of Don Bosco continue his original mission of providing a positive, loving educational environment for those who are underprivileged. Here some young men are receiving free training.

The Salesians of Don Bosco were founded by Saint John Bosco (1815–1888) in Italy in 1859 to serve poor and orphaned boys who otherwise would not have had access to schooling. Saint Bosco was ahead of his time in his belief that a positive, loving educational environment was more beneficial to students than an overly rigid schedule or harsh rules and policies. He brought a healthy, balanced approach to his work with youth. Classes were essential, of course, as were prayer and frequent celebration of the sacraments, especially the Eucharist and Penance and Reconciliation. But leisure and play were also important. Saint Bosco reasoned that if students felt like their school was a second home, then they could relax and be themselves, and they would learn better.

Although Saint Bosco's school originally educated only boys, he later collaborated with Saint Mary Domenica Mazzarello (1837–1881) to found an order of Salesian Sisters—the Daughters of Mary, Help of Christians—to serve in girls' schools. Today, nearly thirty thousand Salesian priests, sisters, and brothers in 130 countries evangelize and educate young people in schools, neighborhood youth centers, and youth ministry programs. They focus especially on serving youth who are at risk due to poverty or family instability.

UNIT 5

Education for Justice: The Jesuits

Founded in 1540 by Saint Ignatius of Loyola (1491–1556), the Society of Jesus, or Jesuits, has more than sixteen thousand members, including priests, brothers, and men who are preparing to take vows. The Jesuits dedicate themselves to the greater glory of God and the good of all humanity. There are Jesuit teachers, lawyers, pastors, chaplains, and doctors. As part of their mission, they operate hundreds of high schools, colleges, and universities throughout the world. Each of these schools strives to graduate "men and women for others"—people who will make a positive difference in the world by putting the needs of others before their own.

In addition to educating students about service and justice, the Jesuits also sponsor social service agencies that seek to create a more just and peaceful world. For example, the Kino Border Initiative provides humanitarian and legal assistance to immigrants on both sides of the U.S.–Mexico border and advocates for humane and just immigration laws. Jesuit Refugee Services (JRS) serves people who are displaced by famine, war, and violence in countries like Colombia, South Sudan, and Syria.

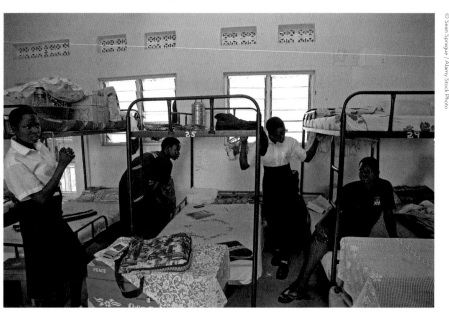

© Sean Sprague / Alamy Stock Photo

The Jesuits also have programs to help those in need. This is a primary school financed by the Jesuit Refugee Service in Sudan

UNIT 5

Health Care: The Religious Sisters of Mercy of Alma, Michigan

Can you imagine going to medical school while also preparing to take vows as a religious sister? Working long into the night in the emergency room as a medical resident, only to rise at the crack of dawn for morning prayer? The Religious Sisters of Mercy of Alma, Michigan, do all this and more. Founded in 1973, this order operates health care clinics in the South and Midwest. Their members minister as primary care physicians, nurses, physical therapists, surgeons, and psychiatrists.

The sisters and the lay health care professionals who work alongside them not only care for their patients' physical ailments but also seek to promote overall health and well-being, including emotional wellness and spiritual wholeness. As part of their commitment to following the example of Jesus and embodying the values of the Gospel, the sisters offer free and low-cost care to people who do not have health insurance. Because they are a relatively new order, their numbers are small—just one hundred members. But they are growing, as many women find the integration of religious life with a career in health care to be a compelling idea and a truly unique vocation.

© Courtesy of Religious Sisters of Mercy of Alma, Michigan

UNIT 5

The Religious Sisters of Mercy are based in Alma, Michigan. You might think that these women spend their days in prayer or perhaps work in schools, but these sisters minister as doctors, nurses, therapists, and surgeons!

CATHOLICS **MAKING** A DIFFERENCE

When Sr. Marilyn Lacey, RSM, answered an ad asking for volunteers to help refugees arriving in the United States from Southeast Asia, she had no idea that the entire course of her life would change. From that quiet beginning in 1980, Sister Marilyn spent more than two decades working in refugee camps around the world. In an effort to alleviate the extreme poverty that often causes people to become refugees, in 2008 she founded Mercy Beyond Borders, which operates in South Sudan and Haiti. Research demonstrates that educating women and girls is the single most effective way to lift families out of poverty. So, Mercy Beyond Borders supports two primary schools for girls. Girls who graduate from eighth grade—a rarity in these countries, where girls often leave school and marry as soon as they reach puberty—can qualify for scholarships to high school and then to nursing school or college.

Changing with the Times

Some religious orders that began with a particular charism have had to shift their ministry to adapt to changing times. For example, the Trinitarians were originally founded to rescue Christians being held captive by Muslim armies during the Crusades. Obviously, once the Crusades ended in the year 1291, the Trinitarians had to reinvent themselves! Today, they follow the spirit of their original charism by seeking to liberate all people who are oppressed by injustice. They have special concern for those who are persecuted because of their religious faith or because they have followed their conscience.

At other times in Church history, new orders have arisen in response to specific needs. For example, in the early twentieth century in the United States, many new orders of religious sisters were founded in order to minister to a rapidly growing Church—growth fueled, in part, by large numbers of Catholic immigrants arriving from Europe. These orders include the Sisters of Charity of Saint Joseph, the Sisters of Loretto, and the Sisters of the Blessed Sacrament.

UNIT 5

Apostolic Orders and You

The apostolic orders are just a few examples of the hundreds of orders that are part of the Church. The sisters, brothers, and priests who belong to these orders have answered a call from God to serve him by serving the world in a particular ministry. Through their work, the Catholic Church has touched hundreds of millions of lives over many centuries. They represent Christ, his Church, and God's love in a very visible and public way.

Consecrated religious life will continue to grow and change in response to the shifting needs of our church and world. You can be a part of this story! Consider whether you may be called to consecrated religious life. Keep your mind and heart open to this possibility as you become a more independent, young adult. However, even if this is not your calling, you can reach out to consecrated religious who serve at your school or parish. Let them know that you appreciate their service to God's people and ask how you can help. Above all, support the ministries of men and women religious by praying that the witness of their lives may draw the whole world toward greater unity in Christ. ✳

Keeping your mind and heart open to God's plan for you is the most important step in discerning your future vocation. You might find yourself called to a lay apostolate, an apostolic order, or even consecrated life!

UNIT 5

HMMMMM. . . What do you think would be the most rewarding part of serving God as a member of a religious order? What do you think would be most challenging?

Article 53

Focus on Pope Francis: "On Care for Our Common Home"

Maritza had joined her school's "Green Team" almost as soon as she arrived on campus in ninth grade. She'd always loved nature and wanted to help protect the environment. Some of the things she read online about starving polar bears, the destruction of coral reefs, rising sea levels, species extinction, and other problems made her so sad and angry—but also motivated her to try to do something before it was too late.

Recycling is just the tip of the iceberg. Pope Francis composed a powerful encyclical called "On Care for Our Common Home" ("*Laudato Si'*") in 2015, in which he stresses our responsibility for the gifts we have been given.

This year, the Green Team was starting a new composting and recycling program in the school cafeteria. At the end of the lunch period, Green Team members stood by the bins to help people sort their trash. To Maritza, it wasn't that complicated. Banana peel = compost. Empty soda can = recycling. Zip-top bag = garbage. But people were in such a rush to get to class that they often just tossed all their stuff without taking the time to sort it. "Ugh!" Maritza thought, as she pulled yet another aluminum can out of the garbage bin. "This is so frustrating! What can I do to get people to understand how *important* this is?"

A Landmark Encyclical

If only Maritza had known that she had a powerful ally behind her: none other than the Pope himself! In 2015, Pope Francis became the first pope to issue an encyclical focused entirely on ecological issues. "On Care for Our Common Home" *("Laudato Si'")* begins by invoking the Pope's own namesake: Saint Francis of Assisi (1181–1226). Saint Francis was known for his love of all God's creatures, animals, people, and plants. He is the patron saint of all who study and work in the area of ecology. In fact, the title of the encyclical was taken from the first line of his famous prayer "Canticle of the Sun": "Praise be to you, my Lord, through our Sister, Mother Earth, who sustains and governs us." After this initial look at Saint Francis of Assisi, Pope Francis discusses the many problems the Earth is facing due to environmental degradation. He also considers how we, as the People of God, might help to solve these problems.

© Purplexsu / Shutterstock.com

UNIT 5

When writing his encyclical, Pope Francis looked to his namesake, Saint Francis of Assisi (c. 1181–1226), for inspiration about discussing our responsibility to care for the Earth that sustains and nurtures us.

Problems: A Planet in Crisis

Pope Francis lists numerous environmental problems that are affecting Earth's ability to sustain life. Foremost among these is pollution of air, water, and soil, which is causing "the earth, our home" to "look more and more like an immense pile of filth" ("On Care for Our Common Home," number 21). Closely related to this is the problem of climate change. Pope Francis supports the "very solid scientific consensus" that "indicates that we are presently witnessing a disturbing warming of the climatic system" (number 23). Observable effects of climate change include rising sea levels and extreme weather events like severe hurricanes and record-setting rainfalls. Other urgent environmental problems include the loss of biodiversity (caused by the extinction of plant and animal species), deforestation, and the depletion of natural resources, including water, access to which is "a basic and universal human right" (number 30). Pope Francis is particularly concerned by the fact that many of these problems mainly affect the poor. He gives three examples to support this idea (see number 48):

- The depletion of fishing reserves hurts people in small fishing communities with no other means to make a living.
- Water pollution harms the poor who cannot afford to buy bottled water.
- Rising sea levels affect impoverished coastal populations who have nowhere else to go.

Pope Francis did not mince words when discussing the potentially serious effects that ocean pollution can have on everyone, but especially those who are poor.

How could you take Pope Francis's advice and develop a more eco-conscious spirituality and lifestyle? Consider the following areas:

- **Your prayer life:** Spend time regularly in nature, simply appreciating the beauty and wonder of all that God has created. Give voice to your praise through poetry or music.

- **Your meals:** Make a commitment to reduce or eliminate food waste. Only buy or cook what you can eat. If you have extra, save it or share it rather than tossing it.

- **Your home:** Work with your family to reduce your home's water consumption or electricity usage.

- **Your school:** Choose one environmental goal and organize your school to meet it. Start a composting program, plant a school garden, or eliminate single-use plastic water bottles.

Whatever you choose to do, you will be putting Pope Francis's message into action and helping to protect the Earth, our common home, for both present and future generations.

Pope Francis believes that human attitudes and behaviors have contributed greatly to many of these environmental problems. He draws particular attention to our wasteful, "throwaway culture" (number 22). For example, how often have you shopped for a new outfit, only to wear it once before it ends up on your closet floor? Or, have you ever bought an electronic device, only to find out six months later that it's already outdated, and now you want a new one? These examples demonstrate the consumerist, materialist mentality that causes us to deplete the Earth's resources, to the point at which the planet is "being squeezed dry beyond every limit" (number 106).

UNIT 5

Solutions

As Pope Francis proposes solutions to these problems, he emphasizes that we must first seek to develop "an ecological spirituality" ("On Care for Our Common Home," number 216), for which Scripture can be a great help. For example, the Creation accounts in the Book of Genesis (see 1:1–2:25) present "a relationship of mutual responsibility between human beings and nature" (number 67). The psalms prompt us to praise God as our Creator (see, for example, Psalms 104, 136, 139, and 148). And, many of the prophetic writings "invite us to find renewed strength in times of trial by contemplating the all-powerful God who created the universe" ("On Care for Our Common Home," number 73; see also Isaiah 40:28b–29 and Jeremiah 32:17).

Prayerful reflection on passages like these can help us to cultivate a spirit of joy, gratitude, and simplicity that moves us toward "a more passionate concern for the protection of our world" ("On Care for Our Common Home," number 216). To our great amazement, we may come to recognize that God's very presence can be found in nature's simple beauty: "in a leaf, in a mountain trail, in a dewdrop" (number 233).

© Dream Perfection / Shutterstock.com

One way to be more mindful of the gifts that God has given us through nature is to intentionally set aside time to reflect on nature's beauty and bounty that it provides for us.

With a firm grounding in ecological spirituality, we can move forward confidently with practical actions. We can make small, yet significant, changes in our daily habits, like reducing our use of paper and plastics, turning off unnecessary lights, and using public transportation or carpools whenever possible. We can promote environmental education for all age-groups and urge both our schools and parishes to stop wasteful practices. We can lobby legislators and other government officials to work toward "enforceable international agreements" ("On Care for Our Common Home," number 173) to address the ecological crisis. Environmental problems like air pollution, climate change, and ocean contamination are not confined by national borders. So they must be solved not by individual nations working alone, but, rather, through international cooperation.

I DIDN'T KNOW THAT!

Is it possible to reduce your energy consumption by more than 80 percent? Is it possible to use 6,200 less gallons of water *per day?* The Sisters, Servants of the Immaculate Heart of Mary know that the answer to these questions is a definite "yes." In the late 1990s, these sisters had a problem. Their seventy-year-old motherhouse—the headquarters of the order—badly needed repairs and renovation. The sisters decided that the renovation of the motherhouse would reflect their order's commitment to eco-justice and environmental sustainability. The overhauled building, which opened in 2003, incorporates many ecologically friendly elements such as: a graywater recycling system, low-flow faucets, and natural heating and cooling, and also takes advantage of natural lighting. In all these ways, the renovated motherhouse beautifully expresses the sisters' mission of trying to live in harmony with all of creation.

UNIT 5

A Community Effort

A variety of organizations offer opportunities for serving along with your friends and co-workers. Many Catholic and interfaith groups share a commitment to ecological justice.

As with other social justice issues, it is most effective, rewarding, and fun to work for environmental justice with other people who share our faith-based commitment and values. If your school has a Green Team, consider joining it or supporting its efforts. Beyond your school, neighborhood, or parish, many Catholic and interfaith organizations promote ecological justice. For example:

Catholic Rural Life	Ministers in rural America advocate for a just and sustainable food supply, foster a sense of stewardship toward all of creation, and seek to preserve and promote the economic and spiritual well-being of farmers and other agricultural workers.
The Global Catholic Climate Movement	This is a group of more than four hundred Catholic member organizations working to turn "On Care for Our Common Home" into concrete action for ecological justice, especially regarding climate change. They urge everyone to take the "On Care for Our Common Home" pledge, which involves promising to pray for and with creation, to live more simply, and to advocate to protect our common home.
Interfaith Power and Light	This is a multi-faith organization that promotes energy conservation, energy efficiency, and renewable energy.

stewardship ➤ The careful and responsible management of someone or something that has been entrusted to a person's care. This includes responsibly using and caring for the gifts of creation that God has given us.

When "On Care for Our Common Home" was released, they collaborated with the Catholic Climate Covenant to produce a "Faith Climate Action Kit" inspired by the main themes of the encyclical.

When we work alone to protect the environment, we can only do so much. However, when we join our individual actions and choices with those of others with whom we share a commitment to Jesus Christ and to his Church, we can trust that God will bless our efforts to protect and preserve the world that he created and that he found to be "very good" (Genesis 1:31). ✳

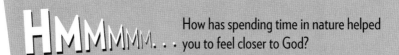

HMMMMM. . . How has spending time in nature helped you to feel closer to God?

1. In what part of the world does Catholic Charities work? What are the three broad areas in which it helps people in need?

2. Where does Catholic Relief Services (CRS) do its work? What are the two main focuses of its work?

3. What is an example of a community-based sustainable development initiative from CRS?

4. What two CRS programs are specifically designed for young people?

5. What is the difference between contemplative religious orders and apostolic religious orders?

6. How has consecrated religious life changed as the Church and world have changed? Give one example.

7. What is the mission of Mercy Beyond Borders?

8. Name five environmental problems that Pope Francis discusses in "On Care for Our Common Home."

9. Name two possible solutions to our environmental problems that Pope Francis discusses in "On Care for Our Common Home."

This modern painting was created by artist A. Vonn Hartung. It is titled
On Earth as It Is in Heaven.

1. What strikes you most about this painting? How does it make you feel?

2. What do the two different sides of the painting represent?

3. What religious symbols do you see? What might their meaning be?

CHAPTER 14
The Gift of Oneself: Gospel-Centered Volunteer Service

HOW CAN I MAKE A DIFFERENCE?

SNAPSHOT

Article 54   Page 347
The Church Unified in Service and Liturgy

Article 55   Page 352
Making a Difference Now

Article 56   Page 359
Making a Difference in the Future

Article 57   Page 364
Being the Church in the World
• Pre-read: Matthew 5:13–16

Article 54
The Church Unified in Service and Liturgy

"Sorry I can't watch the game with you on Saturday. I'm volunteering at that food bank with a bunch of people from school," Reggie said.

"That's alright," Lucas said. "Next Saturday, then. Hey, I didn't know you had to do service hours. I thought that was just a Catholic school thing."

"Nope! We do it too," Reggie said. "At least ten hours a year. I think it's supposed to make us more responsible or teach us to be nice people or something. I'm not sure. It's cool, though. I don't mind it."

Lucas was remembering back to eighth grade, when he and Reggie were classmates at Saint Stephen's. The eighth graders all took turns going to

Share your commitment to service with your friends. The experience of volunteering together can strengthen the bonds of friendship in a way that is different than going to the movies, playing video games, or playing on the same team.

the nursing home to do activities with the residents. The teacher always had them say a prayer together before leaving school to go to the nursing home, and then again when they got back, which Lucas thought was kind of nice.

"Guess you don't say the Hail Mary before you leave, huh? Remember Mrs. Evans would always make us say it a second or even a third time if she thought we weren't being serious enough?"

Laughing, Reggie said, "Of course I remember! Nope, no praying at my school, or at least not out loud."

"Catch you next Saturday, then?"

"For sure. Later, dude."

"Later."

UNIT 5

© Dragon Images / Shutterstock.com

TAKE IT TO GOD

God, when I am pulled in so many different directions,
    you call me to moments of quiet, peace, and prayer.
Help me to root myself firmly in your love and your grace.
Teach me to grow and flourish with you as my strength.
Empower me to bear fruit that pleases you: the fruit of justice,
    integrity, service, charity, and compassion.
Make my whole life a witness of your merciful love.
I ask this in your holy name.
Amen.

Doing Service as the Church

Lucas and Reggie's conversation illustrates an essential point about being a member of the Church, the Body of Christ. Christians are called to works of service and justice and to prayer. If those elements are missing from our life, we really aren't fully living out the Gospel call. When we engage in service, we are doing so not simply to be nice people, or to make the world a better place. We are doing so as part of our commitment to discipleship—to being members of Christ's own body, the Church.

Why are works of service and justice essential to the Church? Because the head of the Church is Jesus Christ, and his life was all about serving others and speaking out for justice. You have studied his many examples and teachings about service and justice. Jesus has set the standard for us to follow. The Church can simply not be the Church, and a Christian cannot be a Christian, if we are not committed to serving others and calling for justice in our world.

This unity with all members of the Church is the basis for our service: all of our good works should aim to protect, preserve, and strengthen that unity. And, as Reggie and Lucas experienced in eighth grade, our works of charity and acts of justice are more likely to foster unity when they are rooted in prayer.

Unity through Liturgy and Sacraments

If unity with all members of the Church is the basis for our service, how do we foster that unity? We must be a part of our Church community. Belonging to the Church is essential because Christ willed the Church to be the ordinary way and means of our salvation. As members of the Church, we participate in the liturgy and sacraments, strengthening our union with God and with one another. Because Christ entrusted the Word and the sacraments to the Church, giving her the fullness of all truth and the totality of the means of salvation; thus we experience Christ's redemption as members of his Body of the Church. Therefore, through the Church, we find union with God, deep within ourselves. And through that inner union with God, we become united with one another, in faith.

This unity with God and with one another is perhaps most obvious when we celebrate the Eucharist. When we receive the Body and Blood of Christ, we are truly united with God. But, we also become united with every other person in the Church—those who are sitting right next to us in the pew, those who are on the other side of the

Participating in service together is not the only way for us to experience unity. Celebrating the Eucharist is a way for us to be united not only with God but also with all other people in the Church.

building, and even those who are on the other side of the world. It's pretty awesome to think about! Sharing in this sacrament truly and deeply connects us with our sisters and brothers in faith all around the world, even though we may never meet them. We are not only connected with the Church on Earth through the Eucharist, but also connected with the Church suffering. These are the faithful departed who have died in Christ but are not yet wholly purified, so that they may enter into the light and peace of Christ. The Eucharist also binds us to the Church glorified. This refers to those in communion with the Blessed Virgin Mary and all the saints. It may be overwhelming to consider, but receiving the Eucharist is powerful and connects us in ways we may not have considered.

UNIT 5

© overki / Shutterstock.com

The Importance of Prayer

Prayer is a necessity for the Christian life. When we pour out our heart to God, we become attentive and responsive to his presence and voice in our hearts and in our world. We grow in holiness and faith and in our ability to persevere in struggle, to avoid temptation and sin, and to put others' needs before our own. Prayer also helps us to understand the teachings of Jesus Christ and his Church more deeply and to live them more fully.

One way the Church helps to direct our prayer is through the **Liturgical Year**. When we join the Church at prayer throughout the Liturgical Year, we remember and celebrate all the mysteries of our Catholic Christian faith. During the Advent and Christmas seasons, we meditate upon the mystery of the Incarnation. During the Lent and Easter seasons, we contemplate the Paschal Mystery. Each year, we can enter into these seasons more and more fully, as our faith grows and deepens. In all our prayer, whether liturgical prayer with others or individual prayer alone, God forms, teaches, guides, consoles, and blesses us. God gives us the strength we need to serve others and to help create a more just, unified, and peaceful world.

© NRedmond / iStock.com

Each of the seasons of the Liturgical Year has a color associated with it. Purple is the color for both Advent and Lent because it symbolizes penance, preparation, and sacrifice.

Liturgical Year ➤ The Church's annual cycle of feasts and seasons that celebrates the events and mysteries of Christ's birth, life, death, Resurrection, and Ascension, and forms the context for the Church's worship.

One day in religious studies class, Ms. Robinson asked, "Why is prayer, personal prayer and liturgical prayer, an important part of Christian life?" Mara's friend Erik commented: "I don't really see the point of going to Church. I don't need holy days of obligation to make me feel like a good Catholic. I can talk to God just fine on my own. I don't really think we need to pray in Church to know God."

This set off a huge debate. But Mara stayed quiet, thinking about her own experience. After class, she found Erik and told him: "I want you to know that I thought a lot about what you said today. I understand that sometimes going to church can feel like a chore, rather than something that builds us up. But for my family, the different seasons and celebrations are part of our history and culture."

Erik stopped walking and seemed to be listening, so Mara explained more: "During Advent, my family goes to Church each week. When we come home, we light the candle on the Advent wreath. We have an Advent calendar in the kitchen. Each day, we open a window of the calendar and say a prayer, do a kind deed, or sometimes get a treat. Its all part of getting ready for Christmas. On Christmas Eve, we go to midnight Mass. I used to fall asleep when I was little, but the music and the candles are so beautiful! I feel like I'm a part of something really special when we go. I can't imagine celebrating Christmas without going to Mass." Erik nodded his head. "I know it is important to my parents too," he said. "I just don't like having to get up and go."

Mara said: "I understand. But when I am in Church, especially during special events of the Liturgical Year, I feel like I have a deeper connection with God . . . one that I wouldn't have if I was talking to him in my bedroom. But the really important thing about praying on my own, or praying during Mass, is that it reminds me who I am. I think about people I can help and how I can be the face of Christ for others." Erik shrugged and started to walk toward his next class. "Maybe Mara is right," he thought. "I don't really think about how I'm connected to other people or how I can help others when I'm playing video games in my room. When I'm at church or youth group, I do. Maybe prayer and liturgy and helping others are all tied together." ✳

UNIT 5

How has prayer strengthened you to engage in charity and service?

Article 55
Making a Difference Now

By this point in this course, you hopefully realize that God is calling you to live the Gospel message, to follow Jesus, and to be of service to God's people. Those stirrings in your heart, that desire to make a difference, and that sense that you want to use your gifts and talents to relieve others' suffering are all signs of God's call to you. Responding to that call is not something to put off until you finish college, have a job, have money saved, or have your life's goals figured out. It's for you to live out right here, right now. Take some time to think creatively about ways you can respond to God's call by serving your school, your parish, and the wider community.

Serving in Your School

One obvious way to be of service at your school is through liturgical ministry. Liturgies do not just happen because the priest shows up and a couple of students volunteer to help. Rather, liturgy requires many people, including lectors, Extraordinary Ministers of Holy Communion, cantors and choir members, and usher Extraordinary Ministers of Holy Communion are another form of service in many schools. It is also possible to serve as a minister. of art and environment, assisting in preparing and decorating your worship space. There are many "behind the scenes" tasks, like creating a worship aid and setting up and

Does your school have a chapel for prayer services and small liturgies? If so, who is responsible for preparing the space for prayer and worship?

cleaning up the worship space. Find out what is most needed at your school and commit to getting involved.

You don't need to look too far to find some inspiration for projects at your school. At Pleasantville High School in New Jersey, students in the school store club organized a drive to collect personal care items to donate to the Atlantic City location of Covenant House. Covenant House provides resources to homeless youth, ages eighteen to twenty-one, in the area. In Nevada, a high school senior collects unwanted school supplies that are otherwise thrown away at the end of the year. She started a group called Students United in Recycling School Supplies and donates the items to homeless youth. If you don't think you could start on your own project, you could always partner with a larger organization. In California, teens partnered with Laura's House, a California-based organization that provides assistance to victims of domestic violence. High school students receive training in order to help their peers who are affected by dating violence.

Are you interested in a service project like the student-run project in Nevada that collects school supplies for homeless youth? How would you go about starting a service project for your school?

UNIT 5

Serving in Your Parish

Just like school, your parish likely needs many ministers for every weekend liturgy. Don't let anyone tell you that you have to wait until you turn eighteen to be a minister. If you are a fully initiated Catholic (that is, if you have received the Sacraments of Baptism, Confirmation, and the Eucharist), then you should be allowed to sign up for your parish's or diocese's training and formation program that will certify you as a liturgical minister.

In fact, one of the most important things Catholics do is celebrate the liturgy. By serving in a leadership role as a liturgical minister, you are doing far more than reading the words of Scripture or singing in the choir. Liturgical ministry benefits both those serving others and those being served. Check out some examples:

Liturgical Ministers	Gain a deep understanding of all facets of the Mass and how all the readings, actions, and rituals are related to one another.
	Assist others in the congregation to have a fuller experience of the Mass through their thoughtful actions, sacred rituals, and compassionate interactions.
Hospitality Ministers	Help all people to feel welcome as they enter the Church.
Extraordinary Ministers of Holy Communion	Share the Body and Blood of Christ with the congregation.
Lectors	Proclaim the Word of God to the assembly.
Choir Members, Musicians, Cantors	Aid the congregation in prayer through song. Sharing their gifts and talents can be the prayerful experience that brings people to the liturgy.

If you are not called to participate as a liturgical minister, there are still more ways that you can participate in the Body of the Church. Consider joining the parish's youth group, or volunteering to help with the children's faith formation program.

- Some parishes have programs like Servant Saturdays. This is a program that gathers people together once a month to do small jobs for the elderly or shut-ins from the parish.
- In Search of a Square Meal is a program that helps to feed people in need. Armed with a grocery list and empty bags, this group from the parish goes door to door asking people to donate one or more items from the list. After a few hours, the groups gather and distribute the food to needy families in the parish or to the Saint Vincent de Paul society.
- Another parish collects items to make Sunshine Packages for those in the hospital or nursing homes. They gather magazines, socks, mints, toothbrushes and toothpaste, and other comfort items, and wrap them in festive packaging. They deliver some "sunshine" to those who may not have many visitors or are in long-term care facilities. There are many people who want to serve within the parish; they only need to be asked!

MAKE IT SO

Do you feel like you can't live without your phone? How many texts do you send and receive every day? twenty or thirty? two hundred or three hundred? Do you check your social media feeds every couple of hours—or every few minutes?

Although technology brings many good things to our lives, it has major drawbacks too. Technology can draw us inward and blind us to the presence and needs of those around us. We seek refuge in an online world instead of seeking connections in the real world. If you'd like to shake the hold that technology has on you, try a tech fast. Choose a certain period—maybe twelve hours, or even twenty-four hours—and power off your phone and other devices. Instead of looking down at your device, look up and greet the people you see. At the end of your fast, thank God for the gift of technology and pray for the grace to use it wisely.

UNIT 5

Serving in the Wider Community

As you have learned throughout this course, our Christian faith demands that we be actively engaged with the wider world. We can't go through our lives staring into our phones. We need to look up and out, opening our eyes to truly notice and participate in the real, flesh-and-blood world around us.

Have you ever volunteered with an organization such as Habitat for Humanity? Do you think it is reasonable for schools to require service hours each year?

Your school probably requires some form of community service—maybe a certain number of hours per year or a certain type of project. Think outside the box about ways that you can exceed this minimum requirement. For example, how about gathering your friends and family for a service day to celebrate your next birthday? As a group, work a shift at Habitat for Humanity or at a hot meal program during the day, and then have a fun birthday celebration that evening. Or, set aside some of your school vacation time (Christmas break, Easter break, or summer vacation) to volunteer. Many agencies count on student volunteer help to remain open and provide essential services. If you've volunteered somewhere during the academic year, it's great if you can maintain your commitment even during breaks from school.

As you grow closer to voting age, it's essential to educate yourself about political issues and candidates, both in your local area and nationally. When the time comes, exercise your right to vote and support candidates whose positions and principles are consistent with Gospel values.

Never Too Young to Be a Saint

Being truly rooted in prayer and truly directed outward toward others, in a spirit of generous service, may seem like a daunting task. For inspiration and direction, we can look to the lives of young saints. All of the canonized saints listed below passed away while in their teens or early twenties. Thanks to advances in health care, an early death is far less likely now than it was when these saints lived! However, their brief lives demonstrate that you don't need to wait until you become older to become holy. With God's grace, through prayer and the sacraments, holiness is within your reach right now.

There are many young people who lived their lives in a way that is inspiring to others. Saint Kateri Tekakwitha (1656–1680) was inspired by a group of missionaries, and devoted her life to prayer, fasting, and teaching.

- Saint Joan of Arc (c. 1412–1431), while still in her teens, was burned at the stake because of her faith in God. She was a child at the time of the Hundred Year's War between France and England. She convinced the French king that she had heard a message from saints telling her to save France. She was given troops to try to defend Orleans and had the honor of leading them into battle. After victory at Orleans and other military successes, Joan was accorded the privilege of standing next to the new king at his coronation. The next year, however, she was captured by the duke of Burgundy and imprisoned. The French king did nothing to save her. She was tried for heresy and convicted. After refusing to deny that the voices she heard were from God, she was condemned to death. Joan was only a teenager when she was burned at the stake, gazing at the cross and calling the name of Jesus.

- Saint Kateri Tekakwitha (c. 1656–1680), born in present-day Auriesville, New York, to a Christian Algonquin mother and a non-Christian Mohawk chief, was the first Native American to be canonized. When she was four years old, smallpox killed her parents and her younger brother, and left her disfigured and partially blind. She met Christian missionaries in later childhood, and through their influence was baptized in 1676. Her new way

UNIT 5

of life made it difficult to remain in her village, so she walked two hundred miles to live in a Christian village near Montreal. Having made a vow not to marry, she led a life of prayer, fasting, teaching, and service until her death at age twenty-four. Kateri surely had the gifts of wisdom and courage.

- Saint Nunzio Sulprizio (1817–1836) died of bone cancer in 1836. When Nunzio was a child, he faithfully attended Mass, prayed, and studied the lives of the saints. Their stories helped him learn how to live a holy, faith-filled life. When both of his parents died, his uncle took custody of him. Unfortunately, his uncle mistreated him, forcing him to work in a blacksmith shop where he had to carry enormous weights over far distances. Nunzio eventually contracted gangrene and was sent to a hospital in Naples. He suffered immensely but found sustenance in the Eucharist, and offered his pain and suffering to God. He eventually recovered and then dedicated himself to be of service to other patients. Ultimately, he died from complications from his injuries just before his twentieth birthday.

- Saint Thérèse of Lisieux (1873–1897), also known as the "Little Flower," was born in Alencon, France, in 1873. While still a young girl, Thérèse longed to enter the Carmelite convent at Lisieux. When she was fifteen, the bishop gave permission, and she joined two of her older sisters there. Her life of prayer and work in the convent was hidden to others, but she became known to the world through her autobiography, *The Story of a Soul*, published in 1899. The book was translated into many languages and became wildly popular. In the book, she describes her life as the "little way"—a simple life of spiritual childhood. Thérèse's little way to holiness emphasizes great love rather than great deeds and has appealed to countless people seeking to be holy in the midst of ordinary life. She died at age twenty-four from tuberculosis, after much suffering.

May the example of these young saints strengthen and inspire you to be a person of holiness and justice, of prayer and service, as you faithfully respond to God's call. ✹

HMMMMM. . .

What is one new, creative way that you could be of service to your school, your parish, or the wider community?

Article 56

Making a Difference in the Future

"Think about your future!" "Don't take any chances with your future!" "Your future is at stake!" Are the adults in your life always giving you advice about your future? Although statements like these can be helpful reminders to consider the long-term consequences of your actions, the simple reality is that the future is unknown. None of us are in total control of how our lives ultimately unfold. However, there are a few things that we can count on, both now and in the future. First of all, we know that God loves us. God loved us into being and will never stop loving us, no matter what. We know that God the Father sent his Son, Jesus Christ, to redeem us and to establish the Church for our salvation. And, we know that God calls each of us to a life of faithful discipleship: a life defined by prayer and service, a life in which we use our gifts and talents to build up the Body of Christ.

One way you can respond to this call in the not-too-distant future is by giving a year or more of full-time volunteer work. Later in your adult life, when you have determined your vocation and established your career, you will find other opportunities to give of yourself in the service of God's Reign.

CATHOLICS **MAKING** A DIFFERENCE

In 1912, Dr. Paluel Joseph Flagg made the long, difficult journey from his home in New York City to the island nation of Haiti, in the Caribbean Sea, to provide medical care to people suffering from leprosy. Overwhelmed by the people's total deprivation, Dr. Flagg decided to start a Catholic organization to promote global health, especially in developing countries. With financial help from the Society for the Propagation of the Faith, the Franciscan Friars of the Atonement, and the Society of Jesus, he founded the Catholic Medical Mission Board (CMMB) and sent its first medical missionary, Dr. Margaret Lamont, overseas.

As times and medical needs have changed, CMMB has adapted. CMMB mobilized in five African countries to prevent mother-to-child AIDS transmission and to care for children orphaned by AIDS. In 2010, when a massive earthquake leveled Port-au-Prince, the capital of Haiti, CMMB staff offered on-the-ground medical care within hours.

Volunteers generally commit to a six- to twelve-month term of service in Haiti, Kenya, Peru, South Sudan, or Zambia.

Full-Time Volunteer Opportunities

Many young adults opt to volunteer full-time for a year (or more) after finishing college, before starting graduate school or looking for a job. This is often an ideal time for long-term volunteer service, because it is relatively free of other commitments. Recent college graduates are probably not yet thinking about getting married and starting a family, and they don't yet own a home. This makes moving relatively easy, because they haven't had time to build up many possessions.

Would you be interested in participating in a mission trip or a long-term service-year immersion program? What do you think would be the pros and cons?

Most full-time volunteer programs, including all those discussed in this article, cover all your basic living expenses during your term of service. You receive a place to live (with roommates who are in the same program), money to buy groceries, transportation to and from work (often a bus pass), health insurance, and a small stipend for personal expenses—usually about $100 per month. So, you don't make any money during the year, but, you don't lose any money either. Most programs also offer deferment of student loans, meaning that you can wait until after your term of volunteer service ends to begin paying back the loan.

Are you open to the possibility of a year or more of full-time service after you finish college? If so, consider the Jesuit Volunteer Corps, the Lasallian Volunteers, the Mercy Volunteer Corps, or the Maryknoll Lay Missioners.

UNIT 5

The Jesuit Volunteer Corps (JVC) is the largest lay Catholic full-time volunteer program in the world. Sponsored by the Society of Jesus (Jesuits), it places volunteers at social service agencies throughout the United States and in Belize, Chile, Micronesia, Nicaragua, Peru, and Tanzania. Volunteers commit to one year of service (with an option to renew for a second year). The year of service is rooted in four key tenets: community, simple lifestyle, social justice, and spirituality. JVC often uses the slogan "ruined for life" to describe the program's long-term effects on volunteers. Their term of service is only a year or two, but their perspective on the world and their awareness of social injustice will never be the same.

Lasallian Volunteers work alongside the De La Salle Christian Brothers to serve the poor in educational ministries through twenty-two ministries in twelve states and one international location in Jerusalem. They may work as teachers, teaching assistants, campus ministers, recreation coordinators, counselors, or social workers. One unique aspect of this program is that volunteers live in community not only with one another but also with vowed Christian Brothers.

Sponsored by the Sisters of Mercy, the Mercy Volunteer Corps places volunteers in ten U.S. cities as well as in Guyana, one of the poorest countries in the western hemisphere. Volunteers serve in one of three broad areas: education (working as a teacher, teacher aide, or after-school program coordinator), health care (working as a nurse or community health advocate), and social services (working in the areas of addiction recovery, community outreach, or immigration and refugee services).

© Sean Sprague / Alamy Stock Photo

UNIT 5

Some volunteer programs, such as the Maryknoll volunteers (seen here), commit to three and a half years of service in Africa, Asia, or Latin America.

The Maryknoll Lay Missioners are a little different from the three programs just discussed. They offer only international volunteer placements throughout Africa, Asia, and Latin America, most of which require a minimum commitment of three and a half years, including in-country orientation and language study. Although they will consider applications from any Catholic who is twenty-one or older, many people find that a few years of work experience after college (or a graduate degree) better prepares them for this more intense, long-term experience. Maryknoll missioners typically work in education, health care, pastoral care, peace and justice ministry, or in sustainable development.

More Ways to Serve

Let's say that you give a year or more of full-time service after college or after graduate school. What then? Does your commitment to Gospel-centered volunteer service end? Absolutely not! God will continue to call you to service in many different ways as your life unfolds. Your response to that call will vary, depending on your vocation, your career, and your location. If you are called to religious life or to priesthood, you will have many opportunities to serve others, to accompany those who suffer, and to witness to God's love. If you are called to marriage, the example of your words and actions will teach your children how to be generous, charitable, and compassionate.

I DIDN'T KNOW THAT!

UNIVERSITY OF NOTRE DAME
founded by the
Congregation of Holy Cross
1842

© Katherine Welles / Shutterstock.com

Have you considered enrolling in a Catholic college or university? No matter what you are looking for in higher education, there is a Catholic institution that meets your needs. Want the excitement of studying in a big city? Try the Catholic University of America or Georgetown University, in Washington, DC. Prefer a smaller city or town? Maybe you're suited to Siena College, in Loudonville, New York, or Briar Cliff University, in Sioux City, Iowa. Want Division 1 sports? Consider Boston College or the University of Notre Dame.

By studying at a Catholic college or university, you will experience not only the rigorous academics and fun activities that you'd find at any college but also an incredible opportunity to nurture your spirituality and grow your faith as a member of the Body of Christ. There's no better way to begin your journey into young adulthood.

Your job, as well, will present you with opportunities to serve. For example, if you become a doctor, nurse, or other health care professional, you may volunteer at a clinic that serves uninsured people. Maybe you will take a week off each summer for a mission trip to provide essential medical services in a developing country. If you become an architect or construction engineer, your expertise would be incredibly helpful to agencies like Habitat for Humanity which build and renovate affordable housing. If you become certified as a counselor or therapist, you could volunteer to provide free or very low-cost services to individuals and families who otherwise wouldn't have access to mental health care.

The Gift of Our Prayer

The one element of our service that can be consistent at every time in our lives and in every circumstance is our prayer. As faithful disciples, we are called to pray for the needs of all people by engaging in **intercessory prayer**. Although we may often pray for the needs of people we know, it is important that we be generous in our prayer. We must pray for all people who are poor, ill, suffering, struggling, dying, and in any kind of need, even if we have never met them. We must pray for people who have no one else to pray for them. By doing this, we expand the circle of our compassionate care, and we ourselves grow in holiness. ✻

Do you think your career might lend itself to serving others? Even without joining an apostolic order or consecrated life, you can still find ways to be involved through your vocation, career, and location.

UNIT 5

HMMMMM. . . How is prayer an act of generosity?

---

intercessory prayer ➤ A prayer form in which we ask God's help for other people's needs; also called intercession.

Article 57
Being the Church in the World

Retreats are a way to pray, reflect, get to know others, and draw closer to God, and maybe even get to know yourself a little better. Have you ever been on a retreat experience with your school or church?

The candle flickered in the center of the circle as Miranda, Russell, Grayson, and Sophia sat quietly, enjoying the room's relaxed, peaceful atmosphere. They had arrived at the retreat center early that morning for their junior overnight retreat, and, now, after dinner, they were finally feeling settled in their small group.

"Well, I'll start," Miranda said. "I'm really glad to be Catholic. I feel like the Church has given me a lot, and I love being a part of it. I've been in Catholic schools forever, and I've always gone to Saint Ambrose Church—since I was born, I guess! It's just part of who I am—an important part."

"Great, Miranda. Thanks," said Mr. Menendez, their small-group leader. He had asked the students to share their thoughts about the Church, and he was glad that they were finally opening up.

"I can go next," Russell said. "I guess my story is a little like Miranda's. I like being Catholic, but I'm not *that* into it. I mean, I'm not gonna try to get others to join the Church or something. It's *my* thing, and if it's not their thing, then that's cool. To each his own, right?"

Grayson cleared his throat. He was so quiet that it was easy to forget he was even there, but he was 100 percent following the conversation. "So, I'm actually not Catholic—I don't know if you all knew that or not. I've been in Catholic school since kindergarten though, so I kind of feel like I am. The Church has its problems, for sure—I mean, it's made up of human beings, and no one's perfect. But, I've actually been thinking about getting baptized."

"That's great, man!" "Awesome." The others in the circle voiced their support.

"I don't know how to explain it exactly," Grayson continued. "It just feels good when I think about being a part of something that Jesus himself started. Plus, having this connection to every other member of the Church—to the whole Body of Christ. It's kind of awe-inspiring. Maybe that's corny. But it's how I feel."

"That's really great, Grayson—good for you," Sophia replied. "I've been Catholic my *entire* life, and I can't imagine being anything else. I mean, I guess if I'd been born into some other family and wasn't raised Catholic, I might feel differently. Who knows?"

"These are all such good reflections—so deep and thoughtful! Thanks so much, everyone," Mr. Menendez said, looking pleased. "I really appreciate your honesty. It's so important to reflect on your relationship with the Church—to think about what the Church means to you. It can make the path ahead a little clearer and help us become more faithful disciples. We'll talk more about all this during tomorrow's sessions. Let's spend a few minutes in silence praying for one another."

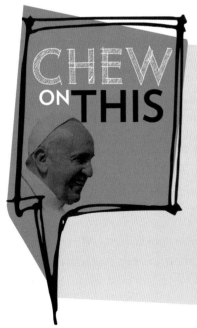

CHEW ON THIS

Young people have engaged and given themselves to the work of building up the Church. When our heart is good soil which receives the word of God, when "we build up a sweat" in trying to live as Christians, we experience something tremendous: we are never alone. We are part of a family of brothers and sisters, all journeying on the same path. We are part of the Church. ("Address of His Holiness Pope Francis on the Occasion of the XXVIII World Youth Day," July 27, 2013)

UNIT 5

Salt and Light

Every member of the Body of Christ has a unique perspective on what it means to be part of the Church. Each person will express his or her relationship with the Church using words or images drawn from his or her own experience. Each person has different thoughts, feelings, and questions about the Church. However, even as we acknowledge these diverse viewpoints, we must never lose sight of Jesus Christ's original vision of what his disciples are to be: salt and light for the world. These powerful, thought-provoking metaphors are found in Matthew's Gospel (see 5:13–16), in the Sermon on the Mount.

Understanding what it means to be "salt" requires a little background about daily life in the time of Jesus. In first-century Palestine, each village had a communal clay oven for baking. Can you guess what the fuel for these ovens was? There weren't a lot of trees in

How can you be the salt of the Earth or the light of the world?

Palestine that could be chopped down for firewood, so what else would be a cheap and plentiful source of fuel? If you guessed animal dung, you're correct! People would collect camel or donkey poop, shape it into patties, and then dry it in the sun before burning it for fuel.

Here's where the salt comes in. In the bottom of the clay oven was a slab of salt. The salt's chemical attributes allowed it to act as a catalyst in the oven. It reacted with the dung and created a fire. However, over time, the salt would lose its catalytic properties. No longer good for making a fire, it would be useless. As Jesus puts it, salt like that is "no longer good for anything but to be thrown out and trampled underfoot" (Matthew 5:13).

UNIT 5

What does that mean for us, as disciples? How are we to be "salt of the earth"? We are called to be catalysts for the Gospel. We are called to help "light the fire" to create change and to make things happen. We are called to share our faith with courage and boldness. We are called to serve others with compassion and total selflessness. We are called to challenge injustice and cooperate with God's grace to create a more equitable society. We are called to be both audacious and tenacious as we nurture the God-given spark within us, using our gifts, our talents, and our very lives to transform the world, for the sake of the Reign of God.

The other metaphor Jesus uses to describe his disciples is "the light of the world" (Matthew 5:14). Two images clarify what kind of light we are to be. We are to be like a city on a mountain, which cannot be hidden (see 5:14). Such a city is a beacon of hope that draws people to it from far and wide. And, we are to be like a lamp that gives light to an entire house (see 5:15). Jesus says that no one would light a lamp (remember, this is way before electricity, so, he's talking about an oil lamp) and then hide it under a basket. Rather, you would want the light of that lamp to be seen, enjoyed, and used by the whole household.

As a shining city on a hill, and as a brilliant, beautiful lamp, we cannot keep our faith a secret. In both word and deed, we must shine brightly, as examples of Christian witness in our schools, parishes, homes, and social circles. We must shine with a passionate commitment to living as Christ calls and teaches us, as known in and through the Church. We must shine with generosity and respect for the dignity of all people. We must shine as we cocreate, with God, a world in which all people may learn, grow, thrive, and hear the Good News preached to them.

When we act as a catalyst for others' faith to grow and blossom, and when we are a shining beacon of Christian commitment, then we are truly living as disciples of Jesus Christ, and we are truly building up his living body, the Church. ✳

UNIT 5

 How can you be a catalyst for positive, Christ-centered change in your family or school? How about in the Church or in the wider world?

1. What is unique about serving others as a member of the Church?

2. Why is belonging to the Church essential?

3. What can we learn from the young saints in this chapter—Saint Thérèse of Lisieux, Saint Nunzio Sulprizio, Saint Kateri Tekakwitha, Saint Joan of Arc?

4. Why is right after graduating from college often an ideal time for full-time volunteer service?

5. Name at least two Catholic long-term volunteer programs.

6. What is one way the Catholic Medical Mission Board has responded to the changing needs of global health?

7. In the Sermon on the Mount, what two metaphors does Jesus use to describe his disciples? Why should they inspire us?

8. How was salt used in the communal clay ovens of first-century Palestine?

The Church Unified in Service and Liturgy

Serve in Your Community

Serve in Your Parish

SOME WAYS TO SERVE

Serve in Your School

COMMUNITY IS THE FOUNDATION FOR SERVICE

UNIT 5

Unity Is Fostered in the Church Community

Unity Is Fostered through Liturgy and Sacraments

1. Where have you experienced unity in the Church?

2. What type of service has brought you closer to others?

CHAPTER 12 ## The Gospel Message of Service and Justice

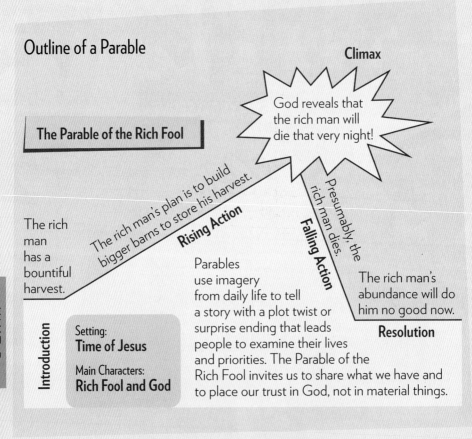

Outline of a Parable

Climax

God reveals that the rich man will die that very night!

The Parable of the Rich Fool

The rich man's plan is to build bigger barns to store his harvest.

Rising Action

Presumably, the rich man dies.

Falling Action

The rich man has a bountiful harvest.

The rich man's abundance will do him no good now.

Resolution

Introduction

Setting: **Time of Jesus**

Main Characters: **Rich Fool and God**

Parables use imagery from daily life to tell a story with a plot twist or surprise ending that leads people to examine their lives and priorities. The Parable of the Rich Fool invites us to share what we have and to place our trust in God, not in material things.

Images: Shutterstock.com

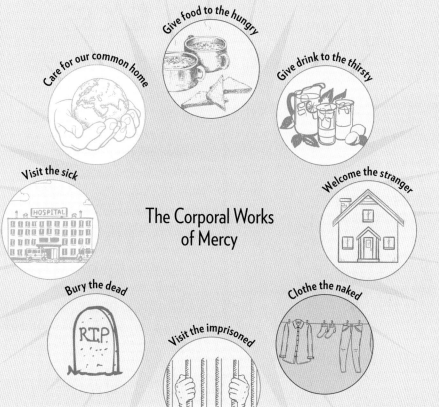

The Corporal Works of Mercy

Give food to the hungry

Give drink to the thirsty

Care for our common home

Welcome the stranger

Visit the sick

Clothe the naked

Bury the dead

Visit the imprisoned

CHAPTER 13 Strength in Numbers:
Catholic Service Organizations

Responding to the Call to Service and Justice

Catholic Charities USA®

The local aid organization of the Catholic Church in the United States.

- Provides service to local people in need and advocates for justice in national, state, and local social structures.

- Each U.S. diocese or region operates a Catholic Charities agency.

- Ministry is focused on:

1. disaster response

2. direct service

3. political advocacy

CRS — CATHOLIC RELIEF SERVICES

The international aid organization of the Catholic Church in the United States.

- Assists impoverished and disadvantaged people overseas.

- Tries to educate Catholics to live their faith in solidarity with the world's poor and vulnerable.

- Serves in more than 100 countries across the globe.

- Is the largest non-governmental relief organization in the world.

- Provides food, shelter, medical care, in times of immediate crisis.

- Focuses on providing community-based, sustainable, development initiatives.

- Promotes global citizenship.

UNIT 5

"On Care for Our Common Home" (*"Laudato Si'"*)

Problems	Solutions
• Pollution of air, water, and soil	• Ecological spirituality
• Climate change	• Recycle and compost
• Loss of biodiversity (species extinction)	• Reduce use of paper and plastics
• Deforestation	• Turn off unnecessary lights
• Depletion of natural resources	• Take public transit or carpool
• Throwaway, consumerist culture	• Conserve water
	• Environmental education for all ages
	• Enforceable international agreements

CHAPTER 14   **The Gift of Oneself:
Gospel-Centered Volunteer Service**

Doing Service as the Church

As members of the Church, service is part of our commitment to discipleship.

Jesus' life was all about serving others and speaking out for justice.

All of our good works should aim to protect, preserve, and strengthen that unity.

Works of service and justice are essential to the Church.

The Church cannot be the Church if we are not committed to service and justice.

Unity with all members of the Church is the basis for our service.

Images: Shutterstock.com

374

How Do We Foster Unity?

Liturgy
We foster unity by participating in the liturgy; this strengthens our union with God and with one another.

Sacraments
Sharing in the Eucharist truly and deeply connects us with our sisters and brothers in faith all around the world.

Unity through Liturgy, Sacraments, and Prayer

Prayer
As we pray together through the Liturgical Year, God gives us the strength to create a more just, unified, and peaceful world.

Making a Difference

Gospel-Centered Service

Making a Difference Now

- Following the example of young saints
- Serving in your school
- Serving in your parish
- Serving in your wider community
- Keeping technology in perspective

Making a Difference in the Future

- Voting
- Enrolling in a Catholic university
- Volunteering full-time
- Serving through your vocation
- Serving through your career

UNIT 5

UNIT 5
BRING IT HOME

HOW IS THE CHURCH CALLED TO SERVE AND TRANSFORM THE WORLD?

UNIT 5

FOCUS QUESTIONS

CHAPTER 12   How am I called to be holy?

CHAPTER 13   How can I best serve others?

CHAPTER 14   How can I make a difference?

COLIN
Father Judge High School

The Church is called to follow Jesus' example, meaning Catholics should live a life of non-violence, honesty, charity, and humility. The Church must do this in the short-term with initiatives that address immediate problems, but also with long-term efforts that transform society itself. Sometimes those efforts get political, but I think that's a good thing. We do not truly grasp Jesus' message if we do not engage in the world. So the Church must fulfill her duty of strengthening and protecting the human family, especially those people that are most vulnerable.

UNIT 5

REFLECT

Take some time to read and reflect on the unit and chapter focus questions listed on the facing page.

- What question or section did you identify most closely with?

- What did you find within the unit that was comforting or challenging?

APPENDIX
Challenge Questions

The content of this course will raise some important questions for those who think seriously about their faith. This is especially true today when many people are asking hard questions about religious beliefs. We are not afraid of these hard questions because an honest search for answers will deepen our faith and understanding of what God has revealed. Here are some common questions with some key points for how to answer them. The references to paragraphs in the *Catechism of the Catholic Church (CCC)* are for further reading if you want to explore these questions more deeply.

QUESTION 1: Why do I have to be a Catholic? Aren't all religions as good as another?

As you learned in chapter 9, ecumenism and interreligious dialogue are of primary importance to the Catholic Church. We explored the depths of the Church's relationship with Judaism, as well as the Church's struggles, commonalities, and commitment to dialogue with Islam. Though we greatly respect both of these faiths, neither believe that Jesus Christ is the incarnate Son of God, a very significant difference in belief. And if Jesus is not both true God and true man, he cannot be the mediator needed to restore us to full communion with God.

We do share more crucial beliefs with our brothers and sisters in other Christian denominations. We share a belief in the Triune God, in the saving power of Jesus Christ as Messiah, and in the necessity of Baptism for example. However, there are some critical differences between Catholicism and other denominations. The Catholic Church recognizes the importance of the entire Deposit of Faith, expressed in both Sacred Scripture and Sacred Tradition. Catholics recognize all Seven Sacraments, experiencing the fullness of sacramental grace. We recognize the primacy of Peter and the authority God has given to the Pope and bishops of the Church. Of course, we find elements of truth in other Christian denominations, but the fullness of God's revealed truth and the fullness of the means of salvation subsists in the Catholic Church (see *CCC*, numbers 816, 836–838).

Christ willed that the Catholic Church be his sacrament of salvation, the sign and the instrument of the communion of God and humanity (see *CCC*, numbers 774–776, 780). The Catholic Church alone can trace its roots to the Apostles. The Church as sacrament is sign and instrument of communion with God and the unity of the human race. What Christ established cannot be replaced or duplicated. Certainly, there have been rifts and disagreements that appeared, and large communities became separated from full communion with the Catholic Church. The Church recognizes the faithful in those communities and accepts them with "respect and affection as brothers . . . all who have been justified by faith in Baptism are incorporated into Christ; they therefore have a right to be called Christians, and with good reason are accepted as brothers in the Lord by the children of the Catholic Church"[1] (*CCC*, number 818). Yet, Christ established his Church as a visible organization through which he communicates his grace, truth, and salvation (see *CCC*, number 771).

So, to answer the question about all religions being as good as others; they are similar in many ways, but they are not the same. The Catholic Church was established by Christ, and functions in a sacramental way—a visible, physical way to experience the fullness of salvation. All members of the Church should share their faith with others. We have a duty to evangelize others (see *CCC*, numbers 849–856). In sharing the Good News, we invite others to experience the possibility of salvation through the Church. We can fulfill our duty and mission to evangelize others by reaching out to those who through no fault of their own do not know Christ or the Catholic Church. They are not excluded from salvation. In a way they are known to God—all people are offered the possibility of salvation through the Church see (*CCC*, numbers 836–848).

QUESTION 2: Isn't the Church being hypocritical in telling other people to be holy and avoid sin when many Catholics, including the clergy, are guilty of terrible wrongs?

Yes, there are members of the Church who are hypocritical. At times, this has been true even of the Church's highest leaders. Like all human beings, members of the Church are guilty of sin. But this doesn't make the Church itself wrong or hypocritical. The Church has both human and divine dimensions. As the Body of Christ, the Church is holy and sinless. Members of the Church share in this holiness. Yet, because the members of the Church are human, individual members of the Church do sin. In other words, the holiness of the members of the Church is real, but it is imperfect. This isn't hypocritical or contradictory! The Church is more than its imperfect members.

The Church teaches what God has revealed about how to be holy and the necessity of avoiding sin. Some members of the Church have failed to live out what God has taught. But their sins do not invalidate the truth of the teaching we have received through the Apostles and their successors. The Church exists to make us holy. This is why all members of the Church, including the Church's leaders and ministers, are invited to continual conversion: a renewal of mind and heart that turns us away from sin and toward God. The Church fosters this conversion, ongoing renewal, and purification in a variety of ways.

We are called to have faith that the Church is guided and animated by the Holy Spirit and, as the Body of Christ, remains sinless even if her members sin. The Church has an invisible dimension as a bearer of divine life, a mystery we can see only with eyes of faith. This invisible mystery builds on the visible reality. The aspects of the Church that we can see put us in touch with her divine dimension. The Holy Spirit assures us that the Church is always carrying out Christ's mission despite the sins and failures of its individual members. Through us, God is doing what we could never do on our own.

QUESTION 3: Who needs organized religion? Isn't it better to worship God in my own way, when and how I want?

Certainly, we can engage in individual prayer, and our experiences of God in nature, relationships, and all of creation are deeply personal. However, belonging to the Church is essential because Christ willed the Church to be the means of our salvation. God desires us to come to him as members of his family, the People of God, so he established the Church to accomplish that purpose (see *CCC*, number 760). Within our Church community, we are unified through the liturgy, sacraments, and service. As human beings we are social in nature, and we need one another's encouragement, support, and example (see number 820). The best place to find that is in the Church. It is here that we find union with God, deep within ourselves. And through that inner union with God, we become united to one another in faith.

This unity with God and with one another is perhaps most obvious when we celebrate the Eucharist. When we receive the Body and Blood of Christ, we are truly united with God. But we also become united with every other person in the Church—those sitting right next to us in the pew, those on the other side of the building, and even those on the other side of the world. Worship of God has both a personal dimension and a communal dimension. Personal, private worship is encouraged to complement communal worship (see *CCC*, numbers 821, 1136–1144). When we spend time in silent prayer, adoration, meditation, or even his creation in nature, our worship takes on a private or personal dimension. But this experience is magnified and deepened when we share that experience with others during the communal worship of the Mass. No one and no community can proclaim the Gospel to themselves (see number 875). Therefore, the relationship we foster with God during our private prayer and worship can only be more authentic when we worship in spirit and in truth, uniting ourselves with Christ's self-offering in the Mass (see numbers 1322–1324).

God taught in the Old and New Testaments that his people should come together and worship in the way that he revealed to them (see *CCC*, numbers 1093–1097). From the very beginning, Jesus taught us how to pray and taught us the importance of community. When he gathered the Apostles, he impressed upon them the value of gathering as a community. This included caring for those in the community who were elderly, widowed, or could not provide for themselves. This is why the Catholic Church has been purposefully structured so that all the members, clergy and laity alike, are accountable to someone and for someone (see numbers 871–879).

Remember in chapter 14 when Erik felt hassled by having to attend Church? He would rather pray alone in his room. His friend reminded him that when we are at Mass, we aren't just thinking about ourselves, we are thinking of and connecting with others and how we can be the face of Christ for them. This rang true for Erik, because when he was playing video games, he certainly wasn't thinking of connecting with or serving others. When we worship and serve in community, our relationships with God and one another grow in authenticity.

QUESTION 4: How is the Catholic Church able to sustain the unity of her members even though they live out their faith in different cultures and sometimes express their faith in different ways?

The Church is able to sustain unity because she has the apostolic teaching office of the Pope and bishops to guide and direct her under the guidance of the Holy Spirit (see *CCC*, number 815). One example of this is when we participate in the Mass. It doesn't matter where in the world we are, all members of the Church across the globe are united with the same profession of faith received from the Apostles. Though it may be in a different language, or the art in the church itself may look different than our own home parish, the Mass is no different. The readings each week are the same in every Catholic church. We will be able to recognize the Liturgy of the Word and the Liturgy of the Eucharist in any language.

The unity of the Church is also sustained through the common celebration of the liturgy and the sacraments (see *CCC*, number 815). The bishops from Guatemala, Mexico, and the United States made a clear statement regarding unity of Church regardless of culture or boundaries. In 2014, they celebrated a bilingual Eucharistic liturgy on both sides of the fence that borders Mexico and the United States. The bishops ministered the Eucharist not only to those gathered with them on the U.S. side of the border but also to those on the Mexican side. Two years later, Pope Francis did something similar during his apostolic journey to Mexico.

The Pope and the bishops are the successors in every age to Saint Peter and the Apostles (see *CCC*, numbers 815, 862). And in that role of authority and teaching, the Pope and bishops work from many different angles to strengthen the unity of the Church. For example, in 2015, Ash Wednesday and the Lunar New Year both fell on February 17. Ash Wednesday would typically be a day of fasting and abstinence. But the Lunar New Year is one of the most important and festive holidays of the year for Asian people—with feasting, not fasting! The bishops declared that the Asian Catholics could celebrate the Lunar New Year as usual, even though it was Ash Wednesday. The bishops asked these Catholics to choose another day of Lent to fast and abstain. They were able to preserve the unity of the Church by ensuring everyone could participate in Lenten traditions, as well as validating the history and traditions of the Asian Catholic people.

GLOSSARY

almsgiving ➤ Freely giving money or material goods to a person who is needy, often by giving to a group or organization that serves poor people. It may be an act of penance or of Christian charity.

Annunciation ➤ The biblical event that includes the angel Gabriel's visit to the Virgin Mary to announce that she is to be the Mother of the Savior.

anti-Semitism ➤ Prejudice against Jewish people.

apostasy ➤ The act of renouncing one's faith.

Apostles ➤ The general term *apostle* means "one who is sent" and can be used in reference to any missionary of the Church during the New Testament period. In reference to the twelve companions chosen by Jesus, also known as "the Twelve," the term refers to those special witnesses of Jesus on whose ministry the early Church was built and whose successors are the bishops.

Apostles' Creed ➤ A profession of faith or statement of Christian belief, the Apostles' Creed developed from the baptism creed of the ancient church of Rome and is considered to be a faithful summary of the faith of the Apostles.

apostolate ➤ The Christian person's activity that fulfills the apostolic nature of the whole Church when he or she works to extend the Kingdom of Christ to the entire world. If your school shares the wisdom of its founder, its namesake, or the charism of the religious order that founded it, it is important to learn about this person or order and his or her charism, because as a graduate you will likely want to incorporate this charism into your own apostolate.

apostolic ➤ To be founded on the Twelve Apostles.

apostolic exhortation ➤ One of several types of documents that are written by the Pope. Its purpose is not to define doctrine, but to encourage people in some aspect of living the faith.

Apostolic Succession ➤ The uninterrupted passing on of apostolic preaching and authority from the Apostles directly to all bishops. It is accomplished through the laying on of hands when a bishop is ordained in the Sacrament of Holy Orders as instituted by Christ. The office of bishop is permanent, because at ordination a bishop is marked with an indelible, sacred character.

Assumption of Mary ➤ The dogma that recognizes that the body of the Blessed Virgin Mary was taken directly to Heaven after her life on Earth had ended.

Baptism ➤ The first of the Seven Sacraments and one of the three Sacraments of Christian Initiation (the others being Confirmation and the Eucharist) by which one becomes a member of the Church and a new creature in Christ.

Beatitudes ➤ The teachings of Jesus that begin the Sermon on the Mount and that summarize the New Law of Christ. The Beatitudes describe the actions and attitudes by which one can discover genuine happiness, and they teach us the final end to which God calls us: full communion with him in the Kingdom of Heaven.

Beloved Disciple ➤ In the Gospel of John, an unnamed disciple who may have been the Apostle John.

bishop ➤ One who has received the fullness of the Sacrament of Holy Orders and is a successor to the Apostles.

C

canon law ➤ The name given to the official body of laws that provide good order in the visible body of the Church.

canonize ➤ The act by which the Church officially recognizes a deceased Catholic as a saint.

Catholic ➤ Along with One, Holy, and Apostolic, Catholic is one of the four Marks of the Church. *Catholic* means "universal." The Church is Catholic in two senses. She is Catholic because Christ is present in her and has given her the fullness of the means of salvation, and also because she reaches throughout the world to all people.

celibacy ➤ The state or condition of those who have chosen or taken vows to remain unmarried in order to devote themselves entirely to the service of the Church and the Kingdom of God.

charism ➤ A special grace of the Holy Spirit given to an individual Christian or community, for the benefit and building up of the entire Church.

chastity ➤ The virtue by which people are able to successfully and healthfully integrate their sexuality into their total person; recognized as one of the fruits of the Holy Spirit. Also one of the vows of religious life.

Church ➤ The term *Church* has three inseparable meanings: (1) the entire People of God throughout the world; (2) the diocese, which is also known as the local Church; and (3) the assembly of believers gathered for the celebration of the liturgy, especially the Eucharist.

circumcision ➤ The act, required by Jewish Law, of removing the foreskin of the penis. Since the time of Abraham, it has been a sign of God's covenant relationship with the Jewish People.

cloistered ➤ Adjective indicating a religious order whose members rarely leave the monastery or convent that is their home.

College of Bishops ➤ The assembly of bishops, headed by the Pope, that holds the teaching authority and responsibility in the Church.

commission ➤ To commission someone is to send him or her on a mission. Jesus commissioned the Apostles to carry out his mission to the world.

common priesthood of the faithful ➤ The name for the priesthood shared by all who are baptized. The baptized share in the one priesthood of Jesus Christ by participating in his mission as priest, prophet, and king.

consecrated life ➤ A state of life recognized by the Church in which a person publicly professes vows of poverty, chastity, and obedience.

conversion ➤ A profound change of heart, turning away from sin and toward God.

Corporal Works of Mercy ➤ Charitable actions that respond to people's physical needs and show respect for human dignity. The traditional list of seven works includes feeding the hungry, giving drink to the thirsty, clothing the naked, sheltering the homeless, visiting the sick, visiting prisoners, and burying the dead.

covenant ➤ A solemn agreement between human beings or between God and a human being in which mutual commitments are made.

creed ➤ An official profession of faith, usually prepared and presented by a council of the Church and used in the Church's liturgy. Based on the Latin *credo*, meaning "I believe."

Crusades ➤ The military expeditions that were launched under Church authority during the eleventh to thirteenth centuries in order to retake the Holy Land from Muslim control.

D

deacon ➤ Along with bishops and priests, one of the three Holy Orders conferred by the Sacrament of Holy Orders. Deacons are entrusted with various ministries, including baptizing, preaching, and witnessing marriages.

denomination ➤ A group of churches or local congregations that are united by a common creed or shared faith under a single governmental structure (for example, the Episcopal Church or the Presbyterian Church).

diocese ➤ Also known as a "particular" or "local" Church, the regional community of believers, who commonly gather in parishes, under the leadership of a bishop. At times, a diocese is determined not on the basis of geography but on the basis of language or rite.

disciple ➤ Follower of Jesus.

doctrine ➤ An official, authoritative teaching of the Church based on the Revelation of God.

dogma ➤ Teachings recognized as central to Church teaching, defined by the Magisterium and considered definitive and authoritative.

E

Eastern Catholic Churches ➤ The twenty-one Churches of the East, with their own liturgical and administrative traditions, which reflect the culture of Eastern Europe and the Middle East. Eastern Catholics are in union with the Universal Catholic Church and her head, the Bishop of Rome.

Ecumenical Council ➤ A gathering of the Church's bishops from around the world convened by the Pope or approved by him to address pressing issues in the Church.

ecumenism ➤ The movement to restore unity among all Christians, the unity to which the Church is called by the Holy Spirit.

Emmanuel ➤ A Hebrew word meaning "God is with us."

encyclical ➤ A teaching letter from the Pope to the members of the Church, or even the whole world, expressing Church teaching on an important topic.

epistle ➤ Another name for a New Testament letter.

eschatology ➤ The area of Christian faith having to do with the last things: the Last Judgment, the particular judgment, the resurrection of the body, Heaven, Hell, and Purgatory.

Eucharist, the ➤ The celebration of the entire Mass. The term can also refer specifically to the consecrated bread and wine that have become the Body and Blood of Christ.

evangelical counsels ➤ The call to go beyond the minimum rules of life required by God (such as the Ten Commandments and the Precepts of the Church) and strive for spiritual perfection through a life marked by a commitment to chastity, poverty, and obedience.

evangelization ➤ The proclamation of the Gospel of Jesus Christ through word and witness.

ex cathedra ➤ A Latin term literally meaning "from the chair," referring to pronouncements concerning faith or morals made by the Pope, acting with full Apostolic authority, as pastor and teacher of all Christians.

F

fasting ➤ The penitential practice of going without food and/or water for a given period of time.

figurative language ➤ A literary form that uses symbolic images, stories, and names to point to a deeper truth.

foreshadow ➤ To represent or prefigure a person before his or her life or an event before it occurs.

G

genealogy ➤ Known as family history, is the study of families and the tracing of their lineages.

genocide ➤ The systematic and planned extermination of a national, racial, ethnic, or cultural group.

Gentile ➤ A non-Jewish person. In Sacred Scripture, the Gentiles were the uncircumcised, those who did not honor the God of the Torah. Saint Paul and other evangelists reached out to the Gentiles, baptizing them into the family of God.

grace ➤ The free and undeserved gift that God gives us to empower us to respond to his call and to live as his adopted sons and daughters. Grace restores our loving communion with the Holy Trinity, lost through sin.

H

heresy ➤ The conscious and deliberate rejection by a baptized person of a truth of faith that must be believed.

hierarchy of truths ➤ The ordering of Catholic doctrines according to their relation to the Trinity, the central foundation of Christian belief.

holiness ➤ The state of being holy. This means to be set apart for God's service, to be devoted to God and united with him and his Church, to live a morally good life, to be a person of prayer, and to reveal God's love to the world through acts of loving service.

Holocaust ➤ In the Old Testament, this refers to a sacrifice consumed by fire. It is now the widely used term to designate the attempted extermination of the Jews by the Nazis during the Second World War (1939–1945).

Holy Orders ➤ The sacrament by which baptized men are ordained for permanent ministry in the Church as bishops, priests, or deacons.

Holy See ➤ This term is a translation of the Latin *sancta sedes*, which literally means "holy seat." The word *see* refers to a diocese or seat of a bishop. The Holy See is the seat of the central administration of the whole Church, under the leadership of the Pope, the Bishop of Rome.

Holy Thursday ➤ The beginning of the Easter Triduum, starting with the evening celebration of the Mass of the Lord's Supper.

human trafficking ➤ Modern-day slavery; the use of force, fraud, or coercion to obtain some type of labor or commercial sex act.

icon ➤ From a Greek word meaning "likeness," a sacred image of Christ, Mary, or the saints, especially in the artwork of the Eastern Churches.

iconostasis ➤ A screen or partition with doors and tiers of icons that separates the bema, the raised part of the church with the altar, from the nave, the main part of the church, in Eastern Churches.

idol ➤ A false god.

idolatry ➤ The worship of other beings, creatures, or material goods in a way that is fitting for God alone.

Immaculate Conception ➤ The Catholic dogma that the Blessed Virgin Mary was free from sin from the first moment of her conception.

inculturation ➤ The process whereby the Gospel becomes incarnate or cultivated within a particular culture. Each culture influences the way the Gospel is understood and practiced.

indefectibility of the Church ➤ The Church's remaining uncorrupted and faithful to Christ's teachings, until the end of human history.

infallibility ➤ The gift given by the Holy Spirit to the Church whereby the pastors of the Church, the Pope and the bishops in union with him, can definitively proclaim a doctrine of faith and morals without error.

infancy narratives ➤ The accounts of Jesus' birth and early childhood.

intercessory prayer ➤ A prayer form in which we ask God's help for other people's needs; also called intercession.

interreligious dialogue ➤ The efforts to build cooperative and constructive interaction with other world religions.

L

laity (laypeople) ➤ All members of the Church with the exception of those who are ordained as bishops, priests, or deacons. The laity share in Christ's role as priest, prophet, and king, witnessing to God's love and power in the world.

Last Judgment ➤ The judgment of the human race by Jesus Christ at his second coming. It is also called the Final Judgment.

lay ecclesial ministers ➤ Those who are not ordained but serve in a leadership capacity by ministering to others in either a full- or part-time capacity within the Church.

Lectionary ➤ The official liturgical book containing the readings of the Mass, the Gospels, the Responsorial Psalms, and the Gospel Acclamations.

Liturgical Year ➤ The Church's annual cycle of feasts and seasons that celebrates the events and mysteries of Christ's birth, life, death, and Resurrection, and Ascension, and forms the context for the Church's worship.

Magisterium ➤ The Church's living teaching office, which consists of all bishops, in communion with the Pope, the Bishop of Rome. Their task is to interpret and preserve the truths revealed in both Sacred Scripture and Sacred Tradition.

Magnificat ➤ This is the first Latin word (from *magnus*, meaning "great," and *facere*, meaning "to make") and the title of the prayer of Mary in response to the Annunciation of the birth of Jesus in the Gospel of Luke (see Luke 1:46–55).

Marks of the Church ➤ The four essential features or characteristics of the Church: One, Holy, Catholic (universal), and Apostolic.

martyr ➤ A person who voluntarily suffers death because of his or her beliefs. The Church has canonized many Christian martyrs as saints.

metaphor ➤ A figure of speech in which a word or phrase that ordinarily designates one thing is used to designate another, making an implied comparison.

monotheism ➤ The belief in and worship of only one God.

new evangelization ➤ A renewed effort, called forth by Pope Saint John Paul II, to bring the Gospel of Christ to individual believers, especially to those who, though baptized, have never fully heard or accepted the Christian message.

Nicene Creed ➤ The formal statement or profession of faith commonly recited during the Eucharist.

Original Sin ➤ The sin by which the first humans disobeyed God and thereby lost their original holiness and became subject to death. Original Sin is transmitted to every person born into the world, except Jesus and Mary.

parable ➤ Generally a short story that uses everyday images to communicate religious messages. Jesus used parables frequently in his teaching as a way of presenting the Good News of salvation.

parish ➤ The local Christian community under the care of a pastor, appointed by the bishop of the diocese. A parish is a local center for celebration of the Eucharist and other sacraments, the preaching of the Gospel, and works of charity and social concern.

Paschal Mystery ➤ The work of salvation accomplished by Jesus Christ mainly through his Passion, death, Resurrection, and Ascension.

Penance and Reconciliation, Sacrament of ➤ One of the Seven Sacraments of the Church, the liturgical celebration of God's forgiveness of sin, through which the sinner is reconciled with both God and the Church.

Pentecost ➤ The fiftieth day following Easter, which commemorates the descent of the Holy Spirit on the Apostles and Mary.

People of God ➤ An image of the Church, based on the Chosen People of the Old Testament and used in the documents of Vatican Council II, to describe the Church as a community of believers chosen by God.

Petrine ministry ➤ This term (an adjective form of Peter) refers to the ministry of the Pope as the successor of Saint Peter and the symbol of the unity and faith of all Christians.

pilgrim church ➤ An expression that came into common use at the time of Vatican Council II as a way of expressing the idea that all Christians are on a pilgrimage toward eternal life, just as the Chosen People were on a pilgrimage to the Promised Land.

Pope ➤ A title used by the Bishop of Rome, who is the successor of Saint Peter and shepherd of the Universal Church.

priest ➤ One who has received the ministerial priesthood through the Sacrament of Holy Orders. The priest serves the community of faith by representing and assisting the bishop in teaching, governing, and presiding at the community's worship.

Protestant Reformation ➤ The movement that began in the early sixteenth century and sought changes to the Roman Catholic Church. This eventually led to the formation of separate Protestant ecclesial bodies.

 Q

Quran ➤ The book of sacred writings accepted by Muslims. Muslims believe the Quran is composed of revelations made to Mohammed by Allah through the angel Gabriel of Christianity; believed by Scripture scholars to be a source for the Gospels of Matthew and Luke.

 R

Reign of God ➤ The reign or rule of God over the hearts of people and, as a consequence of that, the development of a new social order based on unconditional love. The fullness of God's Reign will not be realized until the end of time. Also called the Kingdom of God.

religious communities ➤ A group of men or women religious who are joined by a common charism.

religious vows ➤ The promises made by members of religious communities to follow the evangelical counsels of poverty, chastity, and obedience.

remnant ➤ A prophetic term for the small portion of people who will be saved because of their faithfulness to God.

Roman Catholic Church ➤ Refers to the Western Roman Rite Church that is based in Rome.

 S

Sacred Chrism ➤ Perfumed olive oil consecrated by the bishop that is used for anointing in the Sacraments of Baptism, Confirmation, and Holy Orders.

Sacred Scripture ➤ The sacred writings of the Old and New Testaments, which contain the truth of God's Revelation and were composed by human authors inspired by the Holy Spirit.

Sacred Tradition ➤ Tradition comes from the Latin *tradere*, meaning "to hand on." Sacred Tradition refers to the living process of passing on the Gospel message, and the Gospel handed on. It began with the oral communication of the Gospel by the Apostles, was written down in Sacred Scripture, and is interpreted by the Magisterium under the guidance of the Holy Spirit. Both Sacred Tradition and Sacred Scripture have their common source in the revelation of Jesus Christ and must be equally honored.

saint ➤ Someone who has been transformed by the grace of Christ and who resides in full union with God in Heaven.

salvation history ➤ The pattern of specific events in human history in which God clearly reveals his presence and saving actions. Salvation was accomplished once and for all through Jesus Christ, a truth foreshadowed and revealed throughout the Old Testament.

sanctify ➤ To purify or make holy.

schism ➤ A major break that causes division. A schism in the Church is caused by the refusal to submit to the Pope or to be in communion with the Church's members.

secular ➤ Relating to worldly concerns rather than religion.

secular institutes ➤ Ecclesiastically approved communities whose members commit themselves to the evangelical counsels but work in the world as witnesses to Christ.

servant leadership ➤ A type of leadership based on humble service to all God's people.

Shoah ➤ A Hebrew word meaning "calamity" that is often used to refer to the Holocaust.

societies of apostolic life ➤ Communities whose members strive to live according to the Gospel yet do not take religious vows. They may exercise a particular ministry or sponsor a particular apostolate.

solidarity ➤ Union of one's heart and mind with those who are poor or powerless or who face an injustice. It is an act of Christian charity.

Son of Man ➤ A messianic title from the Book of Daniel, used to describe a figure who receives authority over other nations from God; the only messianic title in the Gospels used by Jesus to describe himself.

stewardship ➤ The careful and responsible management of someone or something that has been entrusted to a person's care. This includes responsibly using and caring for the gifts of creation that God has given us.

Supreme Pontiff ➤ Another title for Pope, the Bishop of Rome, successor to Saint Peter. Comes from the Latin term *pontifex*, meaning "bridge-builder."

symbol ➤ An object or action that points to another reality and leads us to look beyond our senses to consider a deeper mystery.

synod ➤ A group of bishops from around the world who, at the Pope's invitation, gather in Rome to discuss with him matters of concern to the Universal Church.

T

theologian ➤ One who engages in the academic discipline of theology, or the "the study of God." A theologian engages in the pursuit of faith seeking understanding.

third order ➤ People who are affiliated with a religious order; generally, lay or secular members who promise to live according to the spirit of the order and to participate in its ministries to the extent possible.

Torah ➤ A Hebrew word meaning "law," referring to the first five books of the Old Testament. It can also refer to the Law of Moses.

Trinity (or Blessed Trinity) ➤ Often referred to as the Blessed Trinity, the central Christian mystery and dogma that there is one God in three Persons: Father, Son, and Holy Spirit.

V

Vatican Council II ➤ The Ecumenical or general Council of the Catholic Church that Pope Saint John XXIII convened as Pope in 1962 and that continued under Pope Saint Paul VI until 1965.

vocation ➤ A call from God to all members of the Church to embrace a life of holiness. Specifically, it refers to a call to live the holy life as an ordained minister, as a vowed religious (sister or brother), or in a Christian marriage. Single life that involves a personal consecration or commitment to a permanent, celibate gift of self to God and one's neighbor is also a vocational state.

INDEX

Note: Charts and maps are indicated with "C" and "M," respectively.

A

Abraham
  as Church foreshadowing, 151C, 153–155
  as faith model, 269
  in Jesus' genealogy, 201, 202
  Marian prayers referencing, 173
  parables featuring, 304
active orders, 278C, 284
Acts of the Apostles, 31–33, 37–39, 239, 249
Allah, 207, 211C
All Saints, 80
almsgiving, 207, 328
Andrew, 19, 20C
Angrisano, Steve, 255
Annunciation, 92–94, 171
anti-Semitism, 198–200, 205
apostasy, 72
Apostles
  biographical information on, 20
  commission of, 19–21, 121, 122, 126–127, 134–137
  definition, 121
  early Church challenges, 38
  early Church growth and challenges, 36, 38
  martyrdom of, 37–38
  religion on, 197
  Resurrection and appearance of Jesus to, 24
Apostles' Creed, 61–64, 62C
apostolate, 130–133
apostolic exhortations, 44–47
apostolic orders, 278, 330–335
Apostolic Succession, 69
apostolic tradition
  Apostles' mission and origins of, 122, 126–129, 134–137
  definition and descriptions, 121–125
  laity's roles in, 130–133
  leadership succession of, 69
  as Mark of the Church, 57
archdioceses, 234
Assumption of Mary, 94, 246
Augustine of Hippo, 89

B

Babylonian Exile, 156
Bakhita, Josephine, 93

Baptism
  Christian unity through, 59
  Church membership through, 179
  definition, 131
  for grace, 85
  holiness vocation through, 264, 272
  symbolism of, 23, 153
baptismal priesthood, 272
Barber, Michael C., 243
Bartholomew, 20C
Beatitudes, 95, 96
belonging, 179, 239, 349
Beloved Disciple, 161, 174, 176C
Benedict XVI, 43, 108–109, 239
Bible (Sacred Scripture). See also specific books and Gospels
  Church foreshadowing in, 151–156
  Church images in, 157–167, 174
  definition, 123
  early Church development, 38–39, 249
  faith as vocation, 272
  Great Commission, 36
  for holiness and grace, 86–87
  Holy Spirit gifts and fruits, 42C
  Jesus' death, 22
  Judaism in, 201–205
  love, 46
  martyrs, 38
  Pentecost and Holy Spirit, 31–33
  Protestant views of, 76
  sacraments, 23
  unity of Church, 58–60, 239
bishops, 43, 234, 240–243, 245
Body of Christ, 58, 113, 162–163
Bosco, John, 331
Bride of Christ, 162, 165–167
Buddhism, 192, 196
Buonomo, Vincenzo, 257

C

Calungsod, Pedro, 276
Camino de Santiago, 89, 91M
canonize, 88
Canon Law, 257, 275
"Canticle of the Sun" (Francis of Assisi), 337
Care Through Touch Institute, 317

Caritas Christi, 282
catholic (Mark of the Church)
    culture and inculturation, 112–115, 117
    definition, 104–105
    evangelization, 107–111
    as Mark of the Church, 57
Catholic Charities, 136, 243, 257, 323–325, 327
Catholic Extension, 329C
Catholic Foreign Mission Society of America
    (Maryknoll), 282, 362
Catholic Hour, The (radio program), 110–111
Catholic Relief Services (CRS), 326–328
Catholic Rural Life, 342C
Catholic Worker, The, 15, 329C
celibacy, 280–281
charisms, 40–41, 42C, 334
chastity, 279, 280–281
Chosen People, 12, 26, 151, 154–155
Christian Brothers, 40, 278, 361
Church, overview. *See also related topics*
    challenges and conflicts of, 37–39
    definitions and descriptions, 11, 14–15, 47
    diversity of, 60
    domestic, 45
    Eastern *vs.* Latin (Roman) Catholic, 67–68
    establishment of, 16–17
    Gospels of the, 25–27
    mission of, 192, 297
    personal relationship with, 364–367
    sanctification of, 40–42
circumcision, 38
Claire's House, 243
climate change, 338, 341, 342
cloistered life, 330
College of Bishops, 70, 233, 234, 246–247
Colossians, 272
commissions, 19–21, 121, 122, 126–127, 134–137
common priesthood of the faithful, 272
consecrated life
    cloistered, 330
    leadership roles, 255
    religious vows of, 279–281
    service ministries, 330–335
    types of, 278, 282–284
    as vocation, 335
Constantinople, 74, 74M
contemplative orders, 278, 284C
conversion, 82–83, 301–306
Corinthians, 58–59
Corinthians, First Letter of, 42C, 46, 58–59,
    128, 162, 164

Corinthians, Second Letter of, 42C, 58, 269
Corporal Works of Mercy, 96, 309–312
Council of Chalcedon, 73, 247
Council of Jerusalem, 38–39
Counsel, 40, 42C, 266
Courage, 40, 42
covenant
    definition, 12–13
    New, 155, 178, 197, 273
    Old, 151, 153–155, 197, 273
    physical signs of, 38
    symbols of, 152
Covenant House, 353
creeds, 61–64, 62C
Crusades, 208–209, 334
culture, 112–117, 115C
cyberbullying, 96

D
David, 201, 202
Day, Dorothy, 15
deacons, 248, 249, 253
dead, bury the, 310
Decree on Ecumenism (Vatican II), 193, 194
denominations, 195
Diego, Juan, 242
dioceses, 43, 111, 234, 243, 323
disciples
    Church members as, 213, 359
    commission of, 127, 136
    definition, 127
    foot washing, 313–315
    mission descriptions, 366–367
    role models for, 175
doctrine, 72, 195, 245–247
dogma, 72
Dogmatic Constitution on the Church
    (Vatican II), 192, 264, 274, 277
Dominicans, 278
doubting, 135

E
early Church
    challenges of, 38–39, 162
    growth of, 36
    images of, 152, 156, 162–167
    leadership in, 240, 249
Eastern Catholic Churches, 67–68
Eastern Orthodox Christianity, 74–75, 74M,
    75M, 194

Ecumenical Councils, 38–39, 61, 73, 246, 247. *See also* Vatican Council II
ecumenism
about, 193–195
advice on, 214
definition, 192
Eastern Orthodox relationships, 75, 194
evangelization for, 214
Vatican II documents on, 193, 194
Emmanuel, 202
environment, 310–311, 336–343, 342C
Ephesians, Letter to the, 42C, 59, 165, 166
Eucharist, 23, 24, 66, 85, 103, 105, 349
evangelical counsels, 279–281
evangelization, 107–111, 186, 272–277
Examen, 99
ex cathedra, 245–246
Extraordinary Ministers of Holy Communion, 354C

F

faith, 268–271, 272–277
family
Church as, 11, 13, 14, 47, 174, 176C
as domestic Church, 45
love and complexities of, 44–47
Fear of the Lord, 40, 42C
field hospital metaphors, 183–184
figurative language, 150
Flagg, Paluel Joseph, 359
Flood, 151, 152–153
foot washing/massaging, 313–315, 317
foreshadow, 151
Fortitude (Strength), 40, 42C
Francis
Church images, 182–187
ecumenism, 75, 194, 214
environmental issues, 310–311, 337–343
evangelization, 186–187, 213–214
faith as light, 268–271
holiness, 83, 95–98
interreligious dialogue advice, 214, 217
Jewish-Christian relationship, 196, 199–200, 215
lay ecclesial ministry appointments, 257
leadership responsibilities, 43
love, 44–47
Mary as holiness role model, 175
Muslim-Christian relationships, 210, 216
social media, 111
spiritual themes of, 97, 212
United States-Mexico border liturgies, 103
Francis of Assisi, 208–209, 337
Frank, Anne, 199

G

Gabriel, 92–94, 206
Galatians, 42C, 60
genealogies, 201–202
Genesis, 153–155, 340
genocide, 198–199
Gentiles, 36, 38, 39, 239
Gerardi, Juan José, 184
Gies, Miep, 199
Global Catholic Climate Movement, 342C
God
Arabic word for, 207, 211C
call to service, 352
Church as family of, 11, 174, 176C
covenant of, 12–13
praise to, 171–173, 176C
relationship with, 12, 14, 87, 153, 265, 270, 359
unity with, 349
Good Shepherd, 158–160, 161
Gospels
call to conversion, 301–306
call to holiness, 267
Church images in, 157–161
Judaism and Old Testament references in, 201–205
as Word of God, 86–87
grace, 14, 40–41, 76, 85–87, 94
Great Commission, 134–137

H

Habitat for Humanity, 356
heresies, 72
Herod, 37, 204
hierarchy of truths, 241
Hinduism, 192, 196
holiness
Church member imperfection and, 82–83
of daily life, 98
definition, 82
grace, 85–87
light of faith for, 268–271
as Mark of the Church, 57
papal exhortations on, 95–96
role models for, 88–94, 175
service for, 95–96, 97, 173
sharing Jesus's ministry for, 272–277
signs of, 96–98
vocation to, 263–267

Holocaust, 198–199
Holy Orders, 69, 124, 272
Holy See, 233
Holy Spirit
    apostolic tradition roles, 31–33, 123, 124–125
    Church image and soul of, 164
    Church unity in, 58
    early Church guidance of, 36
    for evangelization guidance, 109
    gifts of, 40–42, 42C
    infallibility declarations and guidance of, 247
    for opinion-sharing courage, 275
    for prayer assistance, 42
    service projects and presence of, 33–34
Holy Thursday, 313, 317
hospitality, 313–316, 317
hospitality ministers, 354C

I

Ignatius of Loyola, 99, 332
images of the Church
    Abraham and Chosen People, 151C, 153–155
    Body of Christ, 162–163
    Bride of Christ, 165–167
    faithful remnant, 152C, 156
    field hospitals, 183–184
    Good Shepherd, 158–160, 161
    Marian, 171–175, 176C
    Noah's ark, 151–153, 151C
    Old Testament, 149–156
    People of God, 177, 178–179
    pilgrim church, 177, 180–181
    shepherds, 185–187
    Temple of the Holy Spirit, 162, 164
    vine metaphors, 160–161
Imam, 210, 211C
Immaculate Conception, 92
immigrants, 103, 324, 332, 334
inculturation, 112–117, 115C
indefectibility, 245
infallibility, 245–247
infancy narrative, 201, 202, 204
In Search of a Square Meal, 355
intercessory prayer, 90, 363
Interfaith Power and Light, 342C
interreligious dialogue
    definition, 192
    Jewish-Christian relationship, 196–200, 205, 215
    Muslim-Christian relationship, 206–211, 216
    suggestions for, 214, 217

Iraqi and Syrian Student Project (ISSP), 106
Islam, 206–210, 211C, 216

J

James, son of Zebedee, 19, 20C, 21, 37, 89, 91M
James the Less, 20C
Jesuit Refugee Services (JRS), 332
Jesuits, 261, 278, 332
Jesuit Volunteer Corps (JVC), 361
Jesus
    apostolic commission, 19–21, 121, 122, 126–127, 134–137
    Church as presence of, 137
    Church established by, 16
    Church images on relationship with, 157–163, 174
    discipleship requirements, 366–367
    genealogy of, 201–202
    hospitality modeling, 313–315
    hypocrites, 298–299
    infancy narratives, 201, 202, 204
    ministry of, 272–277
    miracles of, 18, 126, 277
    natures of, 72, 247
    Old Testament connections, 201–205, 269
    parables of, 301–308
    Passion of, 22
    Resurrection of, 24, 267
    teachings of, 17–18
    titles for, 237
    on unity, 71, 193
Jews, 197–205, 215
Joan of Arc, 357
John, 19, 20C, 21
John, Gospel of
    apostolic tradition, 122
    Church as family, 174
    foot washing, 313–315
    Good Shepherd, 158–160
    Jesus' death, 22
    Last Supper and true vine images, 160–161
    overview, 161
    sacraments, 23
John Paul II, 108, 113, 197
Joseph (Jacob/Israel's son), 203
Joseph (Mary's husband), 203
joy, 97, 212
"Joy of Love, The" (Francis), 44–47
"Joy of the Gospel, The" (Francis), 186, 196, 212–215, 217

Judaism, 197–205, 215
Judas Iscariot, 20C
Jude, 20C
justice
　call to, 348
　environmental, 310–311, 336–343
　religious orders for, 332, 334
　social service organizations for, 136, 243, 257, 323–325, 327

K

al-Kamil, Malik, 209
Kino Border Initiative, 332
Kirill, H. H., 75, 194
Knowledge, 40, 42C

L

Lacey, Marilyn, 334
laity, 130–133, 254–259, 283
Lasallian Volunteers, 361
Las Posadas, 112, 114, 115C
Last Judgment, 308, 309
Last Supper, 122, 160–161, 313, 315
Laura's House, 353
lay ecclesial ministers, 256–258
lay ministry, 254–259
Lazarus and the Rich Man (parable), 304–305
leadership
　bishops, 43, 240–243
　deacons, 248, 249, 253
　hierarchy of, 233–235
　lay ministry, 254–259
　Magisterium, 244–247
　popes, 43, 70, 233–234, 236–239, 245–246
　priests, 234, 248–252
　servant, 242
　structure of, 231–235
　unity in, 69–70
Lectionary, 66
Lectors, 352, 354C
Leo I, 247
Leo IX, 74
"Light of Faith, The" (Francis), 268–271
light of the world, 367
liturgical ministers, 352, 354C
Liturgical Year, 350–351
liturgy, 349, 354, 354C

love
　Christ's relationship with Church, 165
　as daily life holiness, 98
　and family, 44–47
　of God, 12, 14, 87, 153, 359
　joy of, 44–47
Luke, Gospel of
　apostolic commission, 126–128
　Church images in, 157
　overview, 129
　parables in, 302–305
　signs of the times, 297–299
Lunar New Year, 241
Luther, Martin, 76

M

Magisterium, 244–247
Magnificat, 171–173, 176C
Marie L'Incarnation, 166
Marks of the Church, 57. *See also* apostolic tradition; catholic; holiness; oneness
marriage, 131, 165–167
martyrs, 37–38, 194, 276
Mary, Mother of God
　heresies on, 72
　as holiness model, 92–94
　inculturated devotion of, 115–116
　as Mother of Church, 174–175, 176C
　prayers of, 171–173, 176C
　religion of, 197
Maryknoll, 282, 362
Maryknoll Lay Missioners, 362
Matrimony, 131
Matthew (apostle), 19, 20C
Matthew, Gospel of
　Church references in, 25–27
　discipleship, 366
　Great Commission, 134–137
　holiness, 267
　Jesus' kingly ministry, 277
　Old Testament references in, 201–205
　parables in, 308
　popes' ministry descriptions, 236–237
　service, 307–308
Maurin, Peter, 15
Mazzarello, Mary Domenica, 331
McAuley, Catherine, 311
Memorial of the Blessed Virgin Mary, Mother of the Church, 175
Mercy Volunteer Corps, 361
metaphors, 150

miracles, 18, 126, 277
Mohammed, 206, 211C
monotheism, 206
Mosaic Covenant, 154
Moses, 154, 204, 269
mosques, 211C
Mother of the Church, 174–175, 176C
Muslims, 206–211, 211C, 216

N

Native Americans, 113, 115C, 166, 242, 357–358
New Covenant, 155, 178, 197, 273
new evangelization, 108–111
Nicene Creed, 61–64, 62C
Noah's ark, 151C, 152–153
non-Christian religions
   Buddhism, 192, 196
   Hinduism, 192, 196
   interreligious dialogue with, 192
   Islam, 206–211, 211C, 216
   Judaism, 197–200, 197–205, 215

O

obedience, 279, 281
Old Covenant, 151, 153–155, 197, 273
"On Care for Our Common Home" (Francis),
   310–311, 337–343
oneness (Mark of the Church)
   biblical references on, 58–60
   in diversity, 60
   divisions and schisms, 72–77, 74M, 75M, 194
   of faith, 61–64
   in leadership, 69–70
   sources of, 58
   in witness, 70–71
   in worship, 65–68
Oratory of Saint Philip Neri, 282
Ordination, 249
Original Sin, 92

P

parables, 17, 301–308, 309
parishes, 111, 234, 354–355
Paschal Mystery, 12, 17, 22, 33, 269, 350
pasos, 114, 115C
Passion, 22
Pastoral Constitution on the Church in the
   Modern World (Vatican II), 299

Paul
   Church images, 162–167
   Church unity, 58
   conversion of, 36
   early Church mission and growth, 36, 38
   faith, 272
   faithful remnant as early Church, 152C, 156
   gifts of God, 197
   religion of, 197
   Resurrection, 267
Penance and Reconciliation, 82–83, 85, 153, 266
Pentecost, 31–33, 125
People of God, 177, 178–179
Peter (Simon)
   biographical information, 19, 20C
   foot washing, 314
   leadership of, 21, 70, 234, 237, 239
   Pentecost and preaching of, 32–33
Petrine ministry, 70
Philip, 20C
Piety, 40, 42C
pilgrim church, 177, 180–181
Pius XII, 246
politics, 297, 300, 356
poor and vulnerable
   apostolic religious orders supporting, 333
   Corporate Works of Mercy, 309–312
   environmental issues impacting, 338
   immigrant assistance, 324, 332
   service organizations providing for,
      322–328, 329C
   support for, 299, 300, 302–308
popes, 43, 70, 233–234, 236–239, 245–246.
   See also specific names of popes
poverty, 279, 280. See also poor and vulnerable
prayer(s)
   call to, 175
   on ecology, 337
   for holiness, 98, 265, 273
   intercessory, 90, 363
   liturgical year and, 350–351
   Marian, 171–173
   as service, 175, 348, 363
   steps for, 99
presbyters, 249
priests, 234, 248–252
Project Rice Bowl, 328
Protestant Reformation, 76, 194

Q

Quran, 206, 216

R

Ramadan, 206, 211C
Reign (Kingdom) of God
  apostolic mission and proclamation of, 126, 127
  as Church's goal, 179, 180, 181
  definition, 17
  Jesus's teachings on, 273
  signs of the times, 298
"Rejoice and Be Glad" (Francis), 95–98
Relation of the Church to Non-Christian Religions (Vatican II), 196, 200, 205, 207
religious communities
  charisms of, 40–41, 334
  cloistered, 330
  consecrated religious life, descriptions, 278
  definition, 40
  leadership roles of, 255
  religious vows, 279–281
  service ministries of, 330–335
  types of, 278, 284
  working with, 335
religious vows, 279–281
remnants, faithful, 152C, 156
Resurrection of Jesus, 24, 267
Reverence (Piety), 40, 42C
Rich Fool (parable), 302–303
Right Judgment (Counsel), 40, 42C, 266
Roman Catholic Church, 67, 74–75
Romans, Letter to the, 156
Romero, Oscar, 89
Ruffino, Paolo, 257

S

sacraments. *See also* Baptism; Eucharist
  for Church leadership, 69, 124, 249, 272
  for conversion and forgiveness, 82–83, 266
  for grace, 85
  matrimony, 131
  unity through, 66, 349
Sacred Chrism, 272
Sacred Scripture, 123. *See also* Bible
Sacred Tradition, 61, 123
saints, 88–90, 113, 357–358. *See also specific names of saints*
Salesians of Don Bosco, 331
salt, 366–367

salvation, 12–15, 76, 104–105, 153, 297
sanctify, 40–42, 131, 242
Sarah, 154–155, 173, 200
schisms, 73–74, 74M, 75M, 194
Schutz-Marsauche, Roger, 67
secular institutes, 282, 284C
Sendler, Irena, 199
Sermon on the Mount, 95, 204, 366
servant leadership, 242
Servant Saturdays, 355
service
  for apostolic mission, 136
  apostolic religious orders and ministries of, 40, 330–335
  Catholic organizations for, 322–328, 329C
  challenges and commitment requirements of, 316
  charitable actions of, 96, 309–312
  Christian call to, 173, 175, 176C, 321–322, 347–348, 359, 362–363
  in community, 356
  experience of, 322
  faith as light for, 271
  for holiness, 87, 95–96, 97, 264, 266–267
  Holy Spirit presence during, 33–34
  hospitality, 313–316, 317
  parables on, 302–308
  in parish, 354
  prayer as, 363
  role models for, 357–358
  at school, 352–353
  volunteer lay ministry for, 258–259
  volunteer programs, full-time, 360–362
Sheen, Fulton J., 110–111
Sheep and Goats (parable), 308
shepherding, 158–160, 161, 185–187
Shoah, 198–199
signs of the times, 297–300, 305–306, 334
Simbang Gabi, 114, 115C
Simon (Peter). *See* Peter
Simon the Zealot, 20C
sinfulness, 82–83, 83, 85, 153, 266
single life, 132, 280, 282
Sisters of Mercy, 40, 278, 333, 361
Sisters of the Presentation, 278
social media, 108, 111, 131, 355
societies of apostolic life, 282, 284C
Society of Jesus (Jesuits), 278, 332, 361
Society of Saint Vincent de Paul, 267
Solemnities, 90, 94
solidarity, 326

Son of Man, 237
Stephen, 36, 38
stewardship, 342
Strength, 40, 42C
structure of Church, 231–235. *See also* leadership
Students United in Recycling School Supplies, 353
Sulprizio, Nunzio, 358
Sun Dance, 113, 115C
Sunshine Packages, 355
Supreme Pontiff, 239
symbols, 150
synods, 44

T

Tawadros II, 194
Tekakwitha, Kateri, 357–358
Temple of the Holy Spirit, 162, 164
theologians, 73, 89, 94, 195
Thérèse of Lisieux, 358
Thering, Rose, 200
third orders, 283, 284C
Thomas, 20C
Timothy, First Letter of, 240, 275
Titus, 240
Tolton, Augustine (Augustus), 37
Trinitarians, 334
Trinity, 58

U

Understanding, 40, 42C
United States Conference of Catholic Bishops (USCCB), 329C
unity. *See also* oneness
    Church as Body of Christ, 162–163
    ecumenism and, 193–195
    Jesus's teachings on, 71, 193
    for service and justice, 347
    through liturgy and sacraments, 349

V

Vanier, Jean, 136
Vatican Council II
    Church images, 177–181
    definition, 177
    ecumenism, 193
    history of, 246
    laity as Church mission instrument, 277
    non-Christian religion relationships, 192, 196, 200, 205, 207
    signs of the times, 299
    vocation to holiness, 264
verbal violence, 96
vine, 160–161
vocations, 130–133, 263–267, 285. *See also* consecrated life
Voluntas Dei, 282
volunteering. *See* service

W

Wisdom, 40, 42C
witnessing, 70–71
Wonder and Awe (Fear of the Lord), 40, 42C
Word of God, 86–87, 123
Workers in the Vineyard (parable), 307–308, 309

Y

youth groups, 355

Z

zema, 114, 115C
Zephaniah, 152, 156
Zumarraga, Juan de, 242

ACKNOWLEDGMENTS

The scriptural quotations in this publication are taken from the *New American Bible, revised edition* © 2010, 1991, 1986, 1970 Confraternity of Christian Doctrine, Inc., Washington, D.C. All Rights Reserved. No part of this work may be reproduced or transmitted in any form or by any means, electronic or mechanical, including photocopying, recording, or by any information storage and retrieval system, without permission in writing from the copyright owner.

The excerpts and quotations throughout this publication marked *Catechism of the Catholic Church* or *CCC* are from the English translation of the *Catechism of the Catholic Church* for use in the United States of America, second edition. Copyright © 1994 by the United States Catholic Conference, Inc.—Libreria Editrice Vaticana LEV. English translation of the Catechism of the *Catholic Church: Modifications from the Editio Typica* copyright © 1997 by the United States Catholic Conference, Inc.— Libreria Editrice Vaticana LEV.

The excerpt by Pope Francis on page 18 is from "Apostolic Journey to Rio De Janeiro on the Occasion of the XXVIII World Youth Day," July 27, 2013, at *http://w2 .vatican.va/content/francesco/en/speeches/2013/july/documents /papa-francesco_20130727_gmg-veglia-giovani.html.* Copyright © LEV.

The quotation on page 23 is from Pope Francis "General Audience," May 17, 2017, at *https://w2.vatican.va/content /francesco/en/audiences/2017/documents/papa-francesco _20170517_udienza-generale.html.* Copyright © LEV.

The excerpts by Pope Francis on pages 34, 63, and 128 are from "Apostolic Journey of His Holiness Pope Francis to Poland on the Occasion of the XXXI World Youth Day," July 30, 2016, at *http://w2.vatican.va/content/francesco/en /speeches/2016/july/documents/papa-francesco_20160730 _polonia-veglia-giovani.html.* Copyright © LEV.

The first quotation by Pope Francis on page 47 is from "The Pastoral Challenges of the Family in the Context of Evangelization" (*"Relatio Synodi"*), Vatican City, 2014," number 28, at *http://w2.vatican.va/content/francesco /en/speeches/2016/july/documents/papa-francesco_20160730_ polonia-veglia-giovani.html.* Copyright © LEV.

The second and third quotations by Pope Francis on page 47 are from "The Joy of Love" (*"Amoris Laetitia,"* April 8, 2016), number 87, at *https://w2.vatican.va/content/dam /francesco/pdf/apost_exhortations/documents/papa-francesco _esortazione-ap_20160319_amoris-laetitia_en.pdf.* Copyright © LEV.

The Apostles Creed and the Nicene Creed on page 62 are from the English translation of *The Roman Missal* © 2010, International Commission on English in the Liturgy Corporation (ICEL) (Washington, DC: United States Conference of Catholic Bishops, 2011), pages 527 and 528. Copyright © 2011, USCCB, Washington, D.C. All rights reserved. Used with permission of the ICEL. Texts contained in this work derived whole or in part from liturgical texts copyrighted by the International Commission on English in the Liturgy (ICEL) have been published here with the confirmation of the Committee on Divine Worship, United States Conference of Catholic Bishops. No other texts in this work have been formally reviewed or approved by the United State Conference of Catholic Bishops. All

rights reserved. Used by permission of the ICEL and the Committee on Divine Worship.

The quotations by Pope Francis on page 75 are from "Joint Declaration of Pope Francis and Patriarch Kirill of All Russia," signed in Havana, Cuba, February 12, 2016, at *https://w2.vatican.va/content/francesco/en/speeches /2016/february/documents/papa-francesco_20160212 _dichiarazione-comune-kirill.html.* Copyright © LEV.

The quotations by Fr. Antonio Spadaro and Pope Francis on page 83 are from "Interview with Pope Francis by Fr. Antonio Spadaro," September 2013, at *https://w2.vatican .va/content/francesco/en/speeches/2013/september/documents /papa-francesco_20130921_intervista-spadaro.html.* Copyright © LEV.

The excerpts by Pope Francis on pages 84 and 269 are from "Apostolic Journey to Rio de Janeiro on the Occasion of the XXVIII World Youth Day, Visit to the Community of Varginha," July 25, 2013, at *http://w2.vatican.va /content/francesco/en/speeches/2013/july/documents /papa-francesco_20130725_gmg-comunita-varginha.html.* Copyright © LEV.

The quotations by Pope Francis on pages 95, 96, 96, 96, 97, 97, 98, 98, and 98 are from "Rejoice and Be Glad" (*"Gaudete et Exsultate,"* March 19, 2018), numbers 14, 110, 111, 115, 127, 135, 147, 149, 145, respectively, at *http://w2.vatican.va/content/francesco/en/apost_exhortations /documents/papa-francesco_esortazione-ap_20180319 _gaudete-et-exsultate.html.* Copyright © LEV.

The excerpt by Pope Francis on page 163 is from "Apostolic Journey to Rio de Janeiro on the Occasion of the XXVIII World Youth Day, Visit of Saint Francis of Assisi to the Providence of God Hospital—V.O.T.," July 24, 2013, at *http://w2.vatican.va/content/francesco/en/speeches/2013/july /documents/papa-francesco_20130724_gmg-ospedale-rio.html.* Copyright © LEV.

The excerpt by Pope Francis on page 173 is from "Address of His Holiness Pope Francis for the XXXII World Youth Day," February 27, 2017, at *http://w2.vatican.va /content/francesco/en/messages/youth/documents /papa-francesco_20170227_messaggio-giovani_2017.html.* Copyright © LEV.

The quotation by Pope Francis on page 183 is from "Interview with Pope Francis by Anthony Spadaro," August, 19, 2013, at *https://w2.vatican.va/content/francesco/en /speeches/2013/september/documents/papa-francesco_20130921_ intervista-spadaro.html.* Copyright © LEV.

The quotation by Pope Francis on page 185 is from "Chrism Mass, Homily of Pope Francis, Saint Peter's Basilica," March 28, 2013, at *http://w2.vatican.va/content/francesco /en/homilies/2013/documents/papa-francesco_20130328 _messa-crismale.html.* Copyright © LEV.

The excerpts by Pope Francis on pages 184 and 186, the quotation on page 196, and the eleven quotations on pages 213–217 are from "The Joy of the Gospel (*"Evangelii Gaudium"*), November 24, 2013, numbers 49, 45, 49, 49, 250, 46, 120, 284, 244, 250, 250, 247, 249, 248, 253, and 251, respectively, at *http://w2.vatican.va/content /francesco/en/apost_exhortations/documents/papa-francesco _esortazione-ap_20131124_evangelii-gaudium.html.* Copyright © LEV.

The quotations from Vatican II on pages 179, 192, 192, 264, 274, and 277 are from *Dogmatic Constitution on the Church* (*Lumen Gentium*, 1964), numbers 9, 8, 8, 42, 35, and 33, respectively, at *http://www.vatican.va/archive/hist _councils/ii_vatican_council/documents/vat-ii_const _19641121_lumen-gentium_en.html*. Copyright © LEV.

The excerpts and quotations throughout this publication marked *Catechism of the Catholic Church* or *CCC* are from the English translation of the *Catechism of the Catholic Church* for use in the United States of America, second edition, number 1565. Copyright © 1994 by the United States Catholic Conference, Inc.—Libreria Editrice Vaticana (LEV). English translation of the *Catechism of the Catholic Church: Modifications from the Editio Typica* copyright © 1997 by the United States Catholic Conference, Inc.—LEV.

The quotation on page 194 is from "Address of His Holiness Pope Francis, Cairo," April 28, 2017, at *http:// w2.vatican.va/content/francesco/en/speeches/2017/april /documents/papa-francesco_20170428_egitto-tawadros-ii.html*. Copyright © LEV.

The quotation by Pope Saint John Paul II on page 197 is from "The Roots of Anti-Judaism in the Christian Environment," April 13, 1986, at *http://www.vatican.va /jubilee_2000/magazine/documents/ju_mag_01111997 _p-42x_en.html*. Copyright © LEV.

The quotations on pages 198 and 199 are from *We Remember: A Reflection on the Shoah*, March 16, 1998, at *http:// www.vatican.va/roman_curia/pontifical_councils/chrstuni /documents/rc_pc_chrstuni_doc_16031998_shoah_en.html*. Copyright © LEV.

The quotation by Pope Francis on page 199 is from "Welcoming Ceremony Address of Pope Francis, Tel Aviv," May 25, 2014, at *http://w2.vatican.va/content/francesco/en /speeches/2014/may/documents/papa-francesco_20140525_ terra-santa-cerimonia-benvenuto-tel-aviv.html*. Copyright © LEV.

The quotations on pages 200, 205, and 207 are from *Declaration on the Relation of the Church to Non-Christian Religions* (*Nostra Aetate*, 1965), numbers 4, 4, and 3, respectively, at *http://www.vatican.va/archive/hist_councils/ii _vatican_council/documents/vat-ii_decl_19651028_nostra -aetate_en.html*. Copyright © LEV.

The excerpt by Pope Francis on page 212 is from "Address of His Holiness Pope Francis on the Occasion of the XXXI World Youth Day," July 31, 2016, at *http://w2 .vatican.va/content/francesco/en/speeches/2016/july/documents /papa-francesco_20160731_polonia-conferenza-stampa.html*. Copyright © LEV.

The excerpt by Pope Francis on page 259 is from "Address of His Holiness Pope Francis on the Occasion of the XXX World Youth Day," January 31, 2015, at *https: //w2.vatican.va/content/francesco/en/messages/youth/documents /papa-francesco_20150131_messaggio-giovani _2015.html*. Copyright © LEV.

The quotations by Pope Francis on pages 268–271 are from his encyclical "The Light of Faith" (*"Lumen Fidei"*),

numbers 5, 8, 15, 18, 20, 69, and 37, respectively, at *http: //w2.vatican.va/content/francesco/en/encyclicals/documents /papa-francesco_20130629_enciclica-lumen-fidei.html*. Copyright © LEV.

The quotation on page 272 is from the English translation of the *Rite of Baptism for Children* © 1969 International Commission on English in the Liturgy (ICEL), as found in *The Rites of the Catholic Church*, volume one, prepared by the ICEL, a Joint Commission of Catholic Bishops' Conferences (Collegeville, MN: The Liturgical Press, 1990), page 429. Copyright © 1990 by the Order of St. Benedict, Collegeville, MN. Used by permission of the ICEL. Texts contained in this work derived whole or in part from liturgical texts copyrighted by the International Commission on English in the Liturgy (ICEL) have been published here with the confirmation of the Committee on Divine Worship, United States Conference of Catholic Bishops. No other texts in this work have been formally reviewed or approved by the United States Conference of Catholic Bishops. All rights reserved. Used by permission of the ICEL and the Committee on Divine Worship.

The quotation on page 275 is from *The Code of Canon Law: A Text and Commentary* (New York: Paulist Press, 1985), canon 212. Copyright © 1985 by the Canon Law Society of America.

The excerpt by Pope Francis on page 306 is from "Address of His Holiness Pope Francis on the Occasion of the XXXIII World Youth Day," February 11, 2018, at *http: //w2.vatican.va/content/francesco/en/messages/youth/documents /papa-francesco_20180211_messaggio-giovani _2018.html*. Copyright © LEV.

The quotation by Pope Francis on page 310 is from "Message of His Holiness Pope Francis for the Celebration of the World Day of Prayer for the Care of Creation," September 1, 2016, at *http://w2.vatican.va /content/francesco/en/messages/pont-messages/2016/documents /papa-francesco_20160901_messaggio-giornata-cura-creato. html*. Copyright © LEV.

The excerpt by Pope Francis on page 325 is from "Address of His Holiness Pope Francis on the Occasion of the XXXIII World Youth Day," February 11, 2018, at *http: //w2.vatican.va/content/francesco/en/messages/youth/documents /papa-francesco_20180211_messaggio-giovani_2018.html*. Copyright © LEV.

The quotations by Pope Francis on pages 338, 338, 338, 339, 339, 340, 340, 340, 340, 340, and 341 are from "On Care for Our Common Home" (*"Laudato Si"*), May 24, 2015, numbers 21, 23, 30, 22, 106, 216, 67, 73, 216, 233, and 173, respectively, at *http://w2.vatican.va/content/francesco /en/encyclicals/documents/papa-francesco_20150524 _enciclica-laudato-si.html*. Copyright © LEV.

The excerpt by Pope Francis on page 365 is from "Address of His Holiness Pope Francis on the Occasion of the XXVIII World Youth Day," July 27, 2013, at *http://w2 .vatican.va/content/francesco/en/speeches/2013/july/documents /papa-francesco_20130727_gmg-veglia-giovani.html*. Copyright © LEV.

Endnote Cited in a Quotation from the *Catechism of the Catholic Church*, Second Edition

1. Unitatis redintegratio 3 § 1.